The Addiction Counselor's
DOCUMENTATION
SOURCEBOOK

The Addiction Counselor's
DOCUMENTATION SOURCEBOOK

The Complete Paperwork Resource for
Treating Clients with Addictions

SECOND EDITION

James R. Finley
Brenda S. Lenz

WILEY

John Wiley & Sons, Inc.

To our spouses, who walk with us every day and are our havens;
to our parents, who came before us and have showed us the way in so many things;
to our children and grandchildren who will follow after us and yet also have much to show us;
to our colleagues, who join us in choosing this work;
and above all to the many clients with whom we have shared so many experiences, who have given us so much, and who will continue to do so in the years ahead.

Contents

Contents

Contents

Contents

CD Contents

CD Contents

CD Contents

CD Contents

Introduction

These are demanding times for substance abuse treatment professionals. Several trends are combining to make the challenges facing clinicians in this field more complex than they have ever been.

Both the scope of the problem and the demand for solutions are greater than ever before. Some promising shifts are taking place; as of June 2004, the incidence of alcoholism is on the decline across the United States, and the downward trend in DWI arrests continues. However, the drop in alcoholism per se has been countered by a rise in alcohol abuse, and problems related to other addictions are increasing again as well. We continue to see easy availability, low prices, and high potency in street drugs and the development and abuse of new pharmaceuticals and club drugs. The mass media continue to sensationalize drug-related crimes and incidents, especially those involving celebrities, even as popular entertainment glamorizes abuse of substances ranging from tobacco and alcohol to heroin.

The state of the practice in treating addiction and alcoholism continues to change. The drive toward greater proof of efficacy and accountability is ongoing, and more sophisticated methods keep emerging from research. Addiction is properly understood as inseparable from other life issues. The life situations of many of our clients or patients grow more difficult as multiple diagnoses are complicated by joblessness, homelessness, and entanglement with the criminal justice system. We must address all these issues in the context of our treatment of addictions.

Resources and standards keep getting scarcer. Funding is harder to find every year, and long-term or residential treatment programs are few and hard to access, with intensive outpatient addiction treatment and brief therapy programs the norms. Implementation of the Health Insurance Portability and Accountability Act (HIPAA) has put a spotlight on protection of client privacy and detailed tracking of clinical work, benefiting the field but increasing the amount of work clinicians must do in addition to the time spent with clients or patients.

To help our colleagues give more of their time and energy to clinical work with the people we serve—the reason we're all in this field in the first place—we offer the resources in this book to save time in documenting our work and in preparing for some aspects of that work. As with the first edition of this book, we have sought to provide clear and well-organized clinical documentation for every phase of treatment, now updated to include HIPAA-required information, and dynamic and effective psychoeducational materials addressing all aspects of the addictive lifestyle and teaching clients about healthy alternatives. These are practical tools you can start using immediately. Our aim is to save time, possibly hundreds of hours of work "reinventing the wheel," and to provide a flexible, comprehensive, and organized set of resources so that carrying out a program and working with clients can be the focus.

This book is divided into three sections. Chapters One through Four provide clinical documentation designed with addiction treatment in mind. All forms are included on the companion CD-ROM and can be reproduced as they are or modified as the user wishes using Microsoft Word. For new programs, these forms may be adopted, modified as necessary, and put into immediate use. Where standing administrative procedures and forms are in place, they may either augment or replace portions of existing documents wherever they offer improvements over forms in current use.

Chapter Five addresses program evaluation including process evaluation and management and outcome evaluation. This chapter offers specific tools and general guidance that can be applied to any treatment program, and includes two forms that can be used in setting up a system for tracking treatment outcomes.

The final section, which includes Chapters Six, Seven, and Eight, is also meant for use in both starting new programs and enriching existing ones. This section contains all the materials needed for over 30 psychoeducational presentations on chemical dependence and related topics. Again, we urge you to take what you want and adapt it as you see fit. All materials in this section are included on the companion CD-ROM; in addition to the facilitator's guides, group member's handouts, and pre-/post-tests in the text of the book, the CD-ROM also contains a Microsoft PowerPoint slideshow file for each presentation, which can be used to print transparencies or handouts.

We hope this combination of materials is useful in a wide variety of settings, and we welcome any feedback you wish to give us about the materials.

James R. Finley, MA
Brenda S. Lenz, MS

Chapter 1

Precontact: Referral Forms

This chapter includes forms to be used to communicate with external sources and clients referred for services. Six forms are included to assist in making the referral process consistent and timely. However, in most cases, external referral sources will have their own processes and forms. You may want to talk with referral sources about possible benefits of providing them with blank forms from your agency.

The pre-contact stage is a brief portion of the process of entering treatment, with the bulk of the paperwork involved in bringing a client into your program taking place in the pretreatment intake and assessment process. These forms are in Chapter Two. The following forms are included in this chapter:

Form 1.1:   Referral for Services

Form 1.2:   Appointment Notification/Confirmation Letter

Form 1.3:   Referral and Treatment Compliance Follow-Up Letter

Form 1.4:   Thank You for Your Referral

Form 1.5:   HIPAA Notice of Privacy Practices and HIPAA Privacy Authorization for Use and Disclosure of Personal Health Information

Form 1.6:   HIPAA—Client Sign-In Sheet

Form 1.1 Referral for Services

Client Name: _____ Date of Birth: _____ Date: _____/_____/_____

Referral Source/Contact: _____

Client Address: _____ Client/ SSN #: _____

_____ Agency Address: _____

Client Phone: (H) _____

(W) _____ Agency Phone: _____ Fax: _____

Parent/Guardian: _____ Agency Contact Person: _____

Emergency Contact Name/Phone: _____

Preferred Focus of Treatment: _____

_____

Service(s)/Program(s) Requested:

( ) Individual counseling   ( ) Case management

( ) Family counseling   ( ) Psychological testing

( ) Group counseling   ( ) Psychiatric assessment

( ) Substance abuse counseling   ( ) Medication monitoring

( ) Medical examination _____

( ) Other: _____

Appointment(s) Will Be Scheduled by:

( ) Client   ( ) Clinician   ( ) Customer service rep.   ( ) Other: _____

Insurance Information:

No insurance: _____

Insurance Company: _____ Blue Cross/Blue Shield _____ CHAMPUS/TriCare _____ Medicare
_____ Aetna _____ Cigna _____ Premier _____ Health Partners
_____ Other: _____

Policy #: _____ Enrollment/Plan/Group Number: _____ Effective Date: _____/_____/_____

Signature of Staff Member Completing Form: _____ Date: _____/_____/_____

Name/Title of Staff Member Completing Form: _____

Individual HIPAA Provider Number of Staff Member Completing Form: _____

HIPAA Organization Number of Staff Member Completing Form: _____

Form 1.2 Appointment Notification/Confirmation Letter

Date: _____/_____/_____

Dear: _____

You have been referred to, or have chosen to receive services from, our agency. You were referred by: _____. Your first appointment is scheduled for the following date and time:

        Date: __/__/__   Day: ___   Time: ___ AM/PM

        You will be seeing: _____

If you are unable to keep this appointment, please call this agency in advance by calling the following number: _____.

- You can expect the first appointment to take approximately _____, as we will need to complete forms and gather additional information to best serve you. This will also allow time to answer any questions you may have.

- In order to complete this initial appointment in a timely fashion, please bring the following information and/or documentation with you: _____

    _____

    _____

    _____

- This will help us work with you in determining insurance coverage, fees for services, and/or who will be billed.

- The fee for your first visit will be $ _____. This agency's policy on payment is

    _____

    _____

However, payment for services is the client's responsibility regardless of what arrangements have been made with other payers.

I look forward to meeting with you!

                Sincerely,

                Name: _____

                Title: _____

Form 1.3 Referral and Treatment Compliance Follow-Up Letter

Date: _____/_____/_____

To: _____

Client Name: _____ Case # / ID #: _____

An authorization for disclosure has been signed by the above named client that permits this communication.

Referral/Treatment Status

(   )   Client met with our intake worker, clinician, doctor on: _____/_____/_____.

(   )   Client failed to attend screening/intake appointment dated: _____/_____/_____.

(   )   Client is scheduled to attend the following: _____ Individual _____ Marital/Family
        _____ Group counseling/therapy program _____ starting _____/_____/_____.

(   )   Client failed to attend his/her scheduled session on _____/_____/_____.

(   )   Client has failed to schedule an appointment as of this date.

(   )   Client enrolled but failed to complete the following program: _____
        Reason for failure: _____

(   )   Client attended sessions but has not fulfilled financial requirements.

(   )   Client completed screening/intake but failed to enroll in the program.

(   )   Client was previously noncompliant but is currently attending sessions.

(   )   Client satisfactorily completed required sessions and other tasks/activities and received a
        certificate of completion dated: _____/_____/_____.

(   )   Client has been contacted and has declined services at this time (reason(s) given if any):
        _____

(   )   Client has been referred for additional services to: _____

Additional Comments: _____

_____

_____

_____

Signature of Staff Member Completing Form: _____ Date: _____/_____/_____

Name/Title of Staff Member Completing Form: _____

Individual HIPAA Provider Number of Staff Member Completing Form: _____

HIPAA Organization Number of Staff Member Completing Form: _____

Form 1.4 Thank You for Your Referral

To: _____ Agency/School/Company: _____

We have processed your referral of _____ for services at this program/agency.

Date Referral Received: _____

The above named individual has given us permission to acknowledge that he/she has made contact with our agency. If additional correspondence is indicated, we will obtain a HIPAA-compliant Authorization of Disclosure.

Please contact us if you have any additional information that may assist us in providing services. Your referral is important to us!

Signed: _____ Name/Title: _____

Program/Service: _____ Phone: _____ Fax: _____

Individual HIPAA Provider Number of Staff Member Completing Form: _____

HIPAA Organization Number of Staff Member Completing Form: _____

This notice describes how medical information about you may be used and disclosed and how you can get access to this information. Please review this notice carefully.

Understanding Your Protected Health Information (PHI)

When you visit us, a record is made of your symptoms, examinations, test results, diagnoses, treatment plan, and other mental health or medical information. Your record is the physical property of the medical health care provider. The information within belongs to you. Being aware of what is in your record will help you to make more informed decisions when authorizing disclosures to others. In using and disclosing your PHI, it is our objective to follow the Privacy Standards of the Federal Health Insurance Portability and Accountability Act (HIPAA) and requirement of state law.

Your Mental Health and/or Medical Record Serves as:

- A basis for planning your care and treatment.
- A means of communication among the health professionals who may contribute to your care.
- A legal document describing the care you received.
- A means by which you or a third-party payer can verify that services billed were actually provided.
- A source of information for public health officials charged with improving the health of the nation.
- A source of data for facility planning and marketing.
- A tool with which we can assess and continually work to improve the care we render and the outcomes we achieve.

Responsibilities of (agency name)

We are required to:

- Maintain the privacy of your PHI as required by law and provide you with notice of legal duties and privacy practices with respect to the PHI that we collect and maintain about you.
- Abide by the terms of this notice currently in effect. We have the right to change our notice of privacy practices and to make the new provisions effective for all protected health information that we maintain, including that obtained prior to the change. Should our information practices change, we will post new changes in the reception room and provide you with a copy.
- Notify you if we are unable to agree to a requested restriction.
- Use or disclose your health information only with your authorization except as described in this notice.

Your Protected Health Information (PHI) Rights

You have the right to:

- Review and obtain a paper copy of the notice of information practices and your health information upon request. A few exceptions apply. Copy charges may apply.
- Request and provide written authorization and permission to release PHI for purposes of outside treatment and health care. This authorization excludes psychotherapy notes and any audio/video tapes that may have been made with your permission for training purposes.
- Revoke your authorization in writing at any time to use, disclose, or restrict health information except

to the extent that action has already been taken.

- Request a restriction on certain uses and disclosures of PHI, but we are not required to agree to the restriction request. You should address your restriction in writing to the Privacy Officer by asking for name of Privacy Officer, address, and phone. We will notify you within 10 days if we cannot agree to the restriction.
- Request that we amend your health information by submitting a written request with reasons supporting the request to the Privacy Officer. We are not required to agree with the requested amendment.
- Obtain an accounting of disclosures of your health information for purposes other than treatment, payment, health care operations, and certain other activities for the past six years but not before April 14, 2003.
- Request confidential communications of your health information by alternative means or at alternative locations.

Disclosures for Treatment, Payment, and Health Operations

(Name of clinic) will use your PHI, with your consent, in the following circumstances:

<u>Treatment</u>: Information obtained by a nurse, physician, psychologist/counselor, dentist, or other member of your health care team will be recorded in your record and used to determine the management and coordination of treatment that will be provided for you.

<u>Disclosure to others outside of the agency</u>: If you give us written authorization, you may revoke it in writing at any time but that revocation will not affect any use or disclosures permitted by your authorization while it was in effect. We will not use or disclose your health information without your authorization, except to report serious threat to health or safety of child and/or vulnerable adult.

<u>For payment, if applicable</u>: We may send a bill to you or to your insurance carrier. The information on or accompanying the bill may include information that identifies you, as well as your diagnosis to obtain reimbursement for your health care or to determine eligibility or coverage.

<u>For health care operations</u>: Members of the mental health staff or members of the quality improvement team may use the information in your health record to assess the performance and operations of our services. This information will be used in an effort to continually improve the quality and effectiveness of the mental health care and services we provide.

We may use or disclose your PHI in the following situations without your authorization: as required by law, public health issues as required by law, communicable diseases, health oversight, abuse/neglect, Food and Drug Administration requirements, legal proceedings, law enforcement, coroners and organ donation, research, or workers' compensation. Under the law, we must make disclosures to you when required by the Secretary of the U.S. Department of Health and Human Services to investigate or determine our compliance with the requirements.

For More Information or to Report a Problem

If you have questions and would like additional information, please ask your clinician. He/she will provide you with additional information or put you in contact with the designated Privacy Officer. If you are concerned that your privacy rights have been violated or you disagree with a decision we have made about access to your health information, you may contact the Privacy Officer. We respect your right to privacy of your health information. There will be no retaliation in any way for filing a complaint with the Privacy Officer of our agency or the U.S. Department of Health and Human Services.

HIPAA Privacy Authorization for Use and Disclosure of Personal Health Information

This authorization is prepared pursuant to the requirements of the Health Insurance Portability and Accountability Act of 1996 (HIPAA) and its implementing regulations as amended from time to time. You may refuse to sign this authorization.

By my signature below, I acknowledge that I have received and read the Notice of Health Information Privacy Practices. I have been provided a copy of, read and understand (agency name) HIPAA Privacy Notice containing a complete description of my rights, and the permitted uses and disclosures of my protected health information under HIPAA. Further, I acknowledge that any information used or disclosed pursuant to this authorization could be at risk for re-disclosure by the recipient and is no longer protected under HIPAA.

Name: _____
          Last   First   MI

Address: _____
          Street   City   State   Zip

Date of Birth: _____

Today's Date: _____

For office use only

I attempted to obtain written acknowledgment of receipt of our Notice of Privacy Practices, but acknowledgment could not be obtained.

Reason: _____

_____   _____
Clinician Signature   Date

Individual HIPAA Provider Number of Clinician Completing Form: _____

HIPAA Organization Number of Clinician Completing Form: _____

Form 1.6 HIPAA—Client Sign-In Sheet

The page that follows can be reproduced on plain paper or on a full sheet of peel-off labels (Avery Standard 5167 Return Address label form), either by photocopying the following page from this book or by printing the Microsoft Word file titled CH0106.DOC on a laser or inkjet printer. If printed, it will produce an entire 8.5" x 11" sheet of entries.

If the page is reproduced on plain paper, it should be placed on a clipboard, and patients/clients should be instructed to sign in and hand the clipboard to a staff member or notify staff that they have signed in. Staff should then note the patient/client's arrival on a paper or computerized schedule/calendar that is positioned so as not to be visible to patients/clients, and mark through the patient/client's initials and time entry with an opaque permanent marker before making the clipboard available to the next patient/client.

If the page is reproduced on a sheet of label forms, patients/clients should again be instructed to sign in and hand the clipboard to a staff member or notify staff that they have signed in. Staff may then peel off the label and stick it on the patient/client's chart or on a paper schedule/calendar, or use it in any other internal tracking system, again ensuring that it is not visible to other patients/clients, and make the clipboard available to the next patient/client.

Initials	Initials	Initials	Initials
Time Arrived	Time Arrived	Time Arrived	Time Arrived
Initials	Initials	Initials	Initials
Time Arrived	Time Arrived	Time Arrived	Time Arrived
Initials	Initials	Initials	Initials
Time Arrived	Time Arrived	Time Arrived	Time Arrived
Initials	Initials	Initials	Initials
Time Arrived	Time Arrived	Time Arrived	Time Arrived
Initials	Initials	Initials	Initials
Time Arrived	Time Arrived	Time Arrived	Time Arrived
Initials	Initials	Initials	Initials
Time Arrived	Time Arrived	Time Arrived	Time Arrived
Initials	Initials	Initials	Initials
Time Arrived	Time Arrived	Time Arrived	Time Arrived
Initials	Initials	Initials	Initials
Time Arrived	Time Arrived	Time Arrived	Time Arrived
Initials	Initials	Initials	Initials
Time Arrived	Time Arrived	Time Arrived	Time Arrived
Initials	Initials	Initials	Initials
Time Arrived	Time Arrived	Time Arrived	Time Arrived
Initials	Initials	Initials	Initials
Time Arrived	Time Arrived	Time Arrived	Time Arrived
Initials	Initials	Initials	Initials
Time Arrived	Time Arrived	Time Arrived	Time Arrived
Initials	Initials	Initials	Initials
Time Arrived	Time Arrived	Time Arrived	Time Arrived
Initials	Initials	Initials	Initials
Time Arrived	Time Arrived	Time Arrived	Time Arrived
Initials	Initials	Initials	Initials
Time Arrived	Time Arrived	Time Arrived	Time Arrived

Chapter 2

Intake and Assessment Forms

Because substance abuse treatment is often combined with treatment for other co-occurring issues, the documentation in this chapter provides a framework for a generalized intake and assessment process with special attention to substance abuse issues. We have incorporated documentation of other clinical issues with the idea that the clinician can use some of these forms in place of, rather than in addition to, existing documentation that does not address issues of addiction as effectively as needed for a substance abuse treatment program. This is done to assist clinicians in keeping their paperwork load manageable, and with an eye toward making this volume comprehensive and useful. The following forms are included in this chapter:

Form 2.1:   Initial Client Information Fact Sheet

Form 2.2:   Confidential Brief Health Information Form

Form 2.3:   Therapist Clinical Assessment

Form 2.4:   Chemical Dependence Assessment Matrix

Form 2.5:   Substance Abuse Assessment Matrix

Intake and Assessment Forms

It is at the intake and assessment stage that you may ask your clients to participate in outcome measurement. Refer to Form 5.2, Informed Consent for Participation in Outcome Assessment, in this manual for that purpose.

Form 2.1 Initial Client Information Fact Sheet

Name: _____   Birth Date: _____ / _____ / _____

Address: _____   Today's Date: _____ / _____ / _____

_____   Phone: (H) _____

Employer: _____   Phone: (W) _____

Address: _____   SSN: _____

Emergency Contact Name: _____   Relationship: _____

Phone Number: _____

Relationship Status: _____ Married _____ Yrs _____ Never married _____ Separated

_____ Committed Relationship _____ Divorced _____ Yrs _____ Widowed _____ Yrs

Children (Names and Ages): _____

_____

Employer/School: _____   Length of current employment: _____

Address: _____

Occupation: _____

Responsible Parent/Guardian/Spouse Info:

Name: _____

Address/Phone: _____

Employer: _____

Who referred you to the clinic? _____

Have you been in treatment before? If so, where and when? _____

Current reason for seeking treatment: _____ AODA   _____ Interpersonal

_____ Academic/Career   _____ Court Ordered

_____ Mood   _____ Referred

_____ Other: _____

Insurance/Billing Information

Primary Insurance Data:

Policy Holder: _____   Employer: _____

Insurance Company: _____

Address: _____

ID #: _____   Group #: _____

Group Name: _____   Effective Date: _____

Insurance Verification Phone: _____

Secondary Insurance Data:

Policy Holder: _____   Employer: _____

Insurance Company: _____

Address: _____

ID #: _____   Group #: _____

Group Name: _____   Effective Date: _____

Insurance Verification Phone: _____

Designated Family Physician: _____

Please print legal name clearly: _____

Signature: _____

Form 2.2 Confidential Brief Health Information Form

Name: _____   Birth Date: _____/_____/_____
Address: _____   Phone: (H) _____
_____   SSN: _____
Primary Care Physician: _____
Today's Date: _____/_____/_____
Month and year of last physical: _____
Please check any of the following for which you have received care:

____ allergies	____ headaches	____ heart disease	____ asthma
____ irritable bowel	____ diabetes	____ sleep problems	____ chronic pain
____ epilepsy/seizures	____ emotional problems	____ arthritis	____ hearing problems
____ vision problems	____ stomach problems	____ cancer	____ thyroid problems
____ blood pressure	____ head injury		

Please list any hospitalizations (dates and reasons): _____
Currently under the care of a physician? If so, for what? _____
Please list any prior mental health services received: _____
For children who are the primary identified client, list immunizations, all developmental milestones, any medications, and health concerns: _____
_____

Please check any area where you think you have a problem:

____ anxiety, nervousness	____ dental health	____ work/academic
____ behavioral problems	____ depression	____ ADHD
____ parenting	____ sleep	____ stress
____ physical health	____ reproduction	____ anger
____ guilt	____ relationships	____ eating/nutrition
____ weight/body image	____ self-esteem	____ alcohol/other drugs
____ compulsive behavior		

Briefly describe your:
Eating habits: _____
Sleep/rest: _____
Use of alcohol/other drugs: _____
Caffeine intake: _____
Smoking: _____
Physical exercise: _____
Hobbies/play: _____
Please describe any medical concerns not listed above that you believe relevant:
_____
_____

_____   _____
Signature   Date

2.4

Form 2.3 Therapist Clinical Assessment

1. Identifying Data:

Name: _____ Date of Birth: ____/____/____ Date of Assessment: ____/____/____

Gender: M ____ F ____ Client ID/Case File #: _____ Primary Language: _____

Referring Agency Staff Member (Name/Title): _____

2. Presenting Problem and History:

Presenting Problem/Reason for Referral/Behavioral Symptoms (onset, frequency, duration):

_____

_____

Mental Health Treatment History (inpatient/outpatient, including date, duration, and outcome):

Date	Location	Problem	Treatment Provider's Name	Duration	Outcome

Family Mental Health Treatment History:

Family Member	Date	Location	Problem	Duration	Outcome

Family History (family of origin, current family constellation, patterns in family relationships):

Genograms:

Family of Origin   Current Family Constellation

_____   _____

Social History/Issues:

Sexual: Gender identity: _____ Currently sexually active?_____

Sexual issues or problems: _____

Spiritual:

Faith group, if any: _____ Active in religious/spiritual activities? _____

Spiritual issues or problems: _____

Housing:

Describe current living situation: _____

Housing issues or problems relevant to treatment: _____

Cultural/leisure/recreational:

Ethnocultural heritage/identity: _____

Hobbies/activities: _____

Cultural issues or problems relevant to treatment: _____

Social/support resources:

Resources in use: _____

Needs, issues, or problems in this area relevant to treatment: _____

_____

Relationships:

Relationship status: _____ Previous marriages: _____

Other significant relationships: _____

Educational/Vocational/Financial/Military History:

Educational: Years of education: _____

Current/past educational issues or problems: _____

_____

Vocational:

Current employment status: _____ Job satisfaction level: _____

Current and past jobs: _____

Vocational issues or problems relevant to treatment: _____

_____

Financial issues or problems relevant to treatment: _____

_____

Military History:

Ever in service? _____ Years served? _____ How did service end? _____

Nature of primary duties: _____ Feelings about service experience: _____

Combat experience, esp. any trauma: _____

Issues or problems related to military service: _____

_____

Developmental History (Unusual events during pregnancy/childbirth, developmental delays/milestones, speech and language development, special skills/talents):

_____

_____

Legal History (current status and past legal involvement, incl. civil cases, divorce/separation/custody issues): _____

_____

For DUI, BAC at arrest: _____   Other substance-related arrest(s) (specify): _____

_____

Trauma/Abuse History:

_____

_____

Significant Losses:

_____

_____

Substance Abuse History (ask about each specifically):

	Age at First Use	Pattern of Use	Frequency of Use	Route of Administration	Date of Last Use	Current Use?
Alcohol	_____	_____	_____	_____	_____	_____
Amphetamine	_____	_____	_____	_____	_____	_____
Methamphetamine	_____	_____	_____	_____	_____	_____
Cocaine/Crack	_____	_____	_____	_____	_____	_____
Heroin	_____	_____	_____	_____	_____	_____
Other IV drug use	_____	_____	_____	_____	_____	_____
Hallucinogens	_____	_____	_____	_____	_____	_____
Cannabis	_____	_____	_____	_____	_____	_____
Methadone	_____	_____	_____	_____	_____	_____
Barbiturates	_____	_____	_____	_____	_____	_____
Inhalants	_____	_____	_____	_____	_____	_____
Steroids	_____	_____	_____	_____	_____	_____
Nicotine	_____	_____	_____	_____	_____	_____
Caffeine	_____	_____	_____	_____	_____	_____
Other rx meds	_____	_____	_____	_____	_____	_____
Other: i.e., OTC	_____	_____	_____	_____	_____	_____

Drug of choice: _____   Most frequent time of use: _____   Morning use: _____

Use to relax or help sleep? _____   Use to relieve pain/discomfort or feel better? _____

Most frequent setting for use (time, place, people): _____

Briefly list experiences of: DTs? _____   Seizures? _____

Tolerance? _____   Withdrawal? _____   Blackouts/memory loss? _____

Vocational/educational/familial/legal/economical changes related to use? _____

_____

Longest and last period of voluntary abstinence   Longest: _____   Last: _____

Family history of substance abuse (blood relatives): _____

Has anyone told you they were concerned about your drinking/drug use or asked you to stop (who/when)? _____   Have you attended AA/NA (when)? _____

Willing to attend AA/NA? _____   Currently attending AA/NA? _____   How often? _____

Have an AA/NA sponsor? _____   Home group? _____   Willing to work with a sponsor? _____

Do you think your drinking/drug use is a problem (if so, why; if not, what evidence do you have)?

_____

_____

Other current/past compulsive/addictive behaviors (gambling, eating, sex, work, caffeine/nicotine, exercise, etc.): _____

_____

Mental Status: _____

General Appearance: Neat _____ Disheveled _____ Formal _____ Casual _____ Seductive _____
Comments: _____
_____

Orientation: Identity _____ Time _____ Place _____ Activity _____
Comments: _____
_____

Behavior: Impulse control adequate _____ Inadequate _____ Describe: _____
_____

Motor Activity: Normal _____ Hyperactive/Agitated _____ Restless _____ Passive/Hypoactive _____
Posturing _____ Tics/Ritualistic actions (including vocal) _____ Rigid _____ Comments: _____
_____

Mood: Appropriate _____ Relaxed _____ Anxious/Fearful _____ Angry _____ Euphoric _____
Guarded _____ Suspicious _____ Sad/Tearful _____ Depressed _____ Withdrawn _____
Labile _____ Apathetic/Indifferent _____ Manic _____ Comments: _____
_____

Affect: Consistent with mood/activity _____ Dissonant with mood/activity _____ Labile _____
Blunted _____ Flat _____ Constricted _____ Comments: _____
_____

Speech: Coherent _____ Incoherent _____ Pressured _____ Halting _____ Idiosyncratic _____
Quality _____ Volume _____ Speed _____ Impediment _____ Comments: _____
_____

Self-Concept: Adequate/Satisfactory _____ Inadequate/Poor _____ Unrealistic _____
Comments: _____

Thought Process: Associations logical _____ Loose _____ Tangential/Incomprehensible _____
Content Realistic _____ Obsessive/Ruminative _____ Delusional _____ Grandiose _____
Phobic _____ Concentration good _____ Fair _____ Poor _____ Inconsistent _____
Comments: _____

Judgment: Unimpaired _____ Uncertain _____ Impaired _____ Comments: _____
_____

Perception: Normal _____ Hallucinations (auditory, visual, tactile, olfactory, taste) _____
Illusions _____ Comments: _____

Memory: Recent: intact ___ not intact ___ selective ___ Remote: intact ___ not intact ___ selective ___
Comments: _____

Suicidal Potential: Current ideation _____ Current intent _____ Has plan _____ Has means _____
Lethality of Plan/Means _____ Prior threats/Gestures/Attempts _____
Willing to contract against self-harm? _____ Comments: _____
_____

Homicidal Potential: Current ideation _____ Current intent _____ Has plan _____ Has means _____
Prior threats/Gestures/Attempts at homicide/Serious harm to others _____
Willing to contract against harming other(s)? _____ Comments: _____
_____
_____

3. Assessment Summary and Recommendations:
DSM-IV-TR Diagnostic Codes:

	Numeric Code	Name of Disorder		
Axis I:	_____	_____	_____	_____
Axis II:	_____	_____	_____	_____
Axis III:	_____	_____	_____	_____
Axis IV:	_____	_____	_____	_____

Axis V: GAF   Current: _____   Past year: _____

Recommendations for treatment and referral(s): _____
_____

Client's desired outcome of treatment: _____
_____

Client's motivation for change: _____
_____

Client's strengths/resources: _____
_____

Client's limitations/obstacles: _____
_____

Other assessments indicated? None indicated _____
    Psychiatric evaluation _____ Specific areas to evaluate: _____
    Psychological testing _____ Specific tests/Types of test: _____
    Medical evaluation _____ Specific areas to evaluate: _____
    Depression inventory _____ Other: _____

Documentation to be obtained:
Medical: _____
_____

School: _____
_____

Other Agencies/Treatment Facilities: _____
_____
_____

Other needed resources or services (legal, medical, financial, social, support groups, etc.):

_____

_____

Assessor's Name/Title: _____ Signature: _____ Date: ___/___/___

Assessor's Individual HIPAA Provider Number: _____

Assessor's HIPAA Organization Number: _____

HCPCS Procedure Code for this clinical assessment: _____

Client/Guardian's Name: _____ Signature: _____ Date: ___/___/___

Form 2.4 Chemical Dependence Assessment Matrix

Diagnosis of dependency requires 3 or more symptoms as patterns over 12-month period				
DSM-IV-TR Dependency Symptoms (as shown by . . .)	Drug of Choice #1	Drug of Choice #2	Drug of Choice #3	Other Drug(s)
Tolerance				
Withdrawal				
Loss of control: Uses more/for longer than intended:				
Persistent desire/efforts to cut down or control use:				
Substantial time devoted to use:				
Important activities given up or reduced due to use:				
Use despite knowledge of adverse physical or psychological consequences:				
TOTAL (3 or more?)				

DSM-IV-TR Diagnostic Criteria Met

Substance Dependence: 3 or more of 7 symptoms present as patterns over a 12-month period

303.90 Alcohol dependence　　_____

304.40 Amphetamine dependence　　_____

304.30 Cannabis dependence　　_____

304.20 Cocaine dependence　　_____

304.50 Hallucinogen dependence　　_____

304.60 Inhalant dependence　　_____

305.10 Nicotine dependence　　_____

304.00 Opioid dependence　　_____

304.90 Phencyclidine dependence　　_____

304.10 Sedative, Hypnotic, or
　　　　Anxiolytic dependence　　_____

304.80 Polysubstance dependence　　_____

304.90 Other (or unknown)
　　　　substance dependence　　_____

Additional Specifiers:

With physiological dependence　　_____
　(tolerance and/or withdrawal seen)

Without physiological dependence　　_____
　(no tolerance or withdrawal)

Early full remission　　_____
　(no dependence/abuse criteria for 1–12 mo.)

Early partial remission　　_____
　(1/more dependence/abuse criteria for 1–12 mo.)

Sustained full remission　　_____
　(no dependence/abuse criteria 12 mo/more)

Sustained partial remission　　_____
　(1/more dependence/abuse criteria 12 mo/more)

On agonist therapy　　_____

In a controlled environment　　_____

Other Indicators Often Connected to Substance Dependence

1. Blackouts (gaps in memory): _____ Y _____ N If Y, about how many times? _____
Describe most recent blackout experience:
_____
_____
_____

2. Repeated falls, fights, work/sports injuries, etc.: _____ Y _____ N If Y, about how many times? _____
Describe most recent occurrence:
_____
_____
_____

3. Substance-related hallucinations/delusional episodes: _____ Y _____ N If Y, describe: _____
_____
_____
_____

4. Negative changes in social circle/recreational activities: _____ Y _____ N If Y, describe: _____
_____
_____
_____

5. Repeated STDs: _____ Y _____ N If Y, how many times? _____

6. Relationship problems/domestic violence: _____ Y _____ N If Y, describe: _____
_____
_____
_____

7. Financial difficulties: _____ Y _____ N

8. Frequent job changes: _____ Y _____ N

9. Frequent geo. moves: _____ Y _____ N

10. Frequent minor legal infractions: _____ Y _____ N

11. Family history of substance abuse problems: _____ Y _____ N If Y, describe: _____
_____
_____
_____

Treatment Referral Based on Diagnostic Criteria, Intensity of Treatment Need Assessment Matrix, and Other Indicators:

No substance abuse treatment needed _____   Intensive outpatient program (IOP) _____
Outpatient abuse/dependence psychoed group _____   Residential treatment program _____
Outpatient dependence/relapse prev. group _____   Other: _____

Assessor's Name/Title: _____ Signature: _____ Date: ____/____/____
Assessor's Individual HIPAA Provider Number: _____
Assessor's HIPAA Organization Number: _____
HCPCS Procedure Code for this clinical assessment: _____
_____

Client/Guardian's Name: _____ Signature: _____ Date: ____/____/____

DSM-IV-TR Substance Drug(s) Abuse Symptoms (as shown by . . .)	Drug of Choice #1	Drug of Choice #2	Drug of Choice #3	Other Drug(s)
Failure in major role obligations:				
Use in hazardous situations:				
Legal problems related to use:				
Continued use despite adverse results:				
One or more?				

DSM-IV-TR Diagnostic Criteria Met

Substance Abuse: 1 or more of 4 symptoms recurring within a 12-month period without meeting criteria for substance dependence

305.00 Alcohol abuse   _____

305.70 Amphetamine abuse   _____

305.20 Cannabis abuse   _____

305.60 Cocaine abuse   _____

305.30 Hallucinogen abuse   _____

305.90 Inhalant abuse   _____

305.50 Opioid abuse   _____

305.90 Phencyclidine abuse   _____

305.40 Sedative, hypnotic, or
          anxiolytic abuse   _____

305.90 Other (or unknown)
          substance abuse   _____

Other Indicators Often Connected to Substance Dependence

1. Blackouts (gaps in memory): _____ Y _____ N If Y, about how many times? _____
   Describe most recent blackout experience:
   _____
   _____
   _____

2. Repeated falls, fights, work/sports injuries, etc.: _____Y _____ N If Y, about how many times? _____
   Describe most recent occurrence:
   _____
   _____
   _____

3. Substance-related hallucinations/delusional episodes: _____Y _____ N If Y, describe: _____
   _____
   _____
   _____

4. Negative changes in social circle/recreational activities: _____ Y _____ N If Y, describe: _____
   _____
   _____
   _____

5. Repeated STDs: _____Y _____ N If Y, how many times? _____

6. Relationship problems/domestic violence: _____Y _____ N If Y, describe: _____
   _____
   _____
   _____

7. Financial difficulties: _____Y _____ N

8. Frequent job changes: _____Y _____ N

9. Frequent geo. moves: _____Y _____ N

10. Frequent minor legal infractions: _____Y _____ N

11. Family history of substance abuse problems: _____Y _____ N If Y, describe: _____
    _____
    _____
    _____

Treatment Referral Based on Diagnostic Criteria, Intensity of Treatment Need Assessment Matrix, and Other Indicators:

No substance abuse treatment needed _____ Outpatient dependence/relapse prev. group _____
Outpatient abuse/dependence psychoed group _____ Other: _____

Assessor's Name/Title: _____ Signature: _____ Date: ____/____/____
Assessor's Individual HIPAA Provider Number: _____
Assessor's HIPAA Organization Number: _____
HCPCS Procedure Code for this clinical assessment: _____
_____

Client/Guardian's Name: _____ Signature: _____ Date: ____/____/____

2.14

Form 2.6 Acuity of Need/Level of Treatment Assessment Matrix

Dimensions	Substance Abuse Psychoeducational Group	Dependence/ Relapse Prevention Psychoeducational Group	Intensive Out-Patient Program	Residential Program
Substance Abuse/ Dependence	Dx of subst. abuse vs. dependence	Dx of substance dependence	Dx of substance dependence	Dx of substance dependence
Suicidal/ Homicidal	No serious danger to self or others	No serious danger to self or others	No serious danger to self or others	Significant danger to self or others
Medical Issues	Nothing interfering with treatment	Nothing interfering with treatment	Nothing interfering with treatment	Needs 24-hr med. care/monitoring
Mental Status	Not significantly impaired, capable of insight	Not significantly impaired, capable of insight	No more than moderately impaired	Significant/ disabling cognitive impairment
Emotional Status	Low/moderate stress/anxiety/ depression, good rehab potential with minimal support	Low/moderate stress/anxiety/ depression, good rehab potential with minimal support	Moderate/high stress/anxiety/ depression, poor rehab potential without daily support	High stress/ anxiety/ depression, unable to manage in outpatient setting
Program Acceptance	Wants help/ change, willing to cooperate with treatment	Wants help/ change, willing to cooperate with treatment	Requires frequent/ daily monitoring for tx compliance	Requires constant monitoring for tx compliance
Relapse Potential	Good potential to stop abuse with psychoed treatment	Good potential to abstain/avoid relapse with psychoed treatment	Relapse risk high without intensive treatment program	Relapse likely without controlled environment
Environmental Stressors	Daily environment supports recovery/ treatment goals	Daily environment supports recovery/ treatment goals	Daily environment indifferent/hostile to recovery/ treatment	Daily environment hostile to recovery/ treatment
Coping Skills/ Support Network	Adequate coping skills/support network	Adequate coping skills/support network	Marginal coping skills/support network	Ineffective coping skills/support network
Commitment to Recovery	At least moderate commitment to recovery	At least moderate commitment to recovery	Ambivalent/ apathetic/mildly to moderately resistant	Actively resistant to treatment/ recovery

1. For each dimension in left column, choose the phrase to its right that best describes the person being evaluated. Put a check or a brief comment in that box. Where two or more columns have the same phrase, use the box farthest to the left.

2. Once all rows are checked, refer the client to treatment in the type of program identified with the marked column farthest to the right. If any boxes are marked under _Residential_, refer to residential treatment; if the farthest-right box marked is under _Intensive Outpatient_, refer to an intensive outpatient program, and so on.

Treatment Referral Based on Acuity of Need/Level of Treatment Assessment Matrix:

Outpatient abuse/dependence psychoeducational group   _____
Outpatient dependence/relapse prevention group   _____
Intensive outpatient program (IOP)   _____
Residential treatment program   _____
Other: _____

Assessor's Name/Title: _____ Signature: _____ Date: ___/___/___
Assessor's Individual HIPAA Provider Number: _____
Assessor's HIPAA Organization Number: _____
HCPCS Procedure Code for this clinical assessment: _____
_____

Client/Guardian's Name: _____ Signature: _____ Date: ___/___/___

Form 2.7 Informed Consent and Payment Agreement for Services

Dear Client:

Welcome to our clinic. We are looking forward to working with you. The following policy statement will help clarify your responsibility in regard to the development of your treatment plan, billing, and insurance.

In regards to insurance, it will be your responsibility to call your insurance company to verify your benefits. You agree that you are responsible for the charges for services provided by this therapist to you, although other insurance carriers may make payments on your account. You understand insurance deductibles, co-payments, or full-fee for services are due at time of services.

You further guarantee that charges for services provided will be paid upon receipt of billing statements from (this therapist/agency) and that the balance will be paid in full unless special arrangements are made for alternative payment scheduling. If such alternative arrangements are made, you guarantee that payment will be made in compliance with those arrangements. You understand that this office will bill insurance companies and other third party payers, but cannot guarantee such benefits, and is not responsible for collection of such payments.

There will be a charge for all appointments that are missed or cancelled without a twenty-four (24) hour notice. Insurance carriers will not pay for missed or cancelled appointments.

Informed Consent

You have been provided with specific, complete, and accurate information about:

1. The benefits and methods of treatment.
2. Options to proposed treatments.
3. Consequences of not receiving proper treatment.
4. The voluntary nature of the proposed treatment.
5. The tentative treatment plan.
6. The client rights, confidentiality, and grievance procedure.

This informed consent is effective until treatment is terminated.

Payment (Fee) Agreement

I, _____ , request that the therapist/agency named above provide professional services to me and I agree to pay fee(s) of:

$ _____ per session for individual therapy.

$ _____ per session for family/marital therapy.

$ _____ per session for group therapy.

I agree to pay a minimum of $_____ of the professional fees at each session.

I have read the client's rights form and reviewed the fee schedule. In signing this form, I understand my rights as a client at this agency and responsibilities for payment.

Client/Guardian's Name: _____ Signature: _____ Date: ____/____/____

Therapist/Agency Representative: _____ Date: ____/____/____

Therapist/Agency Representative's Individual HIPAA Provider Number: _____

Therapist/Agency Representative's HIPAA Organization Number: _____

Form 2.8 Authorization for Disclosure of Information

_____

Last Name   First Name   Middle Initial   Date of Birth

_____

Address

_____

Telephone

I, _____ ,
hereby authorize the release and disclosure of the following clinical and/or therapeutic records for the following purpose(s):

[ ] Authorization to release information regarding counseling and therapy care and treatment.

[ ] Authorization to release information held under the Drug Office and Treatment Act of 1972 (PL-92255) and the Comprehensive Alcohol Abuse and Alcoholism Prevention Treatment and Rehabilitation Act Amendments of 1974. I understand that my records are protected under the federal regulations governing confidentiality of Alcohol and Drug Abuse Patient Records, 42 CFR Part 2, and cannot be disclosed without my written consent unless otherwise provided for in the regulations.

[ ] Authorization to release information related to Human Immunodeficiency Virus (HIV) and Acquired Immune Deficiency Syndrome (AIDS).

Release to:

Name of Provider/Person: _____

Address: _____

Phone: _____

Specific information to be released (client's initials to approve release):

_____ Assessments and evaluations (specify:)   _____ Psychosocial history

_____ Entire mental health record   _____ Discharge summary

_____ Summary of treatment

Correspondence (specify): _____

Other (specify): _____

_____

Purpose(s) for which information is to be released (check all that apply):

_____ continuity of care   _____ referral

_____ consultation   _____ personal

_____ other (please describe): _____

I do not authorize the release of the following information:

_____

Revocation/Expiration: I understand that I may revoke this authorization in writing at any time, except for actions that have already been taken prior to this request. (Forms are available from the therapist.) This authorization will expire ____ days after the signature below. This agency is hereby released from any legal responsibility or liability for disclosure of the above information to the extent indicated and authorized.

Client/Guardian's Name: _____ Signature: _____ Date: ____/____/____

Witness Name: _____ Signature: _____ Date: ____/____/____

Form 2.9 Client Rights and Limits of Confidentiality Handout and Acknowledgment

As a client at our clinic, you have the right to the following:

1. Be informed of your rights verbally and in writing.
2. Give informed consent acknowledging your permission for us to provide treatment.
3. Receive prompt and adequate treatment and refuse treatment that you do not want.
4. Receive written information about fees, payment methods, co-payment, length and duration of sessions and treatment.
5. Be free from unnecessary or excessive medications; to receive clear information pertaining to any recommended medication, its possible benefits, side effects, and alternative medications.
6. Be provided a safe environment, free from physical, sexual, and emotional abuse.
7. Receive complete and accurate information about your treatment plan, goals, methods, potential risks, and benefits and progress.
8. Receive information about the professional capabilities and limitations of any clinician(s) involved in your treatment.
9. Be free from audio or video recording without informed consent.
10. Have the confidentiality of your treatment and treatment records protected. Information regarding your treatment will not be disclosed to any person or agency without your written permission except under circumstances where the law requires such information to be disclosed. You have the right to know the limits of confidentiality and the situations in which the therapist/agency is legally required to disclose information.
11. Have access to information in your treatment records:
    a. With the approval of the clinic director during your treatment.
    b. To have information forwarded to a new therapist following your treatment at this facility.
    c. To challenge the accuracy, completeness, timeliness, and/or relevance of information in your record, and the right to have factual errors corrected and alternative interpretations added.
12. File a grievance if your rights have been denied or limited. You can initiate a complaint either verbally or in writing to the grievance officer. You have the right to receive information about the grievance procedure in writing.

Client Confidentiality

(Name of Clinic   ) has a commitment to keeping the information you provide and your clinical record confidential. Beyond our commitment to Ethical Standards, HIPAA and state law require it. You can give permission to our clinic in writing if you wish your information to be shared with specific persons outside our agency. There are exceptions when we can/must release information without your written permission. Your clinical information will be released without your written consent if: (1) it is necessary to protect you or someone else from imminent physical harm; (2) we receive a valid court order or subpoena that mandates we release your information; or (3) you are reporting abuse to children, the elderly, or persons with a disability.

Clinicians within the agency may, at times, consult with each other regarding your treatment in order to provide you with the best possible services to meet your needs.

If your child is in treatment with our facility and is a minor, we ask that parents/guardians agree that most details of what their child or adolescent tells the therapist be kept confidential. However, parents/guardians do have the right to general information about progress in treatment. The therapist may also have to share information that indicates the child/adolescent is in danger.

This is to acknowledge that I have read, understood, and agreed with the above information.

_____   _____

Signature of Client/Parent/Guardian   Date

This acknowledges that I have reviewed and answered questions about the client's rights and confidentiality as well as our services.

_____   _____

Signature of Clinician   Date

Clinician's Individual HIPAA Provider Number: _____

Clinician's HIPAA Organization Number: _____

Client/Guardian's Name: _____

Signature: _____   Date: ____/____/____

Therapist Name: _____

Signature: _____   Date: ____/____/____

Chapter 3

Treatment Forms

The forms in this chapter include those needed to document contact with the client once treatment has begun. These include forms that are directive, such as treatment planning documents and a behavioral contract, and those used to record actual progress in therapy. The following forms are included in this chapter:

Form 3.1:   Behavioral Contract

Form 3.2:   Contract against Suicide, Self-Harm, or Harm to Others

Form 3.3:   Client Input for Treatment Planning

Form 3.4:   Master Treatment Plan

Form 3.5:   Treatment Plan Update/Revision Form

Form 3.6:   Group Therapy Progress Note

Form 3.7:   Individual/Family Therapy Session Progress Note

Form 3.8:   Telephone Contact Progress Note

Form 3.9:   Therapeutic Materials Loan Record

Treatment Forms

Form 3.1 Behavioral Contract

Name of Client: _____ Client ID #: _____ Date of Birth: ___/___/___

Clinician: _____ Treatment Program: _____ Date of Contract: ____/____/____

I, _____ , understand and agree to comply with the following treatment recommendations. I understand that I must follow these conditions in order to remain in my treatment program. In signing this contract, I agree to meet the following conditions:

_____ 1. I will remain free from all mind-altering substances unless prescribed by a doctor, and if I am taking any prescribed medications, I will take them in the way the doctor instructs me.

_____ 2. I will attend all my therapy sessions on time with one absence allowed for an emergency.

_____ 3. I will attend _____ support group meetings per week and document my attendance.

_____ 4. I will get a support group sponsor and meet with him/her ____ times each week, and if requested will have my sponsor talk with my therapist to confirm I am doing this.

_____ 5. I will call the crisis line, my therapist, or 911 if I feel I might kill or hurt myself or someone else (or this local emergency number _____).

_____ 6. Other condition: _____

_____ 7. Other condition: _____

I am committing myself to honoring this contract for the following time period:
from ____/____/____ to ____/____/____ , or until a specific event takes place as follows: _____
_____

I understand that if I do not comply with these requirements, the consequences will be as follows:
_____
_____

I understand that I will retain a copy of this contract and a copy will be kept by the program staff.

Client/Guardian's Name: _____ Signature: _____ Date: ____/____/____

Staff's Name: _____ Signature: _____ Date: ____/___/____

Staff's Individual HIPAA Provider Number: _____

Staff's HIPAA Organization Number: _____

Form 3.2 Contract against Suicide, Self-Harm, or Harm to Others

I, _____, agree to the following:

1. I understand that my therapist has a legal, ethical, and professional obligation to take all practicable and reasonable measures she/he considers necessary to ensure my safety from suicide and/or self-harm. I agree that this is in my best interest and that I will cooperate with my therapist by providing honest information about any thoughts, desires, or impulses I have to hurt or kill myself. **Initials:** _____

2. I agree not to act on any thoughts, desires, or impulses I may have to hurt or kill myself between _____ and _____. **Initials:** _____
                (date/time or event)   (date/time or event)

3. If, at any time, I feel unable to resist any thoughts, desires, or impulses I may have to hurt or kill myself, I agree that rather than act to hurt or kill myself I will do the following:

   a. Call my therapist at _____ (office) or _____ (pager). If I am unable to reach my therapist, I will:

   b. Call the Suicide/Crisis Hotline at _____. If I am unable to reach the Hotline, I will:

   c. Call 911.

   d. _____ **Initials:** _____

4. If, after talking with my therapist and/or a Suicide/Crisis Hotline worker I still feel unable to resist any thoughts, desires, or impulses I may have to hurt or kill myself, I agree that rather than act to hurt or kill myself I will call 911 and tell the 911 operator that I am thinking of hurting or killing myself, or I will go to the Emergency Room at _____ and tell the staff there that I am thinking or hurting or killing myself. **Initials:** _____

5. I agree that I will either keep this contract with me or where I can quickly get to it at all times while it is in force, and that I will copy down these telephone numbers and keep them with me while this contract is in force. **Initials:** _____

Client/Guardian's Name: _____   Date: ____/____/____

Signature: _____

Therapist Name: _____   Date: ____/____/____

Signature: _____

Therapist's Individual HIPAA Provider Number: _____

Therapist's HIPAA Organization Number: _____

Form 3.3 Client Input for Treatment Planning

I understand that the planning of my therapy is a process that my therapist and I will do together. To help in making sure that my treatment plan includes everything that I feel is important for it to include, I will bring answers to the following questions to my next therapy session:

1. I came to therapy because of _____
_____
_____

2. The things in my life that bother me the most right now are _____
_____
_____

3. The results I am most hoping to get from this therapy are _____
_____
_____

4. The greatest strengths and advantages I can use to achieve my goals for my therapy are _____
_____
_____

5. The greatest challenges I will face in achieving my goals for my therapy are _____
_____
_____

6. The other people who can help me most in achieving my goals are _____
_____
_____

7. The results those people are most hoping I will get from this therapy are _____
_____
_____

8. The best ways other people can help me achieve my goals for this therapy are _____
_____
_____

9. Some methods that I have used successfully to solve problems in the past have been _____
_____
_____

10. Some other things I want to talk about with my therapist are _____
_____
_____

Client/Guardian's Name: _____   Date: ____/____/____
Signature: _____
Therapist Name: _____   Date: ____/____/____
Signature: _____
Therapist's Individual HIPAA Provider Number: _____
Therapist's HIPAA Organization Number: _____

Form 3.4 Master Treatment Plan

Identification Data

Client Name: _____ Admit Date: ____/____/____ Clinician: _____

Client ID#: _____ Age: _____ Gender: _____ Birth Date: ____/____/____

Initial Sessions Authorized: _____ Anticipated Length of Treatment: _____

Status upon Admission: _____ Vol _____ Invol (DTS _____ DTO _____) Mandatory _____

Treatment Modality(ies): _____ Indiv/Fam _____ Psychoed. Group _____ Aftercare _____ Psychiatric

_____ Intensive Outpatient _____ Day Treatment _____ Residential _____ Other: _____

Problem List

Problem #1: _____

      Review Date: ___/___/___ Status: _____ Resolved _____ Improved _____ Unchanged _____ Worse

Problem #2: _____

      Review Date: ___/___/___ Status: _____ Resolved _____ Improved _____ Unchanged _____ Worse

Problem #3: _____

      Review Date: ___/___/___ Status: _____ Resolved _____ Improved _____ Unchanged _____ Worse

DSM-IV-TR Diagnostic Impression

	Code	Description with Qualifiers
Axis I:		
	_____	_____
	_____	_____
Axis II:		
	_____	_____
	_____	_____
Axis III:		
	_____	_____
	_____	_____
Axis IV:		
	_____	_____
	_____	_____
Axis V:	Current functioning: _____	
	Past year functioning: _____	

Primary Diagnosis: _____ Manifested by: _____

_____

Client Strengths: _____

_____

Potential Obstacles to Treatment: _____

_____

_____

Treatment Goals and Interventions

Overall/Long-Term Goal #1 (Related to Problem # _____): _____

    Target date: _____/_____/_____   Date resolved: _____/_____/_____

Measurable Objective 1.A: _____

Intervention 1.A.1: _____

Frequency: _____ Start date: _____/_____/_____ Completion date: _____/_____/_____

Intervention 1.A.2: _____

Frequency: _____ Start date: _____/_____/_____ Completion date: _____/_____/_____

Intervention 1.A.3: _____

Frequency: _____ Start date: _____/_____/_____ Completion date: _____/_____/_____

Measurable Objective 1.B: _____

Intervention 1.B.1: _____

Frequency: _____ Start date: _____/_____/_____ Completion date: _____/_____/_____

Intervention 1.B.2: _____

Frequency: _____ Start date: _____/_____/_____ Completion date: _____/_____/_____

Intervention 1.B.3: _____

Frequency: _____ Start date: _____/_____/_____ Completion date: _____/_____/_____

Measurable Objective 1.C: _____

Intervention 1.C.1: _____

Frequency: _____ Start date: _____/_____/_____ Completion date: _____/_____/_____

Intervention 1.C.2: _____

Frequency: _____ Start date: _____/_____/_____ Completion date: _____/_____/_____

Intervention 1.C.3: _____

Frequency: _____ Start date: _____/_____/_____ Completion date: _____/_____/_____

Overall/Long-Term Goal #2 (Related to Problem # _____): _____

    Target date: _____/_____/_____   Date resolved: _____/_____/_____

Measurable Objective 2.A: _____

Intervention 2.A.1: _____

Frequency: _____ Start date: _____/_____/_____ Completion date: _____/_____/_____

Intervention 2.A.2: _____

Frequency: _____ Start date: _____/_____/_____ Completion date: _____/_____/_____

Intervention 2.A.3: _____

Frequency: _____ Start date: _____/_____/_____ Completion date: _____/_____/_____

Measurable Objective 2.B: _____

Intervention 2.B.1: _____

Frequency: _____ Start date: _____/_____/_____ Completion date: _____/_____/_____

Intervention 2.B.2: _____

Frequency: _____ Start date: _____/_____/_____ Completion date: _____/_____/_____

Intervention 2.B.3: _____

Frequency: _____ Start date: _____/_____/_____ Completion date: _____/_____/_____

Measurable Objective 2.C: _____

Intervention 2.C.1: _____

Frequency: _____ Start date: _____/_____/_____ Completion date: _____/_____/_____

Intervention 2.C.2: _____

Frequency: _____ Start date: _____/_____/_____ Completion date: _____/_____/_____

Intervention 2.C.3: _____

Frequency: _____ Start date: _____/_____/_____ Completion date: _____/_____/_____

Overall/Long-Term Goal #3 (Related to Problem # ____): _____

       Target date: ____/____/____ Date resolved: ____/____/____

Measurable Objective 3.A:

Intervention 3.A.1: _____

Frequency: _____ Start date: ____/____/____ Completion date: ____/____/____

Intervention 3.A.2: _____

Frequency: _____ Start date: ____/____/____ Completion date: ____/____/____

Intervention 3.A.3: _____

Frequency: _____ Start date: ____/____/____ Completion date: ____/____/____

Measurable Objective 3.B.: _____

Intervention 3.B.1: _____

Frequency: _____ Start date: ____/____/____ Completion date: ____/____/____

Intervention 3.B.2: _____

Frequency: _____ Start date: ____/____/____ Completion date: ____/____/____

Intervention 3.B.3: _____

Frequency: _____ Start date: ____/____/____ Completion date: ____/____/____

Measurable Objective 3.C: _____

Intervention 3.C.1:

Frequency: _____ Start date: ____/____/____ Completion date: ____/____/____

Intervention 3.C.2: _____

Frequency: _____ Start date: ____/____/____ Completion date: ____/____/____

Intervention 3.C.3: _____

Frequency: _____ Start date: ____/____/____ Completion date: ____/____/____

Discharge Plan

Projected Date for Resolution of Problems: ____/____/____

Projected No. of Sessions Required: _____

Criteria for Discharge from Treatment:

_____

_____

_____

Aftercare Plan:

_____

_____

Comments:

_____

_____

_____

My/our signature(s) here indicate(s) that I/we have participated in designing this treatment plan, understand it, and accept responsibility to carry out my/our portion(s) of this plan.

Client/Guardian's Name: _____

Signature: _____ Date: ____/____/____

Program Staff's Name: _____

Signature: _____ Date: ____/____/____

Staff's Individual HIPAA Provider Number: _____

Staff's HIPAA Organization Number: _____

Form 3.5 Treatment Plan Update/Revision Form

Client Name: _____ Client ID#: _____ Clinician Name: _____

Date Master Treatment Plan Formulated: ____/____/____   Date of Revision: ____/____/____

Updates/Revisions to Problem List

New Problem: Problem # _____ Description/Status: _____

_____

Revision of Existing Problem # _____ Current Description/Status: _____

_____

Updates/Revisions to Diagnosis

	DSM-IV-TR Code	Description	Manifested by:
New Primary Diagnosis:	_____	_____	_____
New Additional Diagnosis:	_____	_____	_____

Updates/Revisions to Goals, Objectives, and/or Interventions

New Goal: Goal # ____ Related to Problem # _____ Description of Goal: _____

_____

Revision of Goal # ____ Goal as Revised: _____

_____

Revision of Goal # ____ Goal as Revised: _____

_____

New Objective: Objective # ____ Related to Goal # ____ Description of Objective: _____

_____

Revision of Objective # ____ Objective as Revised: _____

_____

Revision of Objective # ____ Objective as Revised: _____

_____

New Intervention: Intervention # ____ Related to Objective # ____ Description of Intervention: _____

_____

   Frequency: _____ Start Date: ____/____/____ Completion Date: ____/____/____

Revision of Intervention # _____ Intervention as Revised: _____

   Frequency: _____ Start Date: ____/____/____ Completion Date: ____/____/____

Revision of Intervention # _____ Intervention as Revised: _____

   Frequency: _____ Start Date: ____/____/____ Completion Date: ____/____/____

Other Update/Revision

_____

_____

My/our signature(s) here indicate(s) that I/we have participated in this treatment plan update/revision, understand it, and accept responsibility to carry out my/our portion(s) of this updated/revised plan.

Client/Guardian's Name: _____ Signature: _____ Date: ____/____/____

Program Staff's Name: _____ Signature: _____ Date: ____/____/____

Staff's Individual HIPAA Provider Number: _____

Staff's HIPAA Organization Number: _____

Form 3.6 Group Therapy Progress Note

Client Name: _____ Client ID#: _____ Birth Date:____/____/____

Program: _____ Session Date: ____/____/____ Session #: _____

Topic: _____ Length of Session: _____

Format: _____ Didactic _____ Process _____ Guided Discussion _____ Other: _____

Training Aids: _____ Videotape _____ Audiotape _____ Written Material _____ Transparencies
_____ Other: _____

Problem & Objective of Session: _____

Level of Participation: _____Active _____ Moderate _____ Minimal _____ Absent

Data (self-report, observations, interventions, current issues/stressors, functional impairment, group
behavior, motivation, progress): _____
_____
_____
_____
_____
_____
_____
_____
_____

Assessment (progress, evaluation of intervention, obstacles or barriers): _____
_____
_____
_____
_____
_____
_____
_____
_____

Plan (tasks to be completed between sessions, objectives for next session, changes, recommendations,
sessions remaining, date of next session, plan for termination): _____
_____
_____
_____
_____
_____
_____
_____

Clinician's Name: _____ Signature: _____ Date: ____/____/____
Clinician's Individual HIPAA Provider Number: _____
Clinician's HIPAA Organization Number: _____
HCPCS Procedure Code for this treatment session: _____
_____

Form 3.7 Individual/Family Therapy Session Progress Note

Client Name: _____ Client ID#: _____ Birth Date:____ / ____ / ____

Program: _____ Session Date: ___ / ___ / ___ Session #: _____

Present in Session: _____ Length of Session: _____

Modality of Treatment: _____

Problem: _____

Objectives of Session: _____

Data (self-report, observations, interventions, current issues/stressors, functional impairment, group behavior, motivation, progress): _____

_____

_____

_____

_____

_____

_____

_____

_____

_____

Assessment (progress, evaluation of intervention, obstacles or barriers): _____

_____

_____

_____

_____

_____

_____

_____

_____

Plan (tasks to be completed between sessions, objectives for next session, changes, recommendations, sessions remaining, date of next session, plan for termination): _____

_____

_____

_____

_____

_____

_____

_____

_____

Clinician's Name: _____ Signature: _____ Date: ____ / ____ / ____

Clinician's Individual HIPAA Provider Number: _____

Clinician's HIPAA Organization Number: _____

HCPCS Procedure Code for this treatment session: _____

Form 3.8 Telephone Contact Progress Note

Client Name: _____   Client ID#: _____

Date of Call: _____   Duration of Call: _____

Outgoing Call   Call Received

Name of Staff Making Call: _____   Call Received From: _____

Call Made to: _____   Relationship to Client: _____

Relationship to Client (if not client): _____

Nature of Call: _____

_____

_____

_____

_____

_____

_____

_____

Action Taken: _____

_____

_____

_____

_____

_____

_____

_____

Follow-Up Contact Person: _____

_____

_____

_____

_____

_____

_____

Clinician's Name: _____   Date: _____/_____/_____

Signature: _____

Clinician's Individual HIPAA Provider Number: _____

Clinician's HIPAA Organization Number: _____

HCPCS Procedure Code for this treatment session: _____

_____

Form 3.9 Therapeutic Materials Loan Record

Date Checked Out	Title of Item	Client #	Format	Length of Loan	Date Returned	Comments
————	————	————	————	————	————	————
————	————	————	————	————	————	————
————	————	————	————	————	————	————
————	————	————	————	————	————	————
————	————	————	————	————	————	————
————	————	————	————	————	————	————
————	————	————	————	————	————	————
————	————	————	————	————	————	————
————	————	————	————	————	————	————
————	————	————	————	————	————	————
————	————	————	————	————	————	————
————	————	————	————	————	————	————
————	————	————	————	————	————	————
————	————	————	————	————	————	————
————	————	————	————	————	————	————
————	————	————	————	————	————	————
————	————	————	————	————	————	————
————	————	————	————	————	————	————
————	————	————	————	————	————	————
————	————	————	————	————	————	————
————	————	————	————	————	————	————
————	————	————	————	————	————	————
————	————	————	————	————	————	————

Format:

B = Book   M = Manual
V = Video   W = Workbook
D = DVD   P = Pamphlet
T = Tape   J = Journal

You have been given this handout because the professional(s) treating you believes you might benefit from receiving a specialized type of therapy called Eye Movement Desensitization and Reprocessing, or EMDR. Before you can decide whether to participate in this treatment, you must understand what is being offered and what you are being asked to do. The purpose of this handout is to explain EMDR and answer questions people often ask about it. If you don't understand the information in this handout or if you have questions that aren't answered here, you should talk to the therapist or other professional who is suggesting this therapy for you and get the information you need to make a fully informed decision.

WHAT EMDR IS

EMDR is a method of therapy that is highly effective at providing relief to people suffering from a variety of emotional problems. In particular, EMDR can be useful in treatment of substance abuse problems, though as you will read later in this handout there are some addictive problems for which it cannot be used and, in any case, special preparation is required.

The EMDR approach is based on the idea that our brains and nervous systems have ways of remembering and handling experiences that are both physical and mental. In other words, some parts of a memory are the physical images, sounds, and feelings stored in our brains and nervous systems, and along with those physical parts, the memories also include the thoughts and emotions connected with them, both what we felt and thought when the experience happened and what we think and feel about it now.

Normally, our brains and nervous systems are able to "process" these physical sensations, thoughts, and feelings so that they become merely memories. The emotional pain and distress fade, so we are able to remember without feeling as strongly upset as we did when the event happened and when it was fresh in our minds. This "processing" of experiences appears to have a physical element to it, often involving rapid eye movements such as we have when we are dreaming. Many researchers believe that when we dream, we are processing experiences in the way described here.

Painful memories sometimes get "stuck" and don't finish being processed, so that they stay as fresh and painful as if they had just happened, sometimes for years or decades. This may happen because the experience is so intense that it overwhelms the processing system's ability to handle it. It leaves the person who has had such an experience feeling that he or she can't get over it. This is sometimes recognized by diagnostic terms such as Posttraumatic Stress Disorder, and at other times may just be indicated by a person continuing to feel emotional pain that does not diminish with time.

EMDR uses guided eye movements or other rhythmic sensory activities such as listening to finger-snaps or feeling taps on a person's hands, combined with training in relaxation and stress management and other mental and emotional therapy, to "unstick" the processing mechanism and let the painful experiences shift from being fresh and painful to becoming memories that no longer cause intense upset. One way to describe it would be to say that on a mental and emotional level, it changes them from unhealed wounds to faded scars.

The process of EMDR is a multistep method. The therapist begins by collecting life history information from the client and evaluating his or her personality, situation, and problems to see whether this therapy is a good idea for this person. If it appears to be a suitable therapy, the therapist explains what is involved in detail, so that the client can decide whether to participate in EMDR. If EMDR looks appropriate and the client, after learning about it, wants to receive the therapy, the therapist prepares him or her by teaching relaxation and stress management methods and having the client practice them, as well as helping the client expand and reinforce his or her emotional support network and resources. Once the client is prepared, typically after devoting at least one entire therapy session and the time between that and the next session to the teaching and support reinforcement mentioned, the therapist goes on to do a current assessment of the type and degree of distress the client is suffering. This is based on the client's descriptions of his or her thoughts and feelings and on detailed self-rating scales. These three steps (history, preparation, and assessment) take place before the EMDR treatment techniques are used.

The EMDR treatment begins with *desensitization*. This is the first time the therapist actually uses the eye movement or other nervous-system-stimulation techniques; this triggers an "unsticking" and acceleration of the brain and nervous system's physical processing of the painful experiences. This typically takes one or two sessions, sometimes more, and results in a significant lessening of distress. One experience or issue is addressed at a time, and for each one, desensitization is followed by an *installation* phase in which a supportive, positive way of thinking and feeling about the experience is reinforced as a replacement for the old painful and negative thoughts and feelings. This takes place during the same session, immediately after completion of desensitization for each experience or issue. Installation is not done until desensitization is complete. If desensitization takes more than one session, the therapist works with the client at the end of each incomplete session to help him or her see the progress made so far, to make sure he or she is not in a crisis, and to help make maximum use of support systems and resources.

Two concluding phases following installation in the processing of each painful memory are the *body scan,* seeking lingering physical signs that the trauma is not fully processed (if such signs are found, the therapist returns to the desensitization phase and finishes the work on that issue); and the *closure* phase, in which the therapist continues the support and education process and gets the client's renewed promise to use his or her support resources including the therapist as needed between sessions.

At the next session, the therapist conducts the final phase, *reevaluation.* In this phase, the client and therapist check for signs that the trauma(s) processed at the previous session have been fully dealt with. If there are signs that the client is still experiencing effects of unresolved trauma, they return to the desensitization phase to help the client complete processing that experience or issue.

WHAT EMDR IS NOT

EMDR is not hypnosis. It is not NeuroLinguistic Programming, another therapy that combines physical, mental, and emotional techniques. EMDR is not a blanket solution for all problems or all people, nor is it a simple technique to be used without careful preparation and follow-up.

WHAT EMDR WILL DO

For many people, EMDR can:

- Give quick and substantial relief and peace of mind from emotional suffering stemming from experiences they "can't get over," whether those are very recent or decades in the past. Typically this relief will generalize to the aftereffects of other, similar experiences.

- Help achieve new understanding and insights about the meanings of experiences, and connections between those experiences and patterns of thought and behavior in a person's life.

- Help change patterns of substance abuse in which a person automatically turns to a chemical to achieve a desired feeling or state of mind, reorienting these impulses or cravings toward healthy substitutes.

- Help people regain memories in greater detail or fill in gaps in their memories—it is important to note that there is no guarantee that any memory "recovered" in this way is true or accurate; often these memories seem to be more symbolic than literally true.

- Lead to a diminished memory of disturbing details in traumatic memories, although there is only one recorded case of a memory disappearing completely.

- Increase the feeling of having control over one's own destiny and actions that is sometimes lost as a result of suffering emotional trauma.

WHAT EMDR WILL NOT DO

EMDR will not:

- Cause painful memories to completely disappear.

- Guarantee that memories will return, or that they will be true and accurate if they do.

- Get rid of anxiety or distress that is appropriate and suitable to the present situation; for example, if a person is currently in danger, it will not make them feel safe.

- Make memories worse or more painful.

CAUTIONS

The following cautions must be considered in deciding whether to participate in EMDR:

- While a specialized EMDR protocol for substance abuse is useful in treating such problems, people with active chemical dependencies, or who are in recovery but do not have strong recovery programs and support systems, may be prone to relapse during or after EMDR therapy unless they receive proper preparation. Some report that they have no craving to use drugs or drink after treatment, but others have had strong cravings. If you have had a drinking or drug problem in the past but you are now clean and sober, before you receive EMDR therapy, you should make sure you have people available to help you through any cravings that might otherwise influence you to start drinking or using again.

  In particular, people who have recently (within 6 months) become clean and sober after long-term use of stimulant drugs such as methamphetamine, other amphetamines, or cocaine, may have extreme and intense reactions that are too much for them to cope with, and may need to be hospitalized. If you have this kind of history, you need to talk with your therapist about this before deciding on EMDR.

- People who are not physically able to tolerate high stress for short periods may not be good candidates for EMDR, as it can be physically very taxing.

- Therapists preparing to use EMDR should not only be trained in this method, they should be prepared by training and experience to help clients through the extreme emotions some people experience during EMDR. These may include rage, panic, intense grief, or reexperiencing disturbing physical sensations that were part of the original traumatic experiences. Only a trained therapist should use EMDR for the safety of the person receiving the therapy, and it should be done only in a setting where any help and support that might be needed is available.

- Therapists should also be generally qualified to work with the specific types of issues and clients they use EMDR to treat. For example, a therapist who had insufficient experience or training to treat a person suffering from Posttraumatic Stress Disorder without EMDR should not attempt to treat that person for that problem with EMDR.

- EMDR should be used only in a situation where the client feels extremely safe and comfortable with the therapist, will be totally honest about what he or she is experiencing during and after therapy, and
will follow through on promises to call on the therapist or other supportive people if he or she experiences emotional disturbances after a therapy session.

- EMDR can be used with people of any age. Procedures are modified for children.

- For clients who have limited coping skills and/or emotional support resources, it is vital to strengthen these abilities and strengths before proceeding with EMDR treatment. The therapist plays a key role in this process by teaching them ways to relax and cope with stress and by helping them increase their support network. This support network may include family members, close friends, the therapist, and organized support groups.

We have given you a lot of basic information about EMDR in this fact sheet, but many people have more questions that are not answered here. Please take your time reading this, then ask your therapist about any other questions that you have, to help you in deciding whether or not you feel this treatment is for you. EMDR is a powerful and effective therapy method that has been very helpful to many people. We hope that if you decide to participate in EMDR therapy, it is equally helpful for you.

QUESTIONS/NOTES:

Form 3.11 Eye Movement Desensitization and Reprocessing (EMDR) Consent for Treatment

Name of Client: _____ Client ID#: _____ Date of Birth: ___/___/___

Clinician: _____ Treatment Program: _____ Date of Consent: ___/___/___

Treatment Diagnosis: *DSM-IV-TR* Code: _____ Description: _____

Manifested by: _____

Treatment Goals/Objectives and Rationale for Use of EMDR: (see attached treatment plan/progress notes)

_____

_____

Clinician's Credentials, Qualifications, and Experience Related to Use of EMDR to Treat This
Disorder/Problem: _____

_____

_____

Name of Session Recommended: _____ Target Completion Date: ___/___/___

Client Initials: _____

1. I understand that I have the right to information about what is involved in EMDR therapy. I have been given written information and have read it and discussed it with my therapist, and I understand the potential benefits and hazards of this therapy. Specifically, I understand the following:

   - EMDR may provide me substantial relief for the problem(s) it is used to treat, but it is not always effective and may not provide any benefit. **Client Initials:** _____

   - I may experience strong cravings or urges to use or drink during or after EMDR therapy, and I will call on my therapist or others to help me cope with these cravings if I experience them and cannot be sure I can maintain my abstinence alone. **Client Initials:** _____

   - I may experience intense and disturbing emotions, thoughts, mental images, or dreams during or after EMDR therapy, although these are normal and temporary and will typically pass fairly quickly. I will call on my therapist or others to help me cope with these things if I experience them. **Client Initials:** _____

   - During or after EMDR therapy, I may remember events and experiences I had not previously recalled. I understand that like dreams, these memories may be symbolic rather than literally true. The fact that I remember an event with EMDR does not mean it happened as I remember it. **Client Initials:** _____

2. I understand that I have the right to information about the professional capabilities, specialization, education and training, certification/licensure, and experience of the above named clinician related to his or her using EMDR to treat my disorder/problem. **Client Initials:** _____

3. In signing this consent, I am stating that I understand and agree to the EMDR treatment I will receive. I understand that I may terminate or withdraw from EMDR treatment at any time. **Client Initials:** _____

Client/Guardian's Name: _____ Signature: _____ Date: ___/___/___

Staff's Name: _____ Signature: _____ Date: ___/___/___

Staff's Individual HIPAA Provider Number: _____

Staff's HIPAA Organization Number: _____

Form 3.12 Eye Movement Desensitization and Reprocessing (EMDR) Progress Note

Session #: _____   Present in Session: _____

Length of Session: _____

Problem: _____

Objectives of Session: _____

Data:

1. Starting stimulus type: ___ Eye movement ___ Horizontal ___ Vertical ___ Diagonal
    ___ Tones   ___ Hand taps ___ Combined eye movement/tones

2. Distancing metaphor: _____

3. Cue word for safe/peaceful place visualization: _____

4. Presenting issue/memory: _____

5. Picture: Mental image representative of the issue/memory: _____

6. Negative cognition: Client's negative self-belief in connection with the presenting issue or memory:
    _____

7. Positive cognition: Positive belief re self client seeks to substitute for negative self-belief:
    _____

8. Validity of Cognition (VOC) check: Client's starting rating of positive cognition on VOC
    scale (1–7):_____

9. Emotion/feeling associated with issue/memory: _____

10. Subjective Units of Disturbance (SUD) check: Client's starting rating of the degree of disturbance at
    these emotions or feelings using the SUDs scale (0–10):_____

11. Location: Client's perception of physical locus of the emotion or feeling: _____

12. Desensitization phase: _____ Complete _____ Incomplete _____ Ending VOC _____ Ending SUD

Summary of events during desensitization phase: _____
_____
_____
_____

13. Installation done: _____ Yes _____ No (if incomplete)   Ending VOC _____
    Body scan clear: _____ Yes _____ No

14. Incomplete session closure: _____ Relaxation exercise(s) _____ Discuss w/client
    _____ Reinforcement of progress

15. Closure/debrief: _____ Discuss w/client _____ Renew agreement to use support system
    Additional comments/observations during session: _____

Client/Guardian's Name: _____   Signature: _____   Date: ___/___/___

Staff's Name: _____   Signature: _____   Date: ___/___/___

Staff's Individual HIPAA Provider Number: _____

Staff's HIPAA Organization Number: _____
HCPCS Procedure Code for this treatment session: _____

_____

Form 3.13 Recovery Program Meeting Review/Critique Form

Directions: DO NOT TAKE THIS FORM WITH YOU TO THE MEETING, and please do not write information that would violate anyone's anonymity or confidentiality!

1. Meeting information:

   Group Name: _____

   Program (AA, NA, etc.): ___   Location: _____   Date/Time: _____

   Meeting format: _____ Tag/Open sharing _____ Speaker _____ Book/Step study

   Other (please describe): _____

   ___ All-male or all-female _____ Mixed   Number of people present: _____

2. What was the main topic of the meeting: _____

3. What were your general thoughts and feelings on that topic? _____

   _____

   _____

   _____

4. In what ways could you relate to the experiences and feelings shared by others at this meeting? Were you unable to relate to some people, and if so what was the difference between them and you that made you unable to relate? _____

   _____

   _____

   _____

5. What other thoughts and feelings did this meeting cause you to have? _____

   _____

   _____

   _____

6. How many people at the meeting did you know? _____

7. Please state your level of participation in this meeting? _____

   _____

   _____

   _____

8. What did you gain from this meeting? _____

   _____

   _____

   _____

Chapter 4

Treatment Forms: Program Administration Documentation

This chapter includes forms to assist clinicians and other staff members of substance abuse treatment programs with program administration. These forms are designed to help with correspondence and communication with referral sources, among agency program staff and among others within the community. Forms for use while clients are in treatment and upon termination are also included. The following forms are included in this chapter:

Form 4.1:   Client Encounter Summary Log Sheet

Form 4.2:   Monthly Progress Note/Report

Form 4.3:   Recovery Program Attendance Verification Form

Form 4.4:   Request/Referral for Extended Services

Form 4.5:   Request/Referral for Additional Services

Treatment Forms: Program Administration Documentation

Form 4.1 Client Encounter Summary Log Sheet

Client Name: _____ Client ID#: _____ Program: _____

Date/Time	Time Spent	Intake	Assess	Indiv. Session	Family Session	Group Session	Phone Call	Corre-spond.	Staffing Meeting	Off-site/In-home	Other	Staff Initials

Form 4.2 Monthly Progress Note/Report

Client Name: _____ Client ID#: _____ Program: _____

Treatment Agency: _____ Referral Source: _____

Admission Date: _____/____/____   Projected Discharge Date: ____/____/____

Date of Report: _____/____/____   Reporting Period: ____/____/____ to ____/____/____

Type/Level of Care: _____ Length of Treatment: _____

Program Attendance

_____ # Individual/Family Sessions Attended

_____ # Group Sessions Attended

_____ Satisfactory (Meets program requirements)

_____ Unsatisfactory

Dates of attendance: _____

Dates of excused absences: _____

Dates of unexcused absences: _____

Degree of participation/involvement: ____ Active ____ Minimal ____ Inactive/passive ____ Absent

Recovery Group Attendance

_____ # AA/NA Attended

_____ Other (please specify)

_____ Satisfactory (Meets program requirements)

_____ Unsatisfactory

Dates of attendance: _____

Dates of excused absences: _____

Dates of unexcused absences: _____

Degree of participation/involvement: ____ Active ____ Minimal ____ Inactive/Passive ____ Absent

Compliance with Other Treatment Program Requirements

Maintaining chemical abstinence/sobriety: _____ Yes _____ No _____ Questionable

Abstinence from other compulsive behavior: _____ Yes _____ No _____ Questionable
(if being addressed in treatment)

# of UAs/other tests this period: _____

Any substance relapses? ____ Yes ____ No   Comments: _____

_____

Any other compulsive behavior relapses? ____Yes ____ No   Comments: _____

_____

Working with support program sponsor: ____ Yes ____ No   Comments: _____

_____

Attending support program home group: _____ Yes _____ No   Comments: _____

_____

Other program requirements satisfied: _____ Yes _____ No   Comments: _____

_____

Treatment goals/objectives revised this period? _____ Yes _____ No   If yes, changes made: _____

_____

Overall Progress toward Treatment Goals/Objectives

_____ Excellent _____ Satisfactory _____ Fair _____ Marginal _____ Unsatisfactory

Comments:

_____

_____

_____

_____

_____

_____ Services continued ____ Terminated: Discharge date: _____/_____/_____ Reason: _____

Comments/recommendations (suggested treatment plan revisions, concerns, etc.): _____

_____

_____

_____

_____

_____

_____

_____

Client/Guardian's Name: _____

Signature: _____ Date: _____/_____/_____

Clinician's Name: _____

Signature: _____ Date: _____/_____/_____

Clinician's Individual HIPAA Provider Number: _____

Clinician's HIPAA Organization Number: _____

Form 4.3 Recovery Program Attendance Verification Form

Date	Time From/To	Program	Group Name	Meeting Location	Signature of Chairperson

Form 4.4 Request/Referral for Extended Services

Provider Information	Client Information

Agency Name: _____   Name: _____

Address: _____   DOB: ___/___/___ SSN:_____

Phone: _____ Fax: _____   Address: _____

Contact Person: _____   Phone: H: _____ W: _____

Initial Date of Service: _____/_____/_____

Requesting Service Dates: ___/___/___ through ___/___/___

Primary Diagnosis (DSM-IV-TR code): _____   Description: _____

Secondary Diagnosis: _____   Description: _____

Type(s) of services requested: _____

Number of units/hours utilized: _____   Number of additional units/hrs. requested: _____

Treatment interventions utilized: _____

Substance abuse history: _____

_____

Other mental health history: _____

_____

Presenting symptoms: _____

_____

Current mental status: _____

_____

Current stressors/functional impairments as result of this disorder: _____

_____

Summary of client progress in treatment; current status in treatment: _____

_____

Documentation of client effort/motivation in treatment: _____

_____

Reasons for requesting an extension: _____

_____

Prognosis with explanation: _____

_____

Other services client is receiving for this disorder (include any medications): _____

_____

Revisions to current treatment plan: _____

_____

Discharge criteria and aftercare/relapse prevention plan: _____

_____

Clinician's Name: _____

Signature: _____   Date:_____/_____/_____

Clinician's Individual HIPAA Provider Number: _____

Clinician's HIPAA Organization Number: _____

Form 4.5 Request/Referral for Additional Services

Client Information

Name: _____   Date of Birth: _____

Social Security Number: _____

Address: _____

_____

Phone: _____

E-Mail: _____

Primary Diagnosis: _____

Secondary Diagnosis: _____

The above named client is requesting/being referred by_____

for the following service: _____   Psychiatric Evaluation

_____   Psychological Testing

_____   Medical Physical

_____   Nutritional/Dietician Assessment

_____   Dental Exam

_____   Other (specify): _____

Reason for the request/referral for additional services: _____

_____

Briefly describe how client will benefit and /or how treatment will be impacted by additional service
being completed: _____

_____

_____

Current treatment the client is receiving: _____

Length of time in current treatment: _____

Name of provider and agency: _____

Will client be continuing with current provider? _____ Y _____ N

Name and address of suggested provider of additional service: _____

_____

_____

_____

_____   _____

(Signature of Client)   (Date)

_____   _____

(Name and Title of Clinician Requesting Additional Service)   (Date)

Signature: _____   Date: _____/_____/_____

Clinician's Individual HIPAA Provider Number: _____

Clinician's HIPAA Organization Number: _____

Form 4.6 Request for Drug Screening by External Providers

Client Information

Name: _____

Address: _____

_____

Phone: _____ E-Mail: _____

Requestor Information

Name: _____

Organization: _____

Address: _____

_____

Phone: _____ E-Mail: _____

Individual HIPAA Provider Number: _____

HIPAA Organization Number: _____

Test(s) Requested:

_____ Blood Alcohol Concentration (BAC)

_____ Tetrahydracannabinol (THC) Metabolites

_____ Opioid/Narcotic Metabolites

_____ Amphetamine or Amphetamine-Like Substance Metabolites

_____ Benzodiazepine Metabolites

_____ Hallucinogen Metabolites

_____ Anabolic Steroid Metabolites

_____ Other: _____

Report Tests Results to:

_____ Requestor Identified Above

_____ Other: Name: _____

Organization: _____

Address: _____

_____

_____

Phone: _____

Signature of Client: _____ Date: _____/_____/_____

Signature of Requestor: _____ Date: _____/_____/_____

Form 4.7 Treatment Program Attendance/Completion Record

Client Name: _____   Case/File ID#: _____

Name/Type of Program   Duration   Frequency

_____   _____ Hrs   _____ Sessions

_____   _____ Hrs   _____ Sessions

Group/Individual Session Attendance

Session 1   (____ hours) Date: ____/____/____   Session 2   (____ hours) Date: ____/____/____

Session 3   (____ hours) Date: ____/____/____   Session 4   (____ hours) Date: ____/____/____

Session 5   (____ hours) Date: ____/____/____   Session 6   (____ hours) Date: ____/____/____

Session 7   (____ hours) Date: ____/____/____   Session 8   (____ hours) Date: ____/____/____

Session 9   (____ hours) Date: ____/____/____   Session 10 (____ hours) Date: ____/____/____

Session 11 (____ hours) Date: ____/____/____   Session 12 (____ hours) Date: ____/____/____

Session 13 (____ hours) Date: ____/____/____   Session 14 (____ hours) Date: ____/____/____

Session 15 (____ hours) Date: ____/____/____   Session 16 (____ hours) Date: ____/____/____

Session 17 (____ hours) Date: ____/____/____   Session 18 (____ hours) Date: ____/____/____

Session 19 (____ hours) Date: ____/____/____   Session 20 (____ hours) Date: ____/____/____

Assignments acceptable and completed on time: _____ Yes _____ No

Appropriate participation in treatment: _____ Yes _____ No

Treatment goals met: _____ Yes _____ No

Exit session note (participation/prognosis): _____

_____

_____

Referred to: _____ Aftercare/Further therapy   _____ Recovery group meetings
                 _____ Back to referring authority   _____ Other: _____

Completion certificate issued: _____ Yes: Dated: ____/____/____   _____ No: Reason: _____

_____

_____

_____

Clinician Name/Title: _____   Date: ____/____/____

Signature: _____   Date: ____/____/____

Clinician's Individual HIPAA Provider Number: _____

Clinician's HIPAA Organization Number: _____

CERTIFICATE OF COMPLETION

This is to certify that

_____

has completed all activities and requirements included in the

Program Title

Conducted at

Name of Agency

Having participated in (____ of hours of program) of

Group Therapy and Education

on Chemical Dependence and Related Issues

Date: ____/____/____   Client ID: _____   Staff Signature: _____

Form 4.9 Case Staffing Record

Date of Case Staffing: ____/____/____

Client Name: _____ **Date of Birth:** ___/___/___ **Client #:** _____

Diagnosis:
Axis I   _____

Axis II   _____

Axis III   _____

Axis IV _____

Axis V (GAF): _____ Current _____ Highest past 6 months

Master Treatment Plan Review:

Goals achieved: _____

_____

_____

Changes to treatment plan: _____

_____

_____

Services outlined in treatment plan not being provided and why: _____

_____

_____

Additional services anticipated: _____

_____

_____

Anticipated discharge date: _____

Next case staffing date: _____

Additional comments: _____

_____

_____

_____

_____

_____

Case Manager/Therapist Signature: _____ Date: ____/____/____

Reviewing Psychiatrist/Psychologist/Clinician: _____ Date: ____/____/____

Clinician's Individual HIPAA Provider Number: _____

Clinician's HIPAA Organization Number: _____

Form 4.10 Treatment Termination Warning

Date: _____/_____/_____

Dear _____:

I am writing because I am concerned:

_____ You _____ the following person for whom you are the legal guardian: _____
have/has failed to keep the following treatment appointment(s):

Date(s):   Type of Appointment(s):

____/____/____   _____

____/____/____   _____

____/____/____   _____

Consistent attendance is a necessary condition of treatment. Please contact this agency at (phone no.
_____) to reschedule the appointment(s) missed. If you are unable to attend
consistently, no longer desire services for yourself and/or your family, or wish me to make a referral for
treatment elsewhere, please contact me immediately.

If I do not hear from you by (date ____/____/____), this agency will discharge you from treatment and
close your file. If you authorized disclosure(s) to a referring agency and/or a specific person, they will be
notified that you are no longer in treatment with this agency at this time. If you are discharged from
treatment, you may be required to re-apply for services with our agency should you decide to return at a
later date. Please contact _____ with questions or concerns about
this letter.

Sincerely,

cc:

Form 4.11 Treatment Termination Notification

Date: _____ / _____ / _____

Dear _____:

This letter is being written as notification that _____ you/_____ your child/_____ ,
for whom you are a legal guardian have/has been discharged from the following services at our agency:

_____

_____

_____

The reason for termination from these services is as follows:

_____ Treatment goals were resolved	_____	Seen for assessment/evaluation only
_____ Lack of contact/attendance	_____	Referred elsewhere
_____ Moved out of the area	_____	Noncompliance with program rules
_____ Withdrew against staff advice	_____	Other: _____

The following authorized persons/agencies will also be notified of this termination from services with our agency:

_____   _____

_____   _____

_____   _____

If you wish to appeal this decision, please contact the clinical director of our agency. The contact information is as follows:

Name of Clinical Director: _____

Phone Number/E-Mail: _____

Sincerely,

cc:

Form 4.12 Treatment Discharge Summary

Date of Report: _____/_____/_____

Client Name: _____ Client ID#: _____ Program: _____

Treatment Agency: _____ Referral Source: _____

Program Admission Date: _____/_____/_____   Program Discharge Date: _____/_____/_____

Type/Level of Care: _____ Length of Treatment: _____ Number of Sessions: _____

Initial reason for treatment: _____

Admitting Diagnosis (DSM-IV-TR Codes)

Axis I: _____   Axis II: _____   Axis III: _____   Axis IV: _____   Axis V: _____

_____   _____   _____   _____   _____

_____   _____   _____   _____   _____

Primary diagnosis manifested by: _____

Discharge Diagnosis (DSM-IV-TR Codes)

Axis I: _____   Axis II: _____   Axis III: _____   Axis IV: _____   Axis V: _____

_____   _____   _____   _____   _____

_____   _____   _____   _____   _____

Reason for Discharge

_____ Treatment plan objectives attained   _____ Moved out of area

_____ Closure against staff advice   _____ Client withdrew

_____ Lack of attendance/contact   _____ Client deceased

_____ Client referred elsewhere   _____ Incarceration

_____ Noncompliance with program rules   _____ Other: _____

Services Provided

_____ Individual   _____ Inpatient   _____ Psychoeducational group

_____ Family   _____ In-home   _____ Intensive/outpatient

_____ Intensive group   _____ Other: _____

Problem Resolution

Status	Problem: _____	Problem: _____	Problem: _____
Resolved	_____	_____	_____
Improved	_____	_____	_____
Same	_____	_____	_____
Problem worse	_____	_____	_____
Unable to determine	_____	_____	_____

Discharge Summary (significant findings, status at discharge, recommendations or referrals for further treatment, aftercare plan): _____

_____

_____

Clinician Name/Title: _____ Signature: _____ Date: ____/____/____

Clinician's Individual HIPAA Provider Number: _____

Clinician's HIPAA Organization Number: _____

Supervisor Name/Title: _____ Signature: _____ Date: ____/____/____

Supervisor's Individual HIPAA Provider Number: _____

Supervisor's HIPAA Organization Number: _____

Form 4.13 Request for an Accounting of Disclosures

Individual Information

Name: _____   Date of Birth: _____

Address: _____   Client #/Social Security No.:_____

_____

_____

_____

Address to send disclosure accounting (if different from above): _____

_____

_____

Dates Requested

I would like an accounting of all disclosures for the following time frame:

From: _____   To: _____

Fee

I understand that there is (check one):   ____   No fee for this request.

____   A fee as indicated below and I wish to proceed.

For requests in the same 12-month period, the charge is $_____.

Response Time

I understand that the accounting of disclosures I have requested will be provided to me within _____ days unless I am notified in writing, then an extension of up to 30 days is necessary.

_____   _____

Requestor Signature or Legal Representative   Date of Request

For Agency Use:

Date request received: _____   *Date accounting sent:* _____

Extension requested: ____ Y   ____ N   *Reason for extension:* _____

Date requestor notified: _____   *Request processed by:* _____

Form 4.14 Disclosure Tracking Log

Client Name: _____   Client #/Social Security No.: _____

Date of Request	Name/Address of Requestor	Purpose	Format	PHI Disclosed	Date/Time Disclosed	By
_____	_____	_____	_____	_____	_____	_____
_____	_____	_____	_____	_____	_____	_____
_____	_____	_____	_____	_____	_____	_____
_____	_____	_____	_____	_____	_____	_____
_____	_____	_____	_____	_____	_____	_____
_____	_____	_____	_____	_____	_____	_____
_____	_____	_____	_____	_____	_____	_____
_____	_____	_____	_____	_____	_____	_____
_____	_____	_____	_____	_____	_____	_____
_____	_____	_____	_____	_____	_____	_____
_____	_____	_____	_____	_____	_____	_____
_____	_____	_____	_____	_____	_____	_____
_____	_____	_____	_____	_____	_____	_____
_____	_____	_____	_____	_____	_____	_____
_____	_____	_____	_____	_____	_____	_____
_____	_____	_____	_____	_____	_____	_____
_____	_____	_____	_____	_____	_____	_____
_____	_____	_____	_____	_____	_____	_____
_____	_____	_____	_____	_____	_____	_____
_____	_____	_____	_____	_____	_____	_____
_____	_____	_____	_____	_____	_____	_____
_____	_____	_____	_____	_____	_____	_____
_____	_____	_____	_____	_____	_____	_____
_____	_____	_____	_____	_____	_____	_____
_____	_____	_____	_____	_____	_____	_____
_____	_____	_____	_____	_____	_____	_____

<u>Purpose of Disclosure:</u>

CC = Continuing Care   REF = Referral   EM = DTO/DTS
LEG = Legal Issues   HOSP = Hospitalization
Explain all others

<u>Format:</u>

V = Verbal   F = Facsimile/Fax
W = Written   E = E-mail
Explain all others

Chapter 5

Program Evaluation

Sometimes thought of as synonymous with *utilization review* or *quality assurance*, program evaluation includes these functions but goes beyond them in important ways. For a clinician working in a substance abuse treatment program, measuring both processes and outcomes is important both for refining and improving a program and for being able to demonstrate its effectiveness to your management, referral sources, and regulatory agencies. This chapter provides basic information about process and outcome measurement and outlines considerations you may want to consider in evaluating both domains within your program or treatment facility.

We provide an overview of process evaluation and management, including basic principles and some specific process measurement tools and methods, and we examine ways to use some of the forms in Chapters Three and Four as tools for process measurement.

We move on to outcome measurement, addressing basic principles first, and previewing ways to measure outcomes employing the pre- and posttest materials included in the psychoeducational presentation materials in Chapters Six, Seven, and Eight. Finally, although we do not include any specific outcome measurement instruments in this volume, we offer pointers directing clinicians to existing tests and surveys that have been validated by rigorous experimentation and extensive use, as well as to further reading for those who want to explore this area in more depth. Included at the end of this chapter are sample forms to be used for tracking outcome evaluation findings and a consent form for outcome measurement.

PROCESS EVALUATION

Process evaluation uses specific tools and methods to document, standardize, and optimize treatment processes. In the context of treatment, the purpose of process evaluation and management is to make sure that treatment interventions are being delivered as intended. This is a necessary foundation; our measurements of an intervention's outcomes have no meaning unless we know that the intervention was delivered at the intended rate and with fidelity, or adherence to its intended design.

Much of process evaluation consists of what is often called *utilization review*. The term *quality assurance* is used to describe practices that are process evaluation, outcome evaluation, or both.

Process Description and Improvement

The first step in evaluating and managing any process is understanding and documenting it. In many organizations, people take it for granted that they and others understand the processes of their work, when often they do not.

Process Descriptions Tools and Methods

The first and most basic tool for describing any process from treatment of substance abuse problems to automobile transmission repairs is the *flowchart*. To create or update an accurate and useful flowchart of the various processes, you need to monitor your treatment program from intake to discharge and follow-up. Be sure to do the following:

1. Flowchart the process the way it *actually* happens, not the way it should happen. If your flowchart is a picture of an ideal that differs from reality, it won't help you find and solve problems.

2. Make sure that each part of the flowchart is created by the people who actually do that part of the work. Where the flowchart depicts an interaction between two people or groups, get both of them involved to confirm that it accurately shows how they interact.

The basic symbols used in the flowchart are:

○   A circle shows a starting or ending point in a process.

▭   A rectangle or box shows a step in the process.

◇   A diamond shows an option or decision point.

These symbols are connected by lines to show the sequence of events. A simple example:

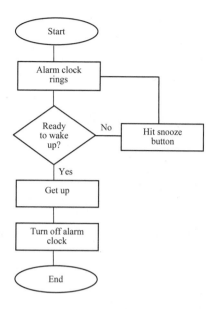

Often when people work together to create a flowchart, their discussion reveals basic misunderstandings that may be the causes of conflicts, situations where referrals or other steps "slip through the cracks," or ways in which people could make processes easier and faster. These insights can then be used to make improvements. This kind of process management greatly facilitates treatment.

Next develop a matrix or table with necessary tasks on one axis and items of information about those tasks on the other axis. It can help identify where people or resources are being over- or underemployed. This is a useful tool for documenting more details about the tasks and decisions identified in a flowchart. A simple example:

Task	By Whom	To Whom	Input	Frequency
Session log	Clinician	Records	Calendar, notes	Weekly
Assessment	Clinician	Records	Intake session, any documentation	As needed
Clinical supervision	Clinical supervisor	Clinicians, records	Supervision session, progress notes, videos	Weekly
Chart audit	Clinicians (audit one another)	Records, clinical supervisor	Client charts, audit checklist	Monthly

A decision tree is a specialized form of flowchart. The *DSM-IV-TR*'s decision trees for differential diagnosis of mental and emotional disorders are good examples. These are useful when the process being studied is a planning process.

Quantitative Process Measurement

Another important part of process evaluation is checking the *throughput* of the process. The main way of doing this is quantitative—measuring the volume of the process in terms such as number of clients served per week, no-show rates, time elapsed from first contact to intake, and so on. Study the process closely enough to understand which quantitative measures are meaningful in evaluating whether the process is working as intended; few things wear out staff and lower morale more than spending time collecting irrelevant data.

Qualitative Process Measurement

This aspect of process evaluation is more concerned with *fidelity,* which is the degree to which the process interventions are being delivered as designed. Often fidelity can be ensured and much useful data for qualitative process measurement collected through careful design of standardized documentation. For example, in the forms included in the first four chapters of this book, there are many examples of required fields that make adherence to intervention requirements automatic and document that adherence.

Feedback and Continuous Process Improvement

A key aspect of process management that is often seen in quality assurance (QA), quality improvement (QI), and other similar functions. When the tools we have been describing are used, the information gained should be provided and explained to the staff who are doing the work, and when processes are changed based on analysis, the results of the changes must be tracked and provided to everyone involved. Quality improvement is an ongoing process carried out in small increments, rather than a process that is done on a large scale and then completed. This is sometimes called the Plan-Do-Study-Act (PDSA), Plan-Do-Check-Act (PDCA), Shewhart, or Deming cycle. The steps are as follows:

Plan: A potential small improvement is identified and a pilot test of small scale and short duration is designed.

Do: The pilot test is carried out, with data being collected on its effects on the process.

Study (or Check): The results of the pilot test are evaluated.

Act: If the improvement worked as intended, act to carry it out on a wider scale, then start a new cycle by planning the next improvement. If it failed, analyze the results, re-fine the improvement, and start a new cycle by identifying another improvement and planning a new pilot test.

OUTCOME EVALUATION

In a treatment setting, *outcome evaluation* is defined as using specifically designed instruments to measure, analyze, and report the results of treatment processes. The basic purpose of outcome measurement is to find out whether, as a result of a treatment process that has been carried out as designed, an observable, measurable behavior change has occurred. This may be an increase in client knowledge, a change toward healthier life functioning, or a change in problematic (in this case, substance abusing) behaviors.

Long-Term and Short-Term Outcome Evaluation

Some outcome measurements are long-term, measuring some variable at the beginning and end of therapy and recording the overall change. Others are short-term or intermediate measures administered during therapy. These short-term measures may track changes using the same indicators as long-term indicators, or they may be subordinate measures that evaluate more narrowly focused indicators, with multiple short-term measures intended to tell whether the work is successfully progressing toward an overall long-term goal. For example, a long term indicator might be success in achieving and maintaining sobriety, as measured at the end of treatment and at six-month intervals thereafter by a report to a drug court. Three monthly (short-term) indicators subordinate to the long-term measure could be the results of drug screenings, documentation of participation in a 12-Step program, and satisfactory participation in treatment program activities.

In substance abuse and mental health treatment, outcomes are often measured using structured surveys or test instruments such as the Minnesota Multiphasic Personality Inventory (MMPI). By asking specific behavioral questions, testing instruments yield information used to assess and quantify changes.

Requirements for Outcome Evaluation

Outcome evaluation is becoming increasingly important in the arena of alcohol and other drug abuse treatment. It may be mandated by legislation, third-party payers, or accrediting bodies; funding is often tied to requirements for objective data about client improvement. Further, with resources continuing to shrink, the demand by providers, government, and payers for high quality in the services provided is driving expectations that this quality be demonstrated by outcome data.

As a result of these trends, you are likely to face requirements that you include outcome evaluation in your program and that you apply the results of that evaluation in the following areas:

- Clinical Practice: Evaluation data showing the results achieved with different treatment approaches will inform your choices of treatment goals, objectives, and interventions, as well as general decisions regarding theoretical orientation and philosophy. Outcome evaluation results can also be useful as integral elements in interventions, such as showing clients the difference in their own levels of functioning as a result of their work in treatment.

- Program Design: Decisions about program design are often assisted, or driven, by outcome evaluation results. For example, a body of outcome research showing that people suffering from paranoid schizophrenia do not benefit from a certain type of group therapy would cause a clinician to steer clear of including such group work in designing a program for a dually diagnosed population containing a large percentage of people with schizophrenia. Many other examples will suggest themselves as you create or modify your program's design.

- Program Administration: Outcome evaluation can drive decisions about program policies. For example, studies showing that many addicts and alcoholics successfully complete treatment and achieve lasting recovery after one or more relapses early in therapy could be crucial in shaping policies on dealing with relapsing clients.

- Marketing: The most effective way to persuade referral sources to send clients to your program is to show them convincing results.

Practical Considerations

You will do outcome evaluation as part of your program; there is no way to avoid it. So the question you must answer is: What will you measure, and how? The following factors are important on a pragmatic level. They will determine what is possible and practical for you to do in this area.

What Is Measured?

A vital consideration in choosing items to measure is validity (i.e., relevance). How closely does the thing we are examining or counting correspond with the life change we seek in the client? The aims of your program, that is, what changes you are trying to bring about, will direct you in your choice of assessment instruments. For substance abuse treatment programs, relevant outcomes can be evaluated in areas including the following:

- Changes in substance abusing behavior, short-term and long-term.
- Changes in symptom frequency.
- Changes in symptom severity.
- Changes in other compulsive behaviors.
- Health-related changes.
- Clinical status as a result of treatment, including changes in other mental health conditions.
- Client satisfaction.
- Changes in marital/intimate relationship status.
- Changes in patterns of interaction with significant others and family members.
- Changes in patterns of interaction with the legal system (DWIs, etc.).
- Changes in work interactions (absenteeism, performance ratings, etc.).
- Level of participation in healthy recreational activities.
- Level of participation in religious/spiritual activities.

How Are Measurements Made?

This is another key question. In the case of a measurement tool, the questions are concerned with *reliability:* does this test, question, or method of observation measure what it is supposed to measure, accurately and consistently? Does it give the same results when different evaluators apply it to the same client or situation? Does a given type of client or group achieve the same results with repeated testing? Some outcome measurements rely on reports from the client or others, while other measures use objective data collected from direct observation or from sources such as schools, the legal system, or objective measures of work performance.

The use of established testing instruments has several advantages, including:

- Availability: They have already been developed and are widely available.

- Validity: It would be impossible for you to replicate the testing that has gone into validating any of the major established research instruments.

- Credibility: Because of their known validity and widespread use, established instruments are respected and their results are more readily accepted than would be the case with a testing instrument you had created yourself.

- Cross-Comparison: Because standardized tests are in use by other treatment programs, if you use them, it is easier to compare your results with those of other clinicians in other programs.

There is also much to be said for developing your own data collection instruments:

- Cost: Some standardized tests are expensive; however, if you develop your own, you don't have to pay anyone a fee to use it.

- Precision: By designing your own instrument, you can zero in on exactly the information you want to obtain, and can customize questions and measures to your community and conditions. It may be difficult to find a standardized test that answers just the questions that are important to you, your regulators, your referral sources, and your clients.

- Speed: Some standardized tests can be scored on site by your own clinical staff, but others must be sent away for scoring, meaning that you may wait weeks for results. If you build your own, you can score it right away if you wish.

There are specific methods for collecting data, including:

- Narrative self-report by client.
- Narrative reports by significant others or family members.
- Questionnaires, surveys, and other paper testing instruments completed by client and/or others.
- Clinical observation.
- Medical examinations and tests.
- Psychiatric evaluation.
- Psychological evaluation and testing.

- Collection of data from the legal system, employers, and other sources.

When Are Measures Used?

Another vital element of designing an outcome evaluation system is obtaining data at the appropriate times to answer the questions your measures are designed to answer. Critical points for data collection are:

- Pretreatment: Studying the client during and after treatment can only yield data about change if a starting baseline has been established. For this reason, you will want to collect starting data on your clients as part of the intake process. To measure learning in a class or psychoeducational group, a pretest is needed to see how much clients know before the information is given to them. Without a pretest, results from posttests can be misleading; a person who knows a subject can sleep through a class and make a perfect score on the posttest, leading the instructor to think he or she has done a fine job when no learning at all took place; or a posttest with every other answer wrong might represent a large improvement.

- During Treatment: Collecting data at various points in the treatment process will give you insight into the relative effectiveness of different components of your treatment program, and may help you justify either including certain elements or making your program of a given duration. Conversely, if you discover that beyond some point in mid-treatment, the improvements your clients experience drop off, you may be able to shorten some part of your program without lessening its effectiveness.

- Completion of Treatment: The only way you can tell whether a client has succeeded in achieving treatment goals is to ask or evaluate and find out. When we have clients submit to drug testing, count the AA meetings they attend, and check their answers on posttests after psychoeducational presentations, we are doing outcomes measurement.

- Posttreatment Follow-Up: Since the ultimate goal of therapy is to restore people to satisfactory functioning on a long-term basis, it is important to measure the durability of the changes achieved. Specifically, in the realm of substance abuse treatment, the first year posttreatment is critical because this is the time when most relapses occur.

Training of Assessors

Avoid choosing a testing methodology that requires training that your staff cannot easily acquire. In many cases, certain measures can only be used with extensive specialized training, as in the case of the many tests that can only be legally administered by a licensed psychologist.

Personnel Turnover

If you anticipate a high rate of turnover, you will not want to rely on a measurement program that requires continuity of individual staff members over long periods.

Time and Resources Available for Testing

Most self-administered standardized tests can be supervised by and scored by office/clinic staff in a relatively short time. However, cost is also a factor; potential users should confirm whether fees are involved before using any standardized measure because some are quite expensive. It is also important to remember legal issues in regard to copyright protection of any standardized instrument.

Planning Questions

Here is a list of 10 questions to guide you in planning your approach to outcome evaluation:

1. What population do you serve? Does the screening instrument chosen or designed fit the individuals you are assessing?

2. Will you use standardized instruments or create your own? Review the benefits and drawbacks of each.

3. What variables do you want to measure? This will influence selection, timing, and frequency of assessments. Do you want to assess only changes in drug consumption patterns, or are you also concerned with related life problems and functional impairments?

4. How much funding do you have for testing, if any? What are the costs in direct fees, required training, and staff time for any instruments you are considering using?

5. Who will administer and score the instruments? What training and qualifications do they have?

6. Will the same staff perform initial baseline testing and follow-ups?

7. What are your intervals of evaluation during treatment and/or posttreatment?

8. What change do you expect to induce in clients through your treatment interventions? How will you know whether that change has occurred?

9. Will you use self-report instruments and/or clinical observation instruments?

10. What will you do with the results? Will you share them with clients, make changes to existing program elements, design new treatment components, use data to explain and justify your program to management and administration, and/or use the data for marketing?

RESOURCES

Government Resources

A wide and useful variety of publications and other resources related to substance abuse treatment outcomes measurement are available from the federal government, many of them at no cost to the user.

The best federal source of information and literature on this topic is the National Clearinghouse for Alcohol and Drug Information (NCADI), P.O. Box 2345, Rockville, Maryland, 20847-2345, (800)729-6686, http://www.health.org. The Clearinghouse will send you a catalog, from which you can select and request materials by mail, telephone, or Internet. By submitting a form included in the catalog, you can be placed on a mailing list to receive updated information as new materials become available in your own areas of special interest.

A related source, whose publications can be obtained through NCADI, is the Substance Abuse and Mental Health Services Administration (SAMHSA). Of particular value and interest to clinicians building treatment programs is the Treatment Improvement Protocol (TIP) series of publications. TIP #14, *Developing State Outcomes Monitoring Systems for Alcohol and Other Drug Abuse Treatment,* bears directly on the subject of this chapter. The other TIP publications also relate to substance abuse research issues and program design, many of them addressing specific client populations and/or treatment issues.

Other Resources

Books that will be useful in establishing this part of your program include those listed below. In addition to these, you may find many more via searches in libraries and on the Internet, and more are published each year.

The Measurement and Management of Clinical Outcomes in Mental Health, by Lyons, Howard, O'Mahoney, and Lish (1997). This includes a chapter on using outcomes in substance abuse treatment. It lists and discusses a number of popular standardized instruments.

Questionnaires and Inventories: Surveying Opinions and Assessing Personality, by Lewis R. Aiken (1997), offers excellent and comprehensive instruction on the art and science of developing assessment instruments.

Rating Scales in Mental Health, 2nd ed., by Martha Sajatovic and Luis F. Ramirez (2003), contains many simple evaluation instruments and guides to their use.

Tracking Mental Health Outcomes, by Donald E. Wiger and Kenneth B. Solberg, (2001), includes a software disk containing several useful process measurement tools.

Forms Included in This Chapter

We are including two forms for your use in integrating outcome evaluation into your substance abuse treatment program:

Form 5.1, the Outcome Measurement Tracking Form: for use with multiple outcome measurement instruments, providing a matrix to track outcomes across several assessment periods and display results from several instruments side by side.

Form 5.2, the Informed Consent for Participation in Outcome Assessment: for use in obtaining and documenting the informed consent of clients for their involvement in your outcome evaluation activities.

Form 5.1 Outcome Measurement Tracking Form

Client Name: _____ Client ID#: _____ Program: _____

Treatment Agency: _____ Program Admission Date: ____/____/____

Reason for Admission: _____ Therapist/Clinician: _____

Admitting Diagnosis (*DSM-IV-TR* Codes):

Axis I: _____ Axis II: _____ Axis III: _____ Axis IV: _____ Axis V: _____

_____ _____ _____ _____ _____

_____ _____ _____ _____ _____

Primary diagnosis manifested by: _____

	Baseline Measurement Date: __/__/__	Treatment Measurement #1 Date: __/__/__	Treatment Measurement #2 Date: __/__/__	Treatment Measurement #3 Date: __/__/__	Treatment Measurement #4 Date: __/__/__
Assessment Tool #1: _____					
Assessment Tool #2: _____					
Assessment Tool #3: _____					
Assessment Tool #4: _____					

Number of Sessions

_____ Individual   _____ Inpatient   _____ Psychoeducational group

_____ Family   _____ In-home   _____ Intensive outpatient

_____ Intensive group   _____ Other: _____

Date Treatment Completed: ___/___/___ Discharge Diagnosis (*DSM-IV-TR* Codes)

Axis I: _____ Axis II: _____ Axis III: _____ Axis IV: _____ Axis V (GAF): _____

_____ _____ _____ _____ _____

_____ _____ _____ _____ _____

Status at Discharge: _____

Additional Comments: _____

_____

Clinician Name/Title: _____ Signature: _____ Date ____/____/____

Clinician's Individual HIPAA Provider Number: _____

Clinician's HIPAA Organization Number: _____

Supervisor Name/Title: _____ Signature: _____ Date ____/____/____

Supervisor's Individual HIPAA Provider Number: _____

Supervisor's HIPAA Organization Number: _____

Form 5.2 Informed Consent for Participation in Outcome Assessment

At different times in the course of your treatment we may be asking you to complete certain question-naires, interviews, tests, or other measurements. These are designed to help us evaluate and improve your treatment plan, progress in treatment, and/or any changes to your plan or referrals to other providers we may need to make. The information we collect will be kept confidential, like the rest of the information in your file at this agency. We will inform you about any decisions or changes that are based on the information we collect in this way. We may also contact you to ask for feedback some time after you have completed treatment with us. This is also to evaluate our program by measuring the long-term benefits we are able to provide our clients. We thank you for your cooperation in this effort.

Please fill out the following form so that we can contact you more easily for this follow-up evaluation and do so in a way that avoids inconveniencing you:

Do you have a phone at home? _____   Phone Number: (____)_____

Do you have a work phone where we may contact you?   Phone Number: (____)_____

Do you have an e-mail address where we may contact you?   E-mail: _____

What is your mailing address? _____

_____

_____

Please indicate the way you would prefer we contact you. Check one or more:

_____ Telephone   _____ E-Mail   _____ Letter   _____ In-person appointment

_____ Other: _____   Do you prefer that we contact you at _____ home or _____ work?

Is it okay to leave a message if you are not available?_____

Is there a time or day that it is more convenient for us to contact you? _____

I understand that all results of outcome measurement completed by _____ will be kept confidential at the level of individual identification and will be shared only with the treatment providers at the above mentioned clinic/agency who are involved with my treatment.

Client Signature: _____   Date: ____/____/____

Chapter 6

Addictive Behaviors: Materials for Use in Psychoeducational Groups

Although chemical dependency treatment programs may be based on a variety of theoretical orientations, nearly all include cognitive or cognitive-behavioral psychoeducational components. The materials included in this chapter consist of detailed lesson plans, participant handouts designed to facilitate note taking, and pre- and posttests to measure effectiveness of the sessions in which the materials are presented. These materials are designed to be used either in conjunction with other teaching aids such as transparencies, videotapes, or audiocassettes, or without additional aids. Drawing on educational learning theory, the use of training aids offers the ideal teaching approach by presenting information in visual (transparencies or other aids), auditory (the presenter's discussion of the material), and tactile/kinesthetic (the act of writing out key points of the information while filling in the blanks on the handouts) formats. These materials are also designed to offer maximum opportunity for group members to participate actively in the teaching/learning process, and are presented from a pragmatic, nontechnical perspective to make it as accessible as possible to a broad range of participants.

The materials included in this chapter address the following six topics regarding addiction and other compulsive behaviors:

Presentation 6.1:   Facilitator's Guide: Psychopharmacology, Part I

Presentation 6.2:   Facilitator's Guide: Psychopharmacology, Part II

Presentation 6.3:   Facilitator's Guide: The Process of Addiction

Presentation 6.4:   Facilitator's Guide: The Process of Relapse

Presentation 6.5:   Facilitator's Guide: Addiction and Contemporary Culture

Presentation 6.6:   Facilitator's Guide: Switching Addictions: Other Compulsive Behaviors

To conserve space and provide more material within the practicable scope of this book, only the facilitator's guide for each presentation is included in the text, but the companion CD-ROM also includes a group member's handout, a pre-/posttest, and a Microsoft PowerPoint slideshow for each presentation, as well as an electronic copy of the facilitator's guide included here.

Presentation 6.1 Facilitator's Guide: Psychopharmacology, Part I

INTRODUCTION

Ask for ideas about the definition of a psychoactive drug. Write responses on a whiteboard or a flip chart. Provide a dictionary definition: A psychoactive drug is one that "influences the mind or mental processes." Invite participants to offer ideas about ways the mind or mental processes could be influenced, write their answers on the board, flip chart, or transparency sheet and briefly discuss them. Possibilities include:

1. Changing of the user's mood
2. Distortion of perceptions of time, space, the user's environment, and the meanings of events
3. Perceptions of things that aren't actually there, with one or more of the senses
4. Actual speeding up or slowing down of thinking processes
5. Changes to the user's judgment and control of impulses
6. Changes to the user's ability to think logically and interpret events accurately
7. Belief in things that aren't true, for example, thinking oneself to be a historical figure
8. Changes to the user's level of motivation to achieve goals

Tell the group that this presentation is about these kinds of changes, about how some kinds of psychoactive drugs affect the human brain, nervous system, and other parts of the body. Ask group members how this subject is important to their lives.

LEARNING GOALS

Explain to the group that they will be evaluated on their accomplishment of the following goals:

1. Upon completion of this presentation, group members will demonstrate understanding of ways psychoactive drugs in the categories of depressants, stimulants, cannabis, and narcotics can affect users by listing, without notes or references, at least six types of psychoactive effects such drugs may have.
2. Upon completion of this presentation, group members will demonstrate with an accuracy rate of at least 80 percent general knowledge of psychoactive drugs in the categories of depressants, stimulants, cannabis, and narcotics and effects common to each category by matching, without notes or references, psychoactive effects with the categories of drugs producing those effects.

QUESTIONS

As the facilitator, you may ask group members to hold their questions until the end or invite them to ask questions during the presentation. If participation is a high priority, we recommend allowing questions at any time; if brevity is more important, it works better to hold questions until the end.

PRETEST/POSTTEST

Pass out the pretest if you choose to use it. You may have the group members fill out and turn in pretests without putting names on them as a general measure of baseline knowledge. Explain that the same test will be given as the posttest at the end of the presentation.

BACKGROUND AND LEAD-IN

Discuss the question: How long have human beings been using psychoactive drugs and what were some of the earliest drugs?

Answer: Since prehistory, people have used drugs. Drugs in use for thousands of years (in other words, since before the modern pharmaceutical industry and synthetic drugs) include:

1. Depressants (alcohol, both fermented and distilled)
2. Stimulants (coca, caffeine, nicotine, sugar, etc.)
3. Cannabis (marijuana, hashish)
4. Narcotics (opium and derivatives)
5. Hallucinogens (psilocybin, peyote, mescaline, ergot)

Discuss the question: What additional types of drugs are now in use (in other words, "modern" drugs)?

Answer: More drugs in each of the categories above, plus benzodiazepines, inhalants, anabolic steroids, and "designer drugs" such as phencyclidine polychloride (PCP), ketamine, gammahydroxybutyrate (GHB), and 3-4 methylenedioxymethamphetamine (MDMA or Ecstasy) that have characteristics of more than one category. Even antihistamines are sometimes considered psychoactive drugs because of some of their effects.

Discuss the question: Why do people use drugs?

Answer: For a variety of reasons, including:

1. *For effect:* The drug's action is pleasant or useful (this includes medical use). It allows people to temporarily feel more pleasure, less pain or discomfort, or both.
2. *For social/popularity reasons:* People use drugs to fit in with their friends, as a shared pleasurable activity, or to show off.
3. *Cultural and religious customs:* Religious practices in many faiths include the ritualized use of psychoactive chemicals; examples range from the communion wine in many Christian services to the use of *ganja* (marijuana) in some Caribbean religious practices (such as those of the Rastafarians) and the use of organic hallucinogens in the spiritual practices of some Native American and other aboriginal peoples.

Discuss the question: These are all good reasons to use drugs, so when and how does drug use become a problem instead of a good thing?

Write down and briefly discuss answers. Offer one answer: Drug use becomes a problem when the drug has harmful effects on a person's life that outweigh the good effects but the person keeps using it anyway. Ask for input and briefly discuss what types of negative effects users might experience.

TYPES OF DRUGS AND THEIR EFFECTS

Depressants

Ask group members to list depressants. Answers include:

1. Barbiturates (Seconal, Nembutal, Amytal, Phenobarbital, etc.)

2. Alcohol

amount of drug, and may include:

Positive Effects	**Negative Effects**
Calming effect: reduced fear, anxiety, anger	Drowsiness
Increased feeling of well-being	Disorientation
Increased confidence	Impaired motor coordination
Sleep-inducing	Impaired judgment and impulse control
Reduced physical pain/discomfort	Blackouts (memory gaps)
	Tremors (shakes) in withdrawal
	Nausea/vomiting with minor overdose (OD)
	Nausea/headache in withdrawal
	Unconsciousness/coma/death with large overdose
	Tolerance and withdrawal with chronic use
	Cross-tolerance with benzodiazepines
	Synergistic (multiplied) effect when mixed with benzodiazepines or other depressants
	Physical and psychological addiction
	Increased risk for cancers, diabetes
	Heart, liver, brain, bowel, other organ damage with heavy/long-term use
	Birth defects

Stimulants

Ask group members to list stimulants. Answers include:

1. Cocaine (including powder cocaine, crack, and basuco, which is incompletely processed cocaine often contaminated with gasoline or other petroleum products)
2. Amphetamines, including methamphetamine ("crystal," "meth," and many other street names)
3. Caffeine
4. Nicotine (also has some calming and antidepressant effects)

Effects of stimulants may last anywhere from 30 minutes to 20 hours, depending on method of use and type and amount of drug, and may include:

Positive Effects	**Negative Effects**
Increased energy, speed, strength	Anxiety, irritability, and paranoia
Increased alertness and concentration	Tremors (shakes)
Increased feeling of well-being	Insomnia
Increased sexual desire	Poor nutrition
Faster reaction time	Headaches
Increased confidence	Impaired judgment and impulse control
Euphoria	Problems with divided attention
Decreased appetite, weight loss	Raised pulse, breathing, temperature, blood pressure
Decreased need for sleep	Hallucinations with OD or prolonged use
Local anesthetic (cocaine and derivatives): medical uses	Convulsions/seizures/stroke with overdose

Vasoconstrictor (shrinks blood vessels): medical uses	Tolerance and withdrawal with chronic use
	Physical and psychological addiction
	Increased tolerance for alcohol, other depressants while using stimulants
	Impaired sexual performance with prolonged use (cocaine)
	Lifelong increased risk for depression/anxiety with chronic use (amphetamines, methamphetamine, cocaine)
	Premature aging of skin due to impaired circulation
	Increased risk for cancer, heart/lung disease (nicotine)
	Birth defects

Cannabis and THC (delta-9-tetrahydracannabinol)

Ask group members to list substances that contain cannabis or THC. Answers include: marijuana, hashish, and hashish oil contain cannabis—each of these substances contains up to 426 separate chemicals, with THC being the main active ingredient—and THC in concentrated form is also a street drug. Effects of these drugs may last anywhere from 2 to 16 hours, depending on method of use and type and amount of drug, and may include:

Positive Effects	Negative Effects
May act either as a stimulant or depressant	Dry mouth, red eyes, decreased body temperature
Calming effect: reduced fear, anxiety, anger	Reduced muscular strength
Treatment for glaucoma: reduces fluid pressure in the eyeball	Weakened immune system
Reduction of physical pain, discomfort, and nausea	Drowsiness
Euphoria	Disorientation
Increased sense of well-being	Dulled senses
Increased confidence	Impaired coordination, time/space perception
	Impaired judgment and impulse control
	Impaired short-term memory
	Impaired concentration, reduced ability to do complex tasks
	Paranoia
	Increased risk of cancers
	Birth defects
	Hormone imbalances with prolonged use
	Damage to lungs, throat with prolonged use
	Psychological addiction with prolonged use

Narcotics/Opiates or Opioids

Ask group members to list opiates or other narcotics. Answers include:

Opium	Codeine	Oxycontin	Vicodin
Morphine	Demerol	Hydrocodone	Darvon

| Heroin | Percodan | Fentanyl | Talwin |
| Methadone | Oxycodone | Dilaudid | |

Effects of narcotics may last anywhere from 4 to 24 hours, depending on method of use and type and amount of drug, and may include:

Positive Effects	**Negative Effects**
Reduction of pain/discomfort	Drowsiness
Euphoria	Disorientation
Increased sense of well-being	Dulled senses
Calming effect: reduced fear, anxiety, anger	Impaired motor coordination
Sleep-inducing	Impaired judgment and impulse control
	Tremors (shakes) in withdrawal
	Nausea, muscle cramps, itching in withdrawal
	Unconsciousness/convulsions/coma/death with OD
	Tolerance and withdrawal with chronic use
	Physical and psychological addiction

CONCLUSION

Review the following key points:

1. Psychoactive drugs are chemicals that have any of these effects:

   - Changing of moods
   - Distortion of perception
   - Perceptions of things that aren't there
   - Speeding up or slowing down
   - Changes to judgment or control of impulses
   - Changes to ability to think logically and interpret events accurately
   - Belief in things that aren't true
   - Changes to levels of motivation to achieve goals

While the method of use and type and amount of the drug used are factors that impact effect, note to clients that there are many other factors, including physical health and personal biology.

2. Since prehistory, people have used drugs, including stimulants, depressants, narcotics, cannabis, and hallucinogens. More recently, new drugs have been discovered in each of these categories, and the additional categories of benzodiazepines, inhalants, steroids, and designer drugs have been added.

3. Reasons people use drugs include for effect, social/popularity reasons, and cultural and religious customs.

4. Drug use becomes a problem when the harmful effects outweigh the benefits.

This presentation has offered information about four categories of drugs—depressants, stimulants, cannabis, and narcotics. The other categories (hallucinogens, inhalants, benzodiazepines, anabolic steroids, and designer or club drugs) will be covered in the next presentation on psychopharmacology.

REVIEW LEARNING GOALS

1. Upon completion of this presentation, group members will demonstrate understanding of ways

psychoactive drugs in the categories of depressants, stimulants, cannabis, and narcotics can affect users by listing, without notes or references, at least six types of psychoactive effects such drugs may have.

2. Upon completion of this presentation, group members will demonstrate with an accuracy rate of at least 80 percent general knowledge of psychoactive drugs in the categories of depressants, stimulants, cannabis, and narcotics and effects common to each category by matching, without notes or references, psychoactive effects with the categories of drugs producing those effects.

QUESTIONS/DISCUSSION BEFORE POSTTEST

ADMINISTER POSTTEST

QUESTIONS/DISCUSSION AFTER POSTTEST

Presentation 6.2 Facilitator's Guide: Psychopharmacology, Part II

INTRODUCTION

Remind the group that this is a continuation of Part I, covering additional categories of drugs not discussed in detail in that presentation. Review the definition of a psychoactive drug as one that "influences the mind or mental processes" in ways including the following:

1. Changing of the user's mood
2. Distortion of perceptions of time, space, the user's environment, and the meanings of events
3. Perceptions of things that aren't actually there, with one or more of the senses
4. Actual speeding up or slowing down of thinking processes
5. Changes to the user's judgment and control of impulses
6. Changes to the user's ability to think logically and interpret events accurately
7. Belief in things that aren't true, for example, thinking oneself to be a historical figure
8. Changes to the user's level of motivation to achieve goals

Review the reasons people use drugs:

1. For effect (to increase pleasure or reduce pain or discomfort)
2. For social reasons
3. For religious or cultural reasons

Review the idea that drug use becomes a problem when the drug has negative effects that outweigh the benefits *but a person keeps using it anyway.* Ask the group to reflect on the first presentation and name ways they can use the information provided.

LEARNING GOALS

Explain to the group that they will be evaluated on their accomplishment of the following goals:

1. Upon completion of this presentation, group members will demonstrate understanding of ways psychoactive drugs in the categories of hallucinogens, benzodiazepines, inhalants, anabolic steroids, and designer drugs can affect users by listing, without notes or references, at least six types of psychoactive effects such drugs may have.
2. Upon completion of this presentation, group members will demonstrate with an accuracy rate of at least 80 percent general knowledge of psychoactive drugs in the categories of hallucinogens, benzodiazepines, inhalants, anabolic steroids, and designer drugs and effects common to each category by matching, without notes or references, psychoactive effects with the categories of drugs producing those effects.

QUESTIONS

As the facilitator, you may ask group members to hold their questions until the end or invite them to ask questions during the presentation. If participation is a high priority, we recommend allowing questions at any time; if brevity is more important, it works better to hold questions until the end.

PRETEST/POSTTEST

Pass out the pretest if you choose to use it. You may have the group members fill out and turn in pretests without putting names on them as a general measure of baseline knowledge. Explain that the same test will be given as the posttest at the end of the presentation.

BACKGROUND AND LEAD-IN

Discuss the question: How did the coming of modern times and the industrial revolution change the reasons and ways people use psychoactive drugs?

Answer: The reasons didn't change much—people still use drugs for effect, because they like the way the drugs make them feel or the things the drugs allow them to do. The old categories and drugs have remained in use:

1. Depressants (alcohol, both fermented and distilled, and now barbiturates and other synthetic depressants)
2. Stimulants (coca, caffeine, nicotine, sugar, etc., with the addition of amphetamines including methamphetamine and other synthetic stimulants)
3. Cannabis (marijuana, hashish, and hash oil)
4. Narcotics (opium and derivatives, with the modern additions of heroin and a wide range of synthetic narcotics including codeine, Demerol, Percodan, and others)
5. Hallucinogens (peyote, mescaline, psilocybin, morning glory seeds, ergot, and a number of synthetics, with lysergic acid diethylamide or LSD being the most widely known)

Some new categories have been added:

6. Inhalants: Drugs used in gas or vapor form
7. Benzodiazepines: Manmade drugs used in psychiatric treatment of anxiety and depression
8. Anabolic steroids: Manmade imitations of natural hormones related to physical growth and development of sexual characteristics for both genders
9. Designer or club drugs: Manmade drugs such as phencyclidine polychloride (PCP), ketamine, gammahydroxybutyrate (GHB), and 3-4 methylenedioxymethamphetamine (MDMA or Ecstasy), which are used illegally for recreational purposes and combine characteristics of more than one of the other drug categories

TYPES OF DRUGS AND THEIR EFFECTS

Hallucinogens (also Called Psychedelics)

Ask group members to list Hallucinogens. Answers include:

1. Natural or organic hallucinogens found in plants, including:
   a. Peyote or mescaline, products of a type of cactus found in northern Mexico
   b. Psilocybin or psylocin, any of three mushrooms also found in Mexico
   c. Morning glory seeds, specifically the species *Rivea corymbosa*, a natural source of LSD
   d. Belladonna alkaloids (atropine, scopolamine, and hyoscyamine), products of the plants jimsonweed, deadly nightshade, henbane, and angel's trumpet
   e. Ergot, a type of fungus that can grow on rye and other grains
   f. Harmine or harmaline, found in a South American vine
   g. Ibogaine, made from a shrub in central and western Africa

h. Fly agaric, a mushroom that grows in forests in Europe, Africa, Asia, and North America

i. Nutmeg, a spice that has hallucinogenic effects but also has harsh side effects

2. Manmade or synthetic hallucinogens, including:

   a. LSD (although it is found in morning glory seeds and is related to the active ingredient in ergot, the man-made version is much more concentrated)

   b. PCP

   c. Ketamine

   d. GHB

   e. MDMA

   f. 2,5-dimethoxy-4-methyl-amphetamine (DOM, also called STP)

   g. 3,4-methylenedioxyamphetamine (MDA)

   h. Dimethyltryptamine (DMT)

   i. Dextromethorphan (found in some cough syrups)

The duration of the effects of hallucinogens may last anywhere from less than an hour to over a day, depending on method of use and type and amount of drug, and may include:

Positive Effects	Negative Effects
Feeling of heightened or expanded awareness	Drowsiness
Hallucinations (if pleasant and desired by user)	Disorientation
	Nausea
	Hallucinations (if unpleasant)
	Distorted perception of time and space
	Panic
	Induced psychosis
	Death with large overdose
	Psychological addiction
	Increased risk for cancers, diabetes
	Birth defects

Inhalants

Ask group members to list inhalants. Answers include:

1. Ether

2. Nitrous oxide (medical, or as aerosol propellant)

3. Amyl and isobutyl nitrite

4. Commercial chemicals (gasoline, paint, glue, etc.)

The duration of the effects of inhalants may last anywhere from less than a minute to one hour, depending on method of use and type and amount of drug, and may include:

Positive Effects	Negative Effects
Euphoria	Lightheadedness
Decreased anxiety	Hallucinations
Anesthetic effect (medical use)	Slurred speech
	Irritability

Nausea/vomiting
Tremors (shakes)
Paranoid delusions
Numbness in extremities
Possible sudden loss of consciousness
Injuries in falls
Damage to brain, liver, heart, lungs, kidneys,
    and peripheral nervous system
Respiratory/heart failure and death

Benzodiazepines

Ask group members to list benzodiazepines. Answers include:

Ativan (lorazapam)
Centrax/Verstran (prazepam)
Dalmane (fluorazepam)
Doral (quazepam)
Halcion (triazolam)

Klonopin (clonazepam)
Librium (chlordiazepoxide)
Paxipam (halazepam)
Prosom (estazolam)
Restoril (temazepam)

Serax (oxazepam)
Tranxene (clorazepate)
Valium (diazepam)
Versed (midazolam)
Xanax (alprazolam)

Effects of benzodiazepines may last anywhere from 30 minutes to a day, depending on method of use and type and amount of drug, and may include:

Positive Effects	Negative Effects
Decreased anxiety	Drowsiness
Induces sleep	Slurred speech
Relaxation before surgical anesthesia	Dizziness
Decreased muscle tension (all medical/	Obesity
psychiatric uses)	Poor muscle tone
	Physical and psychological addiction
	Cross-tolerance for alcohol, other depressants
	Synergistic (multiplied) effect when mixed with
	alcohol or other depressants
	With overdose, unconsciousness and death

Anabolic Steroids

Ask group members to list substances that contain anabolic steroids, or synthetic male sex hormones (make the point that the steroids often used to control swelling or allergic reactions, such as cortisone or prednisone, are corticosteroids and not anabolic steroids, so they don't have the same effects and risks). Answers include:

Anadrol (oxymetholone)
Androstenedione
Deca-Durabolin (nadrolone decanoate)
Dehydroepiandrosterone (DHEA)
Depo-testosterone (testosterone cypionate)

Dianabol (methandrostenolone)
Durabolin (nandrolone phenpropionate)
Equipoise (boldenone undecylenate)
Oxandrin (oxandrolone)
Winstrol (stanozol)

Effects of these drugs are seen in days or weeks and may last a lifetime, depending on method of use and type and amount of drug, and may include:

Positive Effects	Negative Effects
Increased muscle mass	Hormone imbalances
Reduced body fat	Reduced sperm production (men)
Improved athletic performance	Shrinking of the testicles (men)
Euphoria	Baldness
Increased energy	Growth of breasts (men)
Sexual arousal	Shrinking of breasts (women)
	Deepening of voice
	Growth of clitoris (women)
	Growth of body hair plus baldness (women)
	End of bone growth in adolescents
	Heart attack/stroke
	Liver tumors
	Hepatitis and internal bleeding in liver
	Acne and skin cysts
	Infections at injection sites
	Irritability and increased aggression
	Mood swings
	Distractibility, forgetfulness, confusion
	In withdrawal: fatigue, restlessness, loss of appetite, reduced sex drive, depression, anxiety, cravings for more, for up to a year

Designer or Club Drugs

Ask group members to list designer or club drugs. Answers include:

Phencyclidine polychloride (PCP)

Ketamine

Gammahydroxybutyrate (GHB)

3-4 methylenedioxymethamphetamine (MDMA or Ecstasy)

Effects of designer or club drugs may last anywhere from 4 to 48 hours, depending on method of use and type and amount of drug, and may include:

Positive Effects	Negative Effects
Euphoria	Anxiety, emotional outbursts
Decreased sensitivity to pain	Distorted perceptions of time and space
	Hallucinations
	Hostility and violence
	Impaired motor coordination
	Slurred speech
	Tremors (shakes)
	Muscle weakness
	Numbness
	Increased blood pressure
	Rigid muscles
	Vomiting, drooling

Seizures
Muscle damage
Heart attack or stroke
Kidney damage
Brain damage
Death due to extreme drop in blood pressure
Dangerous behavior resulting in accidental death
Induced psychosis
Paranoia
Severe depression
Coma
Amnesia after drug wears off
Psychological addiction

CONCLUSION

Review the following key points:

1. Psychoactive drugs are chemicals that have any of these effects:
   • Changing of moods
   • Distortion of perception
   • Perceptions of things that aren't there
   • Speeding up or slowing down
   • Changes to judgment or control of impulses
   • Changes to ability to think logically and interpret events accurately
   • Belief in things that aren't true
   • Changes to levels of motivation to achieve goals

While the method of use and type and amount of the drug used are factors that impact effect, note to clients that there are many other factors, including physical health and personal biology.

2. Since prehistory, people have used drugs, including stimulants, depressants, narcotics, cannabis, and hallucinogens. More recently, new drugs have been discovered in each of these categories, and the additional categories of benzodiazepines, inhalants, steroids, and designer drugs have been added.

3. Reasons people use drugs include for effect, social/popularity reasons, and cultural and religious customs.

4. Drug use becomes a problem when the harmful effects outweigh the benefits.

This presentation has offered information about four categories of drugs: hallucinogens, inhalants, benzodiazepines, anabolic steroids, and designer drugs. The other categories (depressants, stimulants, cannabis, and narcotics) were covered in Part I.

REVIEW LEARNING GOALS

1. Upon completion of this presentation, group members will demonstrate understanding of ways psychoactive drugs in the categories of hallucinogens, benzodiazepines, inhalants, anabolic steroids, and designer drugs can affect users by listing, without notes or references, at least six types of psychoactive effects such drugs may have.

2. Upon completion of this presentation, group members will demonstrate with an accuracy rate of at least 80 percent general knowledge of psychoactive drugs in the categories of hallucinogens, benzodiazepines, inhalants, anabolic steroids, and designer drugs and effects common to each category by matching, without notes or references, psychoactive effects with the categories of drugs producing those effects.

QUESTIONS/DISCUSSION BEFORE POSTTEST

ADMINISTER POSTTEST

QUESTIONS/DISCUSSION AFTER POSTTEST

INTRODUCTION

Point out to the group that more than half the adult population of the United States drinks alcohol, and many use other drugs as well. But most of these people never become chemically dependent, what is commonly called being alcoholic or addicted. Ask the question: *What causes some people to get addicted?* Write group members' answers on a board or flip chart and facilitate a short discussion.

Point out that everyone in this group either has been diagnosed as chemically dependent, is in an important relationship with someone who is chemically dependent, or is at high risk of becoming chemically dependent based on family history, so this is a personal concern for each member. Note that some members may agree with the diagnosis they've been given and others may not, but either way, because they have been given this label they have more reason than most people to be concerned with what it means to be addicted.

Also, addiction and alcoholism run in families. Group members have reason to learn as much as they can about this to teach their children and other family members and help them as soon as possible if they start to show early signs of becoming addicted to alcohol or other drugs.

LEARNING GOALS

Explain to the group that they will be evaluated on their accomplishment of the following goals:

1. Upon completion of this presentation, group members will demonstrate understanding of the physical and psychological processes of addiction by defining, without notes or references, the terms *addiction, alcoholism,* and *chemical dependence.*

2. Upon completion of this presentation, group members will demonstrate understanding of the physical and psychological processes of addiction by listing, without notes or references, phases of at least one model of addiction and at least two typical events or experiences in each phase.

QUESTIONS

As the facilitator, you may ask group members to hold their questions until the end or invite them to ask questions during the presentation. If participation is a high priority, we recommend allowing questions at any time; if brevity is more important, it works better to hold questions until the end.

PRETEST/POSTTEST

Pass out the pretest if you choose to use it. You may have the group members fill out and turn in pretests without putting names on them as a general measure of baseline knowledge. Explain that the same test will be given as the posttest at the end of the presentation.

BACKGROUND AND LEAD-IN

Discuss the question: What is addiction or alcoholism? Ask group members to name or describe what comes to mind for them when they hear the words *addict* and *alcoholic*; write their answers on the board, flip chart, or transparency sheet, then lead a short discussion (optional, based on time). Then give these definitions:

1. *Addiction* is the same thing as *chemical dependence*: one definition will do for both. Doctors and counselors use the description in the *Diagnostic and Statistical Manual of Mental Disorders, 4th edition, Text Revision (DSM-IV-TR),* which says that a person is addicted to a chemical if he or she has three or more of the following behavior patterns in his or her life over a period of at least a year.

2. *Tolerance*: Need to drink/use more to get same effect, or diminished effect with same amount.

3. *Withdrawal*: Physical/emotional withdrawal symptoms, or drinking/using more to relieve or avoid withdrawal symptoms.

4. *Loss of control*: Drinking/using more, or for longer, than intended.

5. *Attempts to control*: Persistent desire or efforts to cut down or control drinking/use of the substance, including making rules for self about when, where, what to drink/use, and so on.

6. *Time spent on use*: Spending a great deal of time getting the substance, drinking/using it, or recovering from drinking/use.

7. *Sacrifices made for use*: Giving up or reducing social, work, or recreational activities that are important to the person because of conflicts with drinking/using.

8. *Use despite known suffering*: Continuing to drink/use despite knowing one has a physical or psychological problem that is caused or made worse by drinking/using.

9. *Alcoholism* is more specific and means addiction to a specific drug, namely alcohol.

Point out that a person is chemically dependent, addicted, or alcoholic when he or she has at least three of these patterns in his or her life. Chemical dependence is very destructive to a person's health, family, work, social life, finances, and legal status. But many addicts and alcoholics are hard-working, intelligent, and successful (for a while); this is known as being a "functional" alcoholic or addict. The popular image of the addict or alcoholic as homeless or otherwise down-and-out applies only to some.

Ask for group members' thoughts on this. Does this change their feelings about the words addict and alcoholic? Ask for opinions about how information on phases and symptoms of addiction would be useful to a functional addict or alcoholic. Then give this answer: If a person is still at the functional stage, knowing the phases and being able to see the process in action may save him or her from having to go through a lot of suffering before seeing the need to take drastic action to change these patterns.

MODELS AND PHASES OF ADDICTION

Jellinek's Model

Dr. E. M. Jellinek was a pioneer in getting chemical dependence recognized as a disease. Before his work, which was mainly during the 1950s, many people believed dependence was a matter of being weak-willed or being morally defective. Jellinek described chemical dependence as having four phases:

1. *Contact phase:* During this phase, a person has his or her first contact with alcohol or another drug, begins drinking or using, and becomes psychologically dependent. This means that there are no physical withdrawal symptoms if the person doesn't drink or use, but he or she feels the need to drink or use to deal with life. The contact phase may last many years.

2. *Prodromal phase:* In the next phase, tolerance starts to increase. It takes more of the drug to get the same effect. It is often during the prodromal phase that people start experiencing blackouts (if their drug is alcohol); begin to hide from others the amount they're drinking or using; begin drinking/using faster or strictly for the effect; begin avoiding talking about their drinking/use with others; and experience their first loss of control and physical withdrawal.

3. *Crucial phase:* In the third phase, loss of control progresses, so that drinkers or users can't be sure how much they will drink or use once they get started. Alcoholics and addicts in this stage often quit for a while to prove they aren't really dependent, but return to uncontrolled drinking or using when they try to go back to moderate use. They start trying other ways to control their drinking or using,

and to escape the consequences. Addicts or alcoholics in the crucial stage start experiencing more physical and psychological damage because of drinking or using. Other people will notice that their health and personalities are going downhill. Their lives are more and more disrupted and full of conflict as the crucial stage progresses. Prolonged periods of use start—benders for alcoholics, several-day runs for methamphetamine users, and so on.

4. *Chronic phase*: This is the final stage. In the chronic stage, life falls apart, if it hasn't already. This is the stage where people may drop out of their families and social situations, become unemployed, become homeless, be hospitalized due to the effects of drinking/using, and have frequent encounters with the law. This is the stage where some people die and others hit bottom and decide to do whatever it takes to change.

Nonphysiological Model

This model can apply to either substance abuse or other addictive behavior patterns. It has the following four phases:

1. *Contact phase*: As in Jellinek's stages, this is the stage where a person first experiences the drug or behavior and finds that he or she likes it—it either gives him or her pleasure or reduces unpleasant feelings.

2. *Serendipitous phase*: Serendipity means finding something good that you weren't expecting. In this phase, people discover that using the drug or engaging in the behavior helps them deal with situations they had problems with before. For example, a shy person discovers that a drink makes it easier to talk to another person; a depressed person finds that he or she feels less depressed after eating a big meal, or after doing something dangerous.

3. *Instrumental phase*: People begin to deliberately use the drug or behavior for this effect, to cope with difficult situations. In this stage, the use of the drug or behavior becomes a routine and a deliberate coping tool.

4. *Dependent phase*: People come to feel that they can't cope with life without the drug or behavior. They experience loss of control, followed by unpleasant consequences for themselves and others, along with regrets, guilt, and promises not to "do it again." At the same time, they feel trapped because they believe they can't get along without the drug or behavior, and may even feel by this time that it is a part of their basic nature and can't be changed. For this reason, people continue using alcohol or other drugs or engaging in other compulsive patterns in spite of more and more painful results. Nondrug-using behaviors that can fit this pattern may include overeating; bingeing and purging; dieting, with or without physical exercise; physical exercise alone; gambling; spending money; religion; outbursts of rage and violence; sexual acting out; workaholism; and hobbies such as surfing the Internet.

CONCLUSION

Review the following key points:

1. The process of addiction is an important subject for the members of the group because of concerns they may have for themselves and for others, especially family members.

2. The *DSM-IV-TR* definition of chemical dependence includes seven symptoms, and says that if three or more are patterns in a person's life for a year or more, that person is addicted to the substance involved. The words *addiction* and *chemical dependence* mean the same thing, and alcoholism means addiction to alcohol. The symptoms are:
   - Tolerance
   - Withdrawal

- Loss of control
- Attempts to control
- Time spent on use
- Sacrifices made for use
- Use despite known suffering

3. The Jellinek Model of addiction has four phases:
   - Contact phase
   - Prodromal phase
   - Crucial phase
   - Chronic phase

4. The nonphysiological model of addiction also has four phases:
   - Contact phase
   - Serendipitous phase
   - Instrumental phase
   - Dependent phase

REVIEW LEARNING GOALS

1. Upon completion of this presentation, group members will demonstrate understanding of the physical and psychological processes of addiction by defining, without notes or references, the terms *addiction, alcoholism,* and *chemical dependence.*
2. Upon completion of this presentation, group members will demonstrate understanding of the physical and psychological processes of addiction by listing, without notes or references, phases of at least one model of addiction and at least two typical events or experiences in each phase.

QUESTIONS/DISCUSSION BEFORE POSTTEST

ADMINISTER POSTTEST

QUESTIONS/DISCUSSION AFTER POSTTEST

Presentation 6.4 Facilitator's Guide:
The Process of Relapse

INTRODUCTION

Ask the group members why they think a presentation on the process of relapse is important. Record their answers on a board or flip chart and facilitate a brief discussion. Ask how many have tried to stop drinking, using, or engaging in other addictive behaviors and found that they could quit but couldn't maintain abstinence, and ask about the possible impact of relapse of a person's health, freedom, work and finances, relationships, and mental and emotional state. Ask how group members' past experiences might have been different if they had been able to see a relapse coming and take action to avoid it.

Explain that this presentation will define relapse, map its progression, discuss types of relapse, and examine early warning signs of relapse. Other presentations will teach the group to anticipate situations and events that might trigger relapse and develop a plan to avoid or cope with them.

LEARNING GOALS

Explain to the group that they will be evaluated on their accomplishment of the following goals:

1. Upon completion of this presentation, group members will identify, without notes or references, three types of relapse.
2. Upon completion of this presentation, group members will identify, without notes or references, at least six early warning signs of relapse in several areas of a person's life.

QUESTIONS

As the facilitator, you may ask group members to hold their questions until the end or invite them to ask questions during the presentation. If participation is a high priority, we recommend allowing questions at any time; if brevity is more important, it works better to hold questions until the end.

PRETEST/POSTTEST

Pass out the pretest if you choose to use it. You may have the group members fill out and turn in pretests without putting names on them as a general measure of baseline knowledge. Explain that the same test will be given as the posttest at the end of the presentation.

BACKGROUND AND LEAD-IN

Ask group members to define relapse and write their answers on the board. Compare them with a dictionary definition of relapse: *To slip or fall back into a former condition, especially after improvement or seeming improvement; specifically (a) to fall back into illness after recovery or seeming recovery; (b) to fall back into bad habits, wrongdoing, error, etc.; to backslide.* In other words, to relapse is to get sick again. In the case of the recovering addict or alcoholic, this means returning to most or all aspects of an addictive lifestyle, not only to using drugs, including alcohol. *Note:* It may be helpful to compare addiction to other illnesses and diseases that result in people getting sick again if care is not taken (e.g., diabetes).

Ask the question: Is there more than one type of relapse into substance abuse?

Answer: Yes, and they are:

1. *Therapeutic relapse:* A relapse that scares the person so much, or leads to enough insight, that he or she returns to abstinence and becomes more serious and motivated about staying in recovery.
2. *Pathological relapse:* A relapse that leads to a lasting return to addictive behavior—the person returns to out-of-control substance use.
3. *Fatal relapse*: A relapse that results in death by substance-induced accident, suicide, or overdose, or other results of substance abuse.

PROCESS OF RELAPSE AND EARLY WARNING SIGNS: WHERE DOES RELAPSE START?

Discuss the idea that the drug use or drink is the completion of the relapse process, not its start. Relapse is the process of returning to an addictive lifestyle. Just as recovery involves changing not only the substance use but other habits, relationships, and patterns of thoughts and feelings, relapse is a change in all these areas back to their addictive versions. Usually, other changes take place well before the return to actually drinking or using a drug. Those changes can be identified by the recovering person or by others who know what to look for, and used as early warning signs. If group members have not identified this as an important use for the information in this presentation, offer it to them at this time.

Encourage group members to recall past relapses (their own or those of other people) and to compare the following early warning signs with what occurred prior to the actual return to drinking or using. The relapse process takes place in several areas of a person's life:

1. *Thoughts and attitudes:* Several changes in mental state can be part of relapse:
    Increasing denial, minimization, or exaggeration of problems
    Becoming rigid or obsessive about recovery, or avoiding talking or thinking about it
    Unrealistic expectations of situations, oneself, and others
    Becoming apathetic and indifferent
    Justifying or making excuses for past using/drinking
    Nostalgia about using/drinking—the "good old days" effect
    Thinking about alcohol or another drug more and more of the time

2. *Feelings and moods:* Some changes that mean the risk of relapse in progress is high:
    Increased depression, guilt, self-pity, regrets
    Increased anger at oneself or others, general hostility and irritability—"attitude problem"
    Increased boredom
    Increased euphoria—"pink cloud" effect, not being realistic about challenges or problems
    Increased loneliness
    Loss of self-confidence or a false air of superiority and arrogance

3. *Behavior changes:* The most visible outward signs of a relapse in progress:
    Quitting or reducing recovery activities: reducing or giving up meeting attendance and so on
    Increasing self-isolation
    Returning to old using activities, places, and people
    Growing dishonesty and secretiveness
    Growing inconsistency, undependability
    Increased complaining

Creating crises—playing the "drama junkie"

Rejecting help/concern from friends

Eating and sleeping patterns becoming irregular again

Increasing impulsivity

CONCLUSION

Review the following key points:

1. Definition of *relapse:* Getting sick again.
2. In the progression of relapse, the return to using or drinking is the completion of the relapse process, not its start.
3. There are many early warning signs that indicate that a relapse is in process. They occur in the areas of thoughts, emotions, and behaviors.
4. There are three types of relapse: therapeutic, pathological, and fatal.
5. Your own and other people's past experiences of relapse are worth evaluating to spot warning signs and triggers and prevent future relapses.

REVIEW LEARNING GOALS

1. Upon completion of this presentation, group members will identify, without notes or references, three types of relapse.
2. Upon completion of this presentation, group members will identify, without notes or references, at least six early warning signs of relapse in several areas of a person's life.

QUESTIONS/DISCUSSION BEFORE POSTTEST

ADMINISTER POSTTEST

QUESTIONS/DISCUSSION AFTER POSTTEST

Presentation 6.5 Facilitator's Guide:
Addiction and Contemporary Culture

INTRODUCTION

Discuss the question: Are we the products of our heredity, or of our culture, or both, and how do both play a role in shaping our personalities, our beliefs, and our habits? Write group members' responses on a board or flip chart and facilitate a brief discussion, then provide a definition of *culture* from a dictionary: "*the concepts, habits, skills, art, instruments, institutions, etc. of a given people in a given period; civilization.*"

The purpose of this presentation is to guide group members in looking at how cultural influences may also have influenced their views about drinking and using drugs. The aim is not to blame society, but to help each person see where he or she got some basic ideas and beliefs that may be interfering with recovery and replace them with more functional beliefs.

LEARNING GOALS

Explain to the group that they will be evaluated on their accomplishment of the following goals:

1. Upon completion of this presentation, group members will demonstrate understanding of ways culture and substance abuse can be related by listing, without notes or references, at least four examples of ways contemporary culture influences people toward using alcohol or other drugs.
2. Upon completion of this presentation, group members will demonstrate understanding of ways culture and substance abuse can be related by listing, without notes or references, at least four general attitudes or lifestyle values associated with an addictive lifestyle and give one example of how each is encouraged by some aspect of contemporary culture.

QUESTIONS

As the facilitator, you may ask group members to hold their questions until the end or invite them to ask questions during the presentation. If participation is a high priority, we recommend allowing questions at any time; if brevity is more important, it works better to hold questions until the end.

PRETEST/POSTTEST

Pass out the pretest if you choose to use it. You may have the group members fill out and turn in pretests without putting names on them as a general measure of baseline knowledge. Explain that the same test will be given as the posttest at the end of the presentation.

BACKGROUND AND LEAD-IN

Ask the question: What parts of contemporary culture might affect people's behavior with alcohol or other drugs? Write group members' responses on the board or a flip chart and discuss briefly.

Some parts of contemporary culture that might affect people's behavior with alcohol and other drugs include:

1. Views about what is considered normal or acceptable drinking and drug use
2. Mainstream beliefs about what is right and wrong

3. Common attitudes about what things are most important in life
4. Widely held spiritual and religious beliefs
5. Role modeling in popular entertainment
6. Marketing of alcohol and tobacco products
7. Attitudes about what it means to be a man or a woman
8. Traditions about how to celebrate happy or important occasions and how to cope with pain, stress, and hardships

Popular Entertainment

Consider role modeling in popular entertainment as an example and ask the group to describe what behaviors and attitudes related to use of alcohol and other drugs are shown as good or acceptable in movies, TV shows, popular music, and other forms of entertainment.

Point out that these forms of entertainment often encourage use of substances in the following ways, and ask the group for examples of each:

• Many movies and TV programs show appealing and good-looking people drinking, smoking, or using other drugs, often showing substance use as a sign that a character is tough (if a man) or sophisticated (either sex.)

• Drinking and drug use are sometimes glamorized as part of a rebellious, outlaw, or gangster lifestyle.

• Being drunk or high is shown as a funny situation.

• The negative parts of an alcoholic or addicted life are ignored or downplayed; we are seldom shown people having to deal with hangovers (except in comical ways), serious injuries from accidents or fights, other health problems, legal trouble, the financial fallout, and so on.

• Ask the group for more examples.

Marketing of Alcohol and Tobacco

Most of us are exposed to advertising and other forms of marketing of these substances every day, and this also affects our attitudes and behavior. (If it didn't affect people's behavior and increase use of their products, these advertisers wouldn't spend billions of dollars every year on advertising.)

Commercials often show other people being attracted to substance-using behavior, as in commercials in which beautiful women are fascinated by the man who is drinking the brand of beer or liquor being advertised.

Marketing of alcohol and tobacco products is often aimed at a very young audience—young characters are shown in ads, activities are those that appeal to the young, the ads are placed where they target a young audience, and themes are youth-oriented (Joe Camel, etc.)

Advertisers use humor to sell products, including alcohol and tobacco companies, with an example being the beer commercials during the Super Bowl every year.

The physical placement of both advertisements and the products in stores is aimed at increasing our use of alcohol and tobacco. They're often placed in the "impulse buy" area in stores where customers are standing in line to check out, and the sheer number of ads is amazing. (Ask group members to count the advertisements for alcohol and tobacco products on the outside walls, windows, and doors of any convenience store and report back to the group at a later session.)

Ask the group for more examples.

Family and Cultural Traditions

Alcoholism and addiction in parents and other role models increases the risk of the same problems repeating themselves in the lives of those raised in alcoholic or addicted homes. Examples:

• People who grow up in families with a lot of substance abuse often miss out on learning many life skills such as good communication, problem solving, healthy ways to handle anger, financial management, and so on. Lack of these skills raises day-to-day stress levels and the likelihood of self-medicating.

- In many families and cultures it is traditional to use alcohol or other drugs to celebrate special occasions, and to use alcohol in particular as a rite of passage to adulthood.
- Likewise, many people inherit the custom of using alcohol or other drugs to cope with emotionally painful situations.
- Some families have a pattern of multigenerational involvement in gangs that engage in drug-related crime.
- Ask the group for more examples.

Addictive Lifestyle Attitudes Promoted by Contemporary Culture

Our society also promotes other attitudes that are part of an addictive lifestyle and way of thinking, even if they aren't focused directly on use of alcohol or other drugs. Examples:

- *Instant gratification:* Our culture encourages the idea that we should be able to have what we want when we want it, whether by using a credit card to buy a fast food meal or by taking a pill to get into a happy mood.
- *Feeling good:* Our society doesn't do a good job of teaching us how to face pain, accept it, and deal with it. Instead we focus on feeling good. Nothing is wrong with wanting to feel good, but if we believe we *need* to feel good, so much so that we'll choose feeling good now at the price of feeling worse later, we have a problem.
- *Self-centeredness:* In many ways, mainstream society teaches people to be self-centered and inconsiderate of others, from the behavior of corporate executives to the actions of the "heroes" of many movies, TV shows, and music videos.
- *Impulsivity:* Compare the "Just do it" motto that a lot of advertising encourages to the "think the drink or drug through" approach we often hear in recovery programs, and judge whether mainstream society promotes an addictive or sober way of making decisions.
- *Low self-esteem and shame:* Much advertising aims to convince us that something is wrong with us but we can fix it by buying whatever the advertiser is selling, from deodorant to clothes. Compare this with the feeling that many alcoholics and addicts have that something is wrong with them, and the temporary relief they get from that feeling when they take a drink or drug.
- *Emotional isolation:* Alcoholics and addicts are unable to maintain close and healthy relationships with other people, because of the dishonesty, sneakiness, selfishness, and manipulation that are part of the disease of addiction. Our society also encourages us to put up fronts and try to impress and manipulate others rather than being honest and open.
- Ask the group for more examples.

CONCLUSION

Review the following key points:

1. Contemporary society has a strong influence on the way we think about many things including our use of alcohol and other drugs, and in many ways substance abuse is considered normal and acceptable behavior in our society.
2. Popular entertainment promotes the use of alcohol, tobacco, and other drugs in several ways.
3. Marketing of alcohol and tobacco products is widespread and effective.
4. Society also teaches other attitudes that are part of an addictive lifestyle and way of thinking, even when they don't directly involve using alcohol or other drugs.

REVIEW LEARNING GOALS

1. Upon completion of this presentation, group members will demonstrate understanding of ways culture and substance abuse can be related by listing, without notes or references, at least four examples of ways contemporary culture influences people toward using alcohol or other drugs.

2. Upon completion of this presentation, group members will demonstrate understanding of ways culture and substance abuse can be related by listing, without notes or references, at least four general attitudes or lifestyle values associated with an addictive lifestyle and give one example of how each is encouraged by some aspect of contemporary culture.

QUESTIONS/DISCUSSION BEFORE POSTTEST

ADMINISTER POSTTEST

QUESTIONS/DISCUSSION AFTER POSTTEST

INTRODUCTION

Discuss the question: What does it mean to be addicted? Write group members' answers on a board or flipchart, and facilitate a brief discussion. Then present this definition, an alternative to the *DSM-IV-TR* definition in an earlier presentation: *People are addicted when they continue doing things that solve problems for them for a short time but cause them more unhappiness and trouble in the long run, because they believe they can't cope with the short-term problems any other way.* For example, an alcoholic may drink because it solves problems (cravings, withdrawal symptoms, and emotional pain) for a short time, even though the problems are the result of drinking and will be worse when the drinks wear off, and the alcoholic keeps drinking because he or she doesn't know other ways to cope with those problems.

Make the point that people can get addicted to anything that makes them feel better quickly but causes them to feel worse in the long run, and that there are many activities other than drinking or using drugs that can have these effects. Explain that the purpose of this presentation is to help the members of the group understand the risk of switching addictions and avoid getting hooked on nondrug activities that can be just as destructive as their old drinking or drug use.

LEARNING GOALS

Explain to the group that they will be evaluated on their accomplishment of the following goals:

1. Upon completion of this presentation, group members will demonstrate understanding of ways culture and substance abuse can be related by listing, without notes or references, at least six examples of nondrug-using compulsive or addictive behaviors ways that can lure newly abstinent alcoholics and drug addicts into continuing addictive behavior patterns by switching to nonchemical addictions.

2. Upon completion of this presentation, group members will demonstrate understanding of the effects of nondrug-using compulsive behaviors by listing, without notes or references, at least four ways that nonchemical addictions can be destructive to the lives of addicts.

3. Upon completion of this presentation, group members will demonstrate understanding of resources available for recovery from nonchemical addictions by listing, without notes or references, at least four recovery programs or other resources that exist to help people overcome compulsive behaviors that do not involve use of alcohol or other drugs.

QUESTIONS

As the facilitator, you may ask group members to hold their questions until the end or invite them to ask questions during the presentation. If participation is a high priority, we recommend allowing questions at any time; if brevity is more important, it works better to hold questions until the end.

PRETEST/POSTTEST

Pass out the pretest if you choose to use it. You may have the group members fill out and turn in pretests without putting names on them as a general measure of baseline knowledge. Explain that the same test will be given as the posttest at the end of the presentation.

BACKGROUND AND LEAD-IN

Discuss the question: To what compulsive behaviors do people get addicted, even when the behaviors don't involve using alcohol or any other drug?

Answers include:

1. Gambling
2. Compulsive spending, especially with credit cards
3. High-risk or inappropriate sexual activity
4. Involvement in emotionally destructive relationships
5. Workaholism
6. Compulsive overeating
7. Anorexia or bulimia (avoiding eating, or overeating and then vomiting)
8. Compulsive exercising
9. Over-involvement in hobbies (Internet, collections, sports, arts and crafts, or other)
10. Ask the group for suggestions

IMPACTS OF COMPULSIVE BEHAVIORS

These activities can all destroy people's relationships and lives. Provide examples of ways these activities might meet each of the *DSM-IV-TR* criteria for addiction, and ask the group to think of at least three more for each, related to different compulsive behaviors.

1. *Increased tolerance:* For thrill-seeking or comfort-seeking behaviors, it may take more extreme forms of the behavior or doing more of it to have the same emotional effect. For example, a gambling addict might need to risk more money to get the same thrill.
2. *Withdrawal:* This would be the feeling of needing to practice the behavior to feel okay. An example might be a person with an eating disorder who couldn't get to sleep without going on an eating binge first.
3. *Loss of control:* Engaging in the behavior more, or for longer, than planned. For example, a person who stayed late at work planning to put in two extra hours on a project and ended up staying until midnight would be showing loss of control.
4. *Attempts to quit or control the behavior:* This would be seen in a person who repeatedly promised himself or herself to break off an extramarital affair.
5. *Excessive time spent on the behavior:* One example of this might be a person who often stayed on the Internet until late at night, missing out on family time and being tired at work the next day as a result.
6. *Sacrifices made for the behavior:* A person who gave up close friendships and stopped spending time with family members at the demand of a jealous relationship partner would be providing an example of this symptom of addictive behavior.
7. *Continuing to practice the behavior despite known suffering as a consequence:* This could be seen in a person who kept returning to a casino in spite of having been unable to pay his or her bills due to past gambling losses.

The results of these behaviors can include the following:

1. Loss of jobs and careers
2. Bankruptcy or tremendous indebtedness
3. Loss of marriages and other relationships

4. Incarceration

5. Depression, anxiety, and other emotional and psychological problems

6. Injuries, illnesses, or death (HIV/AIDS or other STDs, injuries due to fights or over-exercise, health problems due to eating disorders, suicide)

AVAILABLE RESOURCES

Help is available in several forms for people trying to overcome these compulsive behaviors. Resources include:

1. *Treatment programs:* There are excellent residential and outpatient treatment programs specializing in helping people with non-chemical addictions. If you already have a problem with one of these behavior patterns, your counselor or therapist can help you find the programs that are available for you, and individual therapy can also be very helpful.

2. *12-Step recovery programs:* The programs that deal with chemical dependence, primarily Alcoholics Anonymous, Narcotics Anonymous, and Cocaine Anonymous, make a point in their last Step of saying that members must "practice these principles in all our affairs." This means that they can use the same tools they use to stay abstinent from alcohol and other drugs to avoid getting addicted to other behavior patterns. Gamblers Anonymous, Debtors Anonymous, Overeaters Anonymous, Sex and Love Addicts Anonymous, Codependents Anonymous, and other programs exist specifically to help people apply the 12 Steps to overcoming nonchemical addictions.

3. *Other community groups:* Other groups also exist to help with many issues with which newly clean and sober people may struggle. In many communities, a local newspaper or civic organization may be able to provide a directory of support groups.

4. *Literature:* There are hundreds of books, recordings, and videos on nonchemical compulsive behaviors, especially relationship issues both emotional and sexual. Recovering people can find these in most bookstores or order them through the Internet from online booksellers.

CONCLUSION

Review the following key points:

1. Recovering people are at risk for switching from addictions to alcohol or other drugs to any of several compulsive behavior patterns, which can be just as destructive.

2. These nonchemical compulsive behaviors can have the same behavioral symptoms as addiction to alcohol or other drugs, and can have life-threatening consequences.

3. A variety of resources are available to help recovering people avoid switching addictions and becoming hooked on nonchemical compulsive behaviors or to get help if they already have problems with any of these patterns.

REVIEW LEARNING GOALS

1. Upon completion of this presentation, group members will demonstrate understanding of ways culture and substance abuse can be related by listing, without notes or references, at least six examples of nondrug-using compulsive or addictive behaviors ways that can lure newly abstinent alcoholics and drug addicts into continuing addictive behavior patterns by switching to nonchemical addictions.

2. Upon completion of this presentation, group members will demonstrate understanding of the effects of nondrug-using compulsive behaviors by listing, without notes or references, at least four ways that nonchemical addictions can be destructive to the lives of addicts.

3. Upon completion of this presentation, group members will demonstrate understanding of resources available for recovery from nonchemical addictions by listing, without notes or references, at least four recovery programs or other resources that exist to help people overcome compulsive behaviors that do not involve use of alcohol or other drugs.

QUESTIONS/DISCUSSION BEFORE POSTTEST

ADMINISTER POSTTEST

QUESTIONS/DISCUSSION AFTER POSTTEST

Chapter 7

Recovery Resources and Skills: Materials for Use in Psychoeducational Groups

While Chapter Six focused on problems, Chapter Seven offers materials oriented toward teaching clients about solutions. The presentation materials in this chapter are focused on methods and information chemically dependent people can employ to change the self-destructive patterns that have characterized their lives, both in terms of the use of alcohol and other drugs and in relation to emotional difficulties and self-care skill deficits that accompany an addictive lifestyle and can set the stage for relapse into active addiction.

The materials included in this chapter employ the same multiple-learning-modality approach and cognitive orientation as those in Chapter Six, and address the following topics:

Presentation 7.1:   Facilitator's Guide: The Process of Recovery

Presentation 7.2:   Facilitator's Guide: Recovery Programs and Resources

Presentation 7.3:   Facilitator's Guide: Lifestyle Changes

Presentation 7.4:   Facilitator's Guide: Common Problems and Issues in Recovery

Presentation 7.5:   Facilitator's Guide: Relapse Prevention, Part I

Presentation 7.6:   Facilitator's Guide: Relapse Prevention, Part II

Presentation 7.7:   Facilitator's Guide: Physical and Emotional Self-Care

Presentation 7.8:   Facilitator's Guide: Stress Management

Presentation 7.9:   Facilitator's Guide: Communication Skills

Presentation 7.10:   Facilitator's Guide: Healthy Relationship Skills

Presentation 7.11:   Facilitator's Guide: Setting and Achieving Goals

Presentation 7.12:   Facilitator's Guide: Problem-Solving Skills

Presentation 7.13:   Facilitator's Guide: Coping with Anger and Resentment

Presentation 7.14:   Facilitator's Guide: Coping with Depression and Anxiety

Presentation 7.15:   Facilitator's Guide: Resisting Pressures to Drink or Use

To conserve space and provide more material within the practicable scope of this book, only the facilitator's guide for each presentation is included in the text, but the companion CD-ROM also includes a group member's handout, a pre-/posttest, and a Microsoft PowerPoint slideshow for each presentation, as well as an electronic copy of the facilitator's guide included here.

Presentation 7.1 Facilitator's Guide: The Process of Recovery

INTRODUCTION

Ask the group whether there is anyone who does *not* have questions or concerns about how recovery will work. Explain that this presentation will be about the stages and issues newly recovering people experience and how to cope with them.

LEARNING GOALS

Explain to the group that they will be evaluated on their accomplishment of the following goals:

1. Upon completion of this presentation, group members will demonstrate the ability to define the terms *abstinence, sobriety,* and *recovery.*

2. Upon completion of this presentation, group members will be able to discuss the difference between recovery and being recovered.

3. Upon completion of this presentation, group members will demonstrate understanding of the stages, events, and experiences people typically go through in recovering from chemical dependence.

QUESTIONS

As the presenter, you may ask group members to hold their questions until the end or to ask them at any time during the presentation. If participation is a high priority, we recommend allowing questions at any time; if brevity is more important, it works better to hold questions until the end.

PRETEST/POSTTEST

Pass out the pretest if you choose to use it. You may have the group members fill out and turn in pretests without putting names on them as a general measure of baseline knowledge. Explain that the same test will be given as the posttest at the end of the presentation.

BACKGROUND AND LEAD-IN

Ask group members to define *abstinence, sobriety,* and *recovery.* Write their responses on a board, flip chart, or transparency sheet, then compare them with the following definitions from *Webster's New Universal Unabridged Dictionary:*

Abstinence: The refraining from an indulgence of appetite, or from customary gratification of one's appetites; it denotes a total forbearance, as in fasting or in giving up the drinking of alcoholic liquors.

Sobriety: A two-part definition: the state or quality of being sober; specifically, (a) temperance or moderation, especially in the use of drink; (b) seriousness, solemnity, gravity, or sedateness of manner or appearance.

Recovery: Four definitions. (a) The act or power of regaining, retaking, or conquering again; (b) a getting well again, coming or bringing back to consciousness, revival of a person from weakness; (c) a regaining of balance . . . a return to soundness; (d) the time needed for recovering.

Facilitate a brief discussion of the differences between the definitions for abstinence and sobriety and for recovery. Note that abstinence and sobriety are necessary conditions for recovery, but not everyone who is abstinent is in recovery. Emphasize that recovery indicates changes to lifestyle patterns and interactions. Offer these alternative definitions:

Abstinence: No use of any drug of abuse; in some cases, this may also mean no participation in non-drug compulsive behaviors that have been part of one's addictive pattern.

Sobriety: Usually used in treatment and 12-Step programs to mean the same as abstinence. However, because it can be interpreted to mean only not getting high or drunk, some use it to mislead, telling themselves that even though they used or drank it wasn't enough to get them high or drunk, so they were still sober.

Recovery: Changing from a lifestyle of addiction and other self-destructive, dishonest behavior to one of abstinence and healthy, honest behavior.

Solicit and discuss input on the difference between *recovered* and *recovering.* Comparison to recovery from other illnesses can be useful, for example, a chronic illness, an illness that has no cure but is treatable and can be fatal if not managed (e.g., diabetes). It may be useful to discuss the similarities between diseases such as diabetes, heart disease, and so on, and chemical dependency as a disease. Explain that complete recovery (to be *recovered,* or completely cured) from addiction is an ideal that no one ever achieves, just like any other ideal.

STAGES, EVENTS, AND EXPERIENCES OF RECOVERY

Remind group members that it is important to remember that recovery is a process, much like learning to walk, to play the piano, or to type. As a process, it involves stages that occur over time and build on skills learned in previous stages. It is also important to point out that there is no definitive time frame of recovery that occurs for everyone; many people experience "stuck points" or "backslides" when they must find new ways to continue making progress forward. Further, some things simply get better with time, and only with time.

Early Recovery: Turning Things Around

This stage typically lasts for the first few months of recovery and involves the following:

- *Getting physically clean:* Getting through withdrawal; coping with life without chemical filters/distortion/insulation; regaining physical balance from rebound effects. This may last for days or for as long as several months depending on the drug(s) and the length and amount of use.

- *Growing awareness:* As the "clearing of the fog" continues, newly recovering people often feel the following:

  1. *Hope and exhilaration:* Sometimes called the "pink cloud effect," this is the sometimes giddy feeling that comes from having hope after having felt despair.

  2. *Enthusiasm and determination:* Often, drug-dependent people have spent a long time, maybe all their lives, feeling that there is something basically wrong with them, or that there is no explanation for what is going on in their lives, or that substance-abusing behavior is part of their basic nature and therefore unchangeable. Newly recovering people find explanations for their behavior that make sense, that don't label them as defective, and that offer solutions. The natural reaction is to latch on with both hands.

  3. *Letdown and fear:* At the same time, most people feel: "Quitting was supposed to make my life better, and now I have more problems than before! I don't know if I can deal with all these problems!" What is really happening: They're starting to see problems to which they were blind before (though others may have tried to point the problems out) and realizing the size of the mess they must now clean up. The work ahead may look overwhelming.

4. *Frustration:* "Nobody respects what I'm trying to do. They won't believe I've changed." Because part of the addictive lifestyle has usually involved lying to and hurting themselves and others, newly recovering people may find that others are reluctant to trust them, thinking that this is just another lie, another promise that will be broken or attempt at sobriety that will fail. Also, because many people don't understand addiction and think it is a sign of weak will or defective character, they may think the recovering person is unable to change. Either way, it hurts to go to people to seek support, and to start making amends, and be rejected or scorned.

5. *Connection to others:* "I finally fit in somewhere." After a lifetime of feeling out of place and misunderstood, newly recovering people find themselves surrounded by others who can relate to them and have had similar experiences. They often feel as if they've finally found their real families or that they're home at last.

6. *Loneliness:* At the same time, they may feel: "All my old friends still use/drink!" Human beings are drawn to connect with other people, and part of recovery is usually building a new network of friends and activities. At the beginning, this new social network doesn't exist yet.

7. *Feeling strange or out of place:* "I don't know how to act!" Because psychoactive drug abuse tends to stop emotional growth and development of social skills at the age when heavy use begins, people in their 20s, 30s, or older may be picking up where they left off as adolescents, and feel the same confusion as teenagers trying to figure out how to stop being children and become adults.

- *Ongoing cravings and urges to use/drink:* Habits take time to change, and drug habits are among the strongest—they have actually made physical changes in the body and brain. These cravings may hit at times of stress, or they may hit with no apparent reason at a time when things seem to be going well or nothing seems to be going on. Either way, cravings are normal, and people can learn skills to cope with them without using or drinking.

- *Questions about spirituality and values:* The 12-Step programs emphasize a relationship with a higher power, and recovery involves a shift in values and ethics in daily life. At the same time, many newly recovering people feel they have been hurt or deeply disappointed by the God they may have been taught about as children, and they may have reason to doubt or reject the proclaimed religion, values, and ethics others have urged on them so far in their lives. This phase may see newly recovering people seeking answers to these questions in a variety of places, including 12-Step programs, other self-help programs, churches, books, and the guidance of others they trust.

- *12-Step work during early recovery:* During this early stage, newly recovering people are laying the foundation for a new life and beginning to build on that foundation. In the 12-Step programs, this process is given structure by Steps 1 through 7. In these steps, people come to a realistic view of themselves and their situations; break through their isolation to start establishing healthy relationships with other people and with a higher power; and begin the process of changing the patterns in their lives that have been destructive.

Middle Recovery: Solidifying Change and Putting One Foot in Front of the Other

During this time, the *new patterns* established in early recovery are being strengthened and becoming habits themselves. The old life had a structure built on drug and alcohol use and impulsive and compulsive behavior; the new life also needs a structure, and one built on new routines and new ways of coping with life is becoming stronger and more comfortable. Experiences and feelings during this stage include:

1. *Settling in:* As new practices become habits, they become automatic, and recovering people find themselves noticing that they are doing different things and responding differently to people, places, and situations, without having to stop and think about it as often. Others also notice and comment. New acquaintances who find out about the past may be surprised and say that sounds unlike the people they see.

2. *Growing strength and confidence*: Recovering people at this middle stage find themselves less fearful and anxious and start noticing the distance they have come, especially when they see newcomers who remind them of their earlier selves. They find they have much to offer others. They may need to be on guard at this stage against overconfidence.

3. *Overconfidence*: It can be tempting to think that they have changed and gained control over their lives to such a degree that they can now handle either some drug use or other behaviors that they were unable to control before. They may think to themselves, "Maybe I'm not really an addict or alcoholic after all—maybe it just got away from me before." It is a good idea at this stage to talk with a trusted friend who knows them well and understands how their addiction works. At the same time, however, there may be new awareness of addictive behaviors.

4. *New awareness of addictive behavior in other areas*: As people continue to grow in emotional and mental health and experience of recovery, they may realize additional ways they are still acting like addicts and alcoholics, usually in family, work, and social situations.

Continued improvements in quality of life are seen in several areas:
- Physical health and feeling of well-being
- *Improvement of moods*: relief of chronic depression, anxiety, anger
- *Rebuilding or improving relationships with others*: family, work, social
- Financial situation
- Relationship with spiritual side of life or higher power
- Plans, goals, and prospects for the future

During middle recovery, recovering people are continuing the process of change begun in early recovery and extending it into more areas of their lives. In the 12-Step programs, this continuation is supported by steps 8 through 10. In these steps, people continue to clean up the wreckage of their past and work daily to avoid losing ground gained in the areas of honesty and creating new patterns during early recovery.

Long-Term Recovery: Maintenance and Continued Growth

1. *Maintenance activities:* During this stage, the emphasis for most people is on relapse prevention, avoiding falling back into old patterns:
   - Continued participation in meetings
   - Feedback from others, especially sponsors
   - Continued study and emphasis on recovery (Step study groups, etc.)

2. *Greater focus on helping others*: Helping others, with addiction-related issues and in general, comes to feel more and more natural and necessary:
   - Others seek out advice.
   - Sponsorship, speaking at meetings, starting new groups, and service tasks.

3. *Tackling new problems and issues*: As people integrate new values and attitudes into their basic outlook on life, they find themselves acting on the new awareness they found in middle recovery in areas where they need to make changes. They often seek to apply the same methods that have helped them overcome addiction.
   - Using known tools (12-Step program, other resources) on new issues.
   - Starting participation in other programs. This may have started earlier.

4. *12-Step work in long-term recovery*: During this stage, the focus is on maintenance, as noted above, and on gradual continued growth. In the 12-Step programs, this is supported by steps 10 (which also fits into middle recovery) through 12. In these steps, people work to strengthen and deepen the habits and values that have changed their personalities and to bring their lives into closer harmony with these principles.

CONCLUSION

Review the following key points:

1. Recovery is a process in which people coping with substance abuse and chemical dependency learn to live life without chemicals and other self-defeating behaviors.

2. People learn that there is hope as well as challenge to managing life in more productive ways.

3. Recovery encompasses the substance-abusing behavior, and also provides hope that other life areas will improve.

4. There are stages to recovery, and each stage includes its own experiences, activities, and challenges.

REVIEW LEARNING GOALS

1. Upon completion of this presentation, group members will demonstrate the ability to define the terms *abstinence, sobriety,* and *recovery.*

2. Upon completion of this presentation, group members will be able to discuss the difference between recovery and being recovered.

3. Upon completion of this presentation, group members will demonstrate understanding of the stages, events, and experiences people typically go through in recovering from chemical dependence.

QUESTIONS/DISCUSSION BEFORE POSTTEST

ADMINISTER POSTTEST

QUESTIONS/DISCUSSION AFTER POSTTEST

INTRODUCTION

Solicit input from group members about why they think it is important to know about and use recovery programs and resources. Write their answers on a board, flip chart, or transparency sheet and facilitate a brief discussion. If it has not come up in discussion, point out that most addicts and alcoholics know they have problems and have done their best to solve them alone. If they succeed, they succeed—if not, they end up in treatment programs, or elsewhere.

Quote an anonymous member of a 12-Step program: "My best thinking and hardest efforts got me where I was when I started this program."

Discuss the fact that most people can't recover alone through insight or willpower, but most addicts and alcoholics who work together with others are able to recover if they make a wholehearted effort and don't hold anything back. Most need tools and support.

Explain that this presentation is about where to find those resources and how to use them. Also point out that people frequently consult with professionals for legal problems, when buying a home, and so forth, rather than making a major life change without help, and there's no reason for this change to be different.

LEARNING GOALS

Explain to group members that they will be evaluated on their accomplishment of the following goals:

1. Upon completion of this presentation, group members will demonstrate knowledge of recovery programs available to help people overcome both chemical dependence and other problems.

2. Upon completion of this presentation, group members will demonstrate knowledge of resources, techniques, and practices for making most effective use of recovery programs.

QUESTIONS

As the presenter, you may ask group members to hold their questions until the end or to ask them at any time during the presentation. If participation is a high priority, we recommend allowing questions at any time; if brevity is more important, it works better to hold questions until the end.

PRETEST/POSTTEST

Pass out the pretest if you choose to use it. You may have the group members fill out and turn in pretests without putting names on them as a general measure of baseline knowledge. Explain that the same test will be given as the posttest at the end of the presentation.

BACKGROUND AND LEAD-IN

Ask group members to name programs for chemical dependence available in their community; then ask them to name other addictive patterns and other mental or emotional problems that people have that don't have to be connected with chemical dependency (i.e., depression), and list programs for those problems available in the community.

List the group's answers to these questions on a board, flip chart, or transparency sheet, and facilitate a brief discussion. Point out that this presentation will discuss the services on the list as well as others they may not have been aware of and what each serves to address.

RECOVERY GROUPS AND PROGRAMS FOR CHEMICAL DEPENDENCE

12-Step Programs

These programs are all based on the same twelve steps of recommended action that provide a structure to guide people in changing their behaviors to become free of substance abuse and the patterns of thought and behavior that are part of addiction. 12-Step programs make a point of being free of charge, welcoming all who want to join, and giving suggestions but not requirements for participation. They include Alcoholics Anonymous, Narcotics Anonymous, and Cocaine Anonymous. These programs have more members than others and claim the highest success rates. There are meetings available within most communities (inform group members of the local availability of each program).

The key parts of participation in a 12-Step program are:

1. Working the Steps

2. Establishing a relationship with a higher power

3. Attending meetings frequently

4. Working with a sponsor, a mentor with experience in the program

5. Studying program literature such as the *Big Book, 12 Steps and 12 Traditions,* etc.

6. Having at least one home group

7. Applying the Steps to all areas of life as well as to chemical use

Advantages a 12-Step group provides that are unavailable to people working alone include:

1. Guidance about what to do from others who are successful

2. Frequent feedback to correct distorted thinking and perceptions

3. Knowledgeable peer group or "family" (both support and peer pressure for efforts to maintain recovery)

4. Frequent activities to help restructure daily routine and social life

5. Commonsense answers to many questions and issues that trouble most chemically dependent people

6. Worldwide availability at no cost

Here is some additional information about 12-Step programs:

1. Types of meetings:

    (a) Open: Meetings open to the public

    (b) Closed: For alcoholics and addicts only

    (c) Speaker: One speaker or several share their "story"

    (d) Discussion: Invites group participation; people are either called on by the chairperson or volunteer to share

    (e) Stag: Men-only or women-only meetings; members are more comfortable talking about some issues in a single-gender group; a very important support for men and women

    (f) Book or Step study: Members read from and discuss literature

    (g) Birthday: Usually held monthly, meetings at which members celebrate sobriety anniversaries

    (h) Group conscience: A business meeting at which a group votes on decisions about finances, special events, and other subjects

The Concept of Anonymity

This is for the protection both of individual members and of the program. It allows the meetings to be a safe place to share, and means that no one may identify himself or herself as a member in any mass media, or identify other members at all, or reveal who else was at a meeting or what they said during that meeting.

The Concept of Sponsorship

This means working closely with a more experienced recovering person who is willing to guide a member in working the program. It is typical for a member to seek a sponsor with whom there is no potential of romantic feelings getting in the way, who has a greater length of time in the program, and who has worked all the Steps at least once.

The Concept of Fellowship

Shared activities such as parties, dances, and picnics help people find sober friendships and social life. Also, when one's sponsor is unavailable, there are others who are available. This is based on founder Bill W.'s realization that he needed to help other alcoholics to stay sober himself.

OTHER NONPROFESSIONAL RECOVERY PROGRAMS FOR CHEMICAL DEPENDENCE

Rational Recovery (RR)

This is for people who either can't accept the 12-Step programs' views on a higher power or choose an individual self-help approach to recovery. RR is based on rational-emotive therapy (RET), the idea that all dysfunctional actions are based on mistaken beliefs and that correcting those beliefs will correct the actions. It may be useful to provide a simplified lesson on RET here or create another lesson to teach in more detail. Include the following components:

   A = Activating Event (situation, event, feeling)

   B = Belief (irrational or rational)

   C = Consequence (thoughts, feelings, actions)

Many people believe that A causes C. In RET, it is taught that it is a person's beliefs (B) about A that cause C. Provide a general example and then relate it to substance-abusing behavior. It is also helpful to provide a sample of irrational beliefs people may hold that support substance-abusing behavior. Point out that this is a useful way to address substance-abusing behavior separate from a specific support group.

   This program is centered primarily on alcohol abuse, but its principles can be applied to other chemical dependence as well. Report if any of these meetings are available in the community or how to access information via the Internet.

1. *Faith-based programs*: Many areas offer faith-based recovery programs operated by various churches, mosques, synagogues, or other faith communities. These programs vary widely in the ways they function. If a person belongs to a faith group that offers such a program, he or she may benefit from participation.

Formal Chemical Dependence Treatment Programs

Four basic types of treatment exist. These treatment programs often have patients participate in 12-Step programs as a part of treatment.

1. *Inpatient or residential treatment*: This is the most intensive type of treatment program. In this program, usually located in a hospital or similar institution, people are not free to come and go. They

may receive medical and psychiatric treatment for other problems in addition to being treated for addictions. This is usually for people who either have medical problems that would endanger them if they were not closely monitored, or are so likely to relapse that they must be denied any chance to use or drink. For obvious reasons, it is the most expensive type of treatment and may last anywhere from several days to several months. Components included are medically supervised detoxification, psychiatric or psychological therapy, and medical monitoring.

2. *Intensive outpatient treatment*: This is less intensive than inpatient treatment but is still much more thorough than the other two types to follow. In an intensive outpatient program, the staff seeks to "saturate" people and provide a lot of therapeutic impact and education in a short time. This type of program is aimed at people who do not need inpatient treatment but appear to need more intensive treatment than the other types below. This type of treatment may last as long as inpatient treatment but is less expensive because it does not provide housing, food, and medical supervision, and the movements of people are generally not restricted.

3. *Other outpatient group treatment*: The typical format for less intensive outpatient treatment is for people to attend a group once or twice a week for several weeks, and sometimes to have homework assignments between sessions. This is designed for people who need some treatment and education but appear to have a good chance for success with fairly limited supervision and support. This is the least expensive form of treatment in most cases.

4. *Individual treatment*: Individual therapy may be used in some cases where a person is not required and not willing to participate in a group or is not expected to succeed in a treatment group for any of a number of reasons such as mental disorders that would cause them to be disruptive in a group. This is not the preferred method for treating addictions but may be the only approach available in some cases.

Other Types of Programs and Resources

A variety of books, workbooks, audiotapes, videotapes, and so on offer recommended ways to overcome addiction, usually based on research or existing treatment programs. Many of these are available at large bookstores, typically located in the self-help or psychology sections. There are also bookstores that specialize in recovery-type resources, and online bookstores. It is also useful to ask others at support group meetings about other resources that they recommend.

RECOVERY GROUPS AND PROGRAMS FOR PROBLEMS THAT CAN ACCOMPANY CHEMICAL DEPENDENCE

The 12-Step approach is successfully applied to several other problems with compulsive behavior that do not necessarily involve drugs, but to which recovering alcoholics and addicts are especially vulnerable. Some of these are:

- Overeaters Anonymous: For people who eat compulsively or suffer other eating disorders.

- Gamblers Anonymous: For compulsive gamblers.

- Debtors Anonymous: For compulsive spenders.

- Sex and Love Addicts Anonymous: For people addicted to high-risk sexual behavior and/or dysfunctional relationships.

- Emotions Anonymous: For people with severe depression or anxiety.

- Parents Anonymous: For parents who have lost control of their anger and abused their children or who are afraid they will.

- Al-Anon, Nar-Anon, Gam-Anon: For adult partners, family members, and close friends of alcoholics, addicts, gamblers, and so on.

- Ala-Teen: Similar to Al-Anon, except that it is for adolescent children of alcoholics.

- Adult Children of Alcoholics: For people whose adult lives are troubled by emotional problems from their childhoods in alcoholic families.
- CoDependents Anonymous: For people obsessed with the lives of others and feeling that their own lives are out of control as a result.

MAKING THE MOST EFFECTIVE USE OF RECOVERY RESOURCES

Some of these are already covered in the information about the 12-Step programs. However, for both those and other programs, the following may be helpful and may make the programs more effective:

- Keeping journals or diaries
- Learning additional information about the subject
- Participating in a spiritual, church, or worship group if this is consistent with beliefs
- Asking trusted friends and relatives for support and feedback
- Setting aside time daily to think, meditate, reflect, pray
- Using affirmations (positive self-talk)
- Planning ahead, in writing, to either cope with or avoid stressful situations
- Rewarding oneself for successes in healthy ways
- Combining support group participation work with personal therapy
- Spending time on helping others with similar issues

CONCLUSION

Review the following key points:

1. A variety of support groups and therapies exist for individuals coping with chemical dependency and other issues. Many of these programs are available in most communities.

2. Most support groups are free of charge and have no specific membership requirements, but individuals may want to research this before they attend.

3. We have also discussed ways to make the most effective use of other resources.

4. It is sometimes helpful to point out to class group members that if they put as much time and effort into recovery as they put into substance-abusing behavior, they will likely do very well.

REVIEW LEARNING GOALS

1. Upon completion of this presentation, group members will demonstrate knowledge of recovery programs available to help people overcome both chemical dependence and other problems.

2. Upon completion of this presentation, group members will demonstrate knowledge of resources, techniques, and practices for making most effective use of recovery programs.

QUESTIONS/DISCUSSION BEFORE POSTTEST

ADMINISTER POSTTEST

QUESTIONS/DISCUSSION AFTER POSTTEST

INTRODUCTION

Ask how many group members think they had good reasons to use drugs, including alcohol. Then offer the suggestion that people do use drugs for good reasons, that a drug meets some need in every case, but the problem is that the price is too high. The key to recovery is not denying one's needs, but finding other ways to meet them without paying such a high cost in health, freedom, relationships, money, and self-respect.

LEARNING GOALS

Explain to group members that they will be evaluated on their accomplishment of the following goals:

1. Upon completion of this presentation, group members will demonstrate awareness and acceptance of personal needs that were met in the past by using drugs, including alcohol.

2. Upon completion of this presentation, group members will demonstrate knowledge of alternative ways to meet the same personal needs.

QUESTIONS

As the presenter, you may ask group members to hold their questions until the end or to ask them at any time during the presentation. If participation is a high priority, we recommend allowing questions at any time; if brevity is more important, it works better to hold questions until the end.

PRETEST/POSTTEST

Pass out the pretest if you choose to use it. You may have the group members fill out and turn in pretests without putting names on them as a general measure of baseline knowledge. Explain that the same test will be given as the posttest at the end of the presentation.

BACKGROUND AND LEAD-IN

Ask group members to name some needs drugs meet for people. Write their answers on a board, flip chart, or transparency sheet, and facilitate a short discussion of how drugs meet the needs identified.

Personal Needs Leading People to Use Drugs

The reasons can be divided into two main categories: seeking pleasure and reducing pain. These are basic survival instincts possessed by all creatures. Without them we would die. Drugs can meet these needs, at least in the short run, in ways including the following (compare with group members' responses):

1. Seeking Pleasure/Reward

   - Emotional pleasure—euphoria, bliss, rush, feeling of well-being, excitement

   - Physical pleasure—intensified sensory awareness, hallucinations (for some)

   - Social pleasure—shared activity with others, status, acceptance

2. Reducing Pain

- Reducing emotional pain—relief for depression, anxiety, fear, anger
- Reducing physical pain—aspirin to morphine
- Reducing social pain—overcoming loneliness and inhibitions and fitting in

Experiential Exercise: Cost-Benefit Analysis

On the board/flip chart/transparency sheet, set up four columns: benefits of drug use, costs of drug use, benefits of abstinence from drugs, and costs of abstinence from drugs. For each, ask group members to list as many things as they can; write their answers on the board, then guide a discussion of the "balance sheet" and the decisions it suggests.

Alternatives to Substance Abuse

Without erasing previous material, ask group members to list other ways they have found, or are considering, to achieve the benefits listed.

Guide them in a discussion of the costs of these alternatives, and compare to the costs listed for drug use. Alternatives include:

Talk to non-using friends, loved ones	Martial arts	Going to a meeting
Music (playing or listening)	Swimming	Talking to a sponsor
Movies	Biking	Playing with one's children
Camping, hiking	Rock climbing	Playing with a pet
Church/Spiritual gatherings	Join a club	Taking flying lessons
Prayer, meditation	Reading	Taking scuba lessons
Cooking, eating a favorite meal	Writing	Painting or drawing
Taking a nap	Dancing	Taking a vacation
Running	Fishing	Existing hobbies—collections, etc.
Lifting weights	Going for a drive	Finding a new hobby

Ask each group members to identify which three alternative activities are most interesting to him or her, and to say what he or she has done or can do to pursue those alternatives.

Follow-Through

Ask group members to discuss what they learned about their own needs met by substances and the possibility of alternative activities to incorporate from this point on, then ask what commitments they are willing to make to the group to try one alternative activity during the following week and report back to the group on what the experience was like.

CONCLUSION

Review the following key points:

1. People use drugs to meet legitimate needs, such as to seek pleasure or reward and to reduce pain.

2. The problem in addiction is that the cost of drug use becomes greater than the benefits.

3. The key to overcoming addiction is not to deny these needs but to find safer ways to meet them.

4. There are many alternative ways to find pleasure or reduce pain.

REVIEW LEARNING GOALS

1. Upon completion of this presentation, group members will demonstrate awareness and acceptance of personal needs that were met in the past by using drugs, including alcohol.

2. Upon completion of this presentation, group members will demonstrate knowledge of alternative ways to meet the same personal needs.

QUESTIONS/DISCUSSION BEFORE POSTTEST

ADMINISTER POSTTEST

QUESTIONS/DISCUSSION AFTER POSTTEST

INTRODUCTION

Ask each group member to identify the biggest problem he or she is experiencing in connection with recovery, other than just staying chemical-free. Write their answers on a board, flipchart, or transparency sheet. Tell the group that this presentation will be about problems and issues of this type and ways to cope with them.

LEARNING GOALS

Explain to group members that they will be evaluated on their accomplishment of the following goals:

1. Upon completion of this presentation, group members will demonstrate understanding of common problems and issues in recovery by listing, without notes or references, at least four common problems encountered by many newly recovering alcoholics and addicts.

2. Upon completion of this presentation, group members will demonstrate understanding of common problems and issues in recovery by listing, without notes or references, at least one coping skill and/or resource to use in handling each problem/issue they list in their answers to the first learning goal.

QUESTIONS

As the presenter, you may ask group members to hold their questions until the end or to ask them at any time during the presentation. If participation is a high priority, we recommend allowing questions at any time; if brevity is more important, it works better to hold questions until the end.

PRETEST/POSTTEST

Pass out the pretest if you choose to use it. You may have the group members fill out and turn in pretests without putting names on them as a general measure of baseline knowledge. Explain that the same test will be given as the posttest at the end of the presentation.

BACKGROUND AND LEAD-IN

Facilitate a brief discussion of how each of the problems the group listed could affect a newly recovering person's abstinence from substance use or other addictive/compulsive behaviors. Guide members in considering whether the problems identified can be overcome by abstinence from substance use without other changes in lifestyle. Explain that the information in this presentation is based on the experiences of many others who have had to get clean and sober, and will increase the group members' chances of success and help them improve their quality of life.

COMMON PROBLEMS AND ISSUES IN RECOVERY

Dislike of Meetings

This may be a common complaint for group members who are required to attend AA, NA, or other community recovery program meetings. Many people find they initially dislike 12 Step meetings and attend only because they are required to do so, but later find that they come to enjoy and value the meetings. This process often takes weeks or months. Many people have used the following methods to make meetings more enjoyable:

- *Shop around:* Go to as many different groups as possible, and find the ones you like best. Try other programs as well as groups in your main program. Every group has its own personality, and some will fit for you while others won't. Find people you have a lot in common with and ask which meetings they like best.

- *Go with friends:* Attending a meeting with friends or family members, then discussing it afterward, makes it a more interesting and enjoyable experience. This is sometimes described as "the meeting after the meeting" which takes place in the car or van on the way home (or back to a treatment center). Going with friends can also help if you are nervous about going to meetings you have not attended before.

- Participate—Read, help out, and speak up at meetings: Even if you only bring someone a cup of coffee, or give your name and a brief comment—for example, mentioning that you could relate to something someone said—you'll probably leave the meeting feeling better than if you do and say nothing to interact with others.

- *Find the type of meeting you prefer:* Some people prefer Step study or book study meetings, some like speaker meetings, some like open topic/sharing meetings; pick the format you like best and seek out meetings with that format. You may also find that you are most comfortable in a meeting that is small or large, smoking or nonsmoking, open or closed, stag (one sex only) or mixed, oriented toward a certain age range, gay/lesbian, in a language other than English, or some other type of group.

- *Go a little early/Stay a little late:* Most meetings include some socializing before and after, and people are usually friendly but not nosy. This is a good chance to meet people one-on-one and ask questions you might not want to share with the whole room.

- *Pick a home group:* A home group is like a second family, where you are known, accepted, expected, and missed if you aren't there. That's a good feeling for most of us.

- *Help start a new meeting:* If you are one of a small group that gets in at the beginning of a group's formation, that group's personality will be partly based on your personality and preferences. If you are looking for a particular type of meeting or one at a certain time, chances are some other people are, too. It is a good idea to have at least a couple of people with a few years of recovery to help launch a new meeting, but you can do a lot to help and put your own stamp on it.

- Give the meetings some time: For most people, meetings feel strange at first. Give yourself a chance to get used to the experience, and you may come to look forward to them.

Higher Power Issues

Most people have trouble with the idea of surrendering to a Higher Power. It doesn't fit with our beliefs and values, it doesn't seem to make sense, and it doesn't fit with the pattern many addicts have of trying to control and manipulate everything and everyone around them. Here are some methods that have worked for many people to solve their problems with the idea of a Higher Power:

- *Read the words "as we understood Him" and think about their meaning:* The 12 Steps don't ask anyone to believe in a particular version of God, Allah, Buddha, the Great Spirit, the Force, or whatever. If you can believe that there *could* be a power greater than you, that's all you need to start with. People have chosen as their Higher Power any of the following things, or many more:

  1. Their principles of right and wrong

  2. Their groups

  3. Their conscience or "inner voice"

  4. The God they were raised to believe in

  5. A mystery they hope to understand later on

6. Nature

7. Time

- *Find someone at a meeting you can relate to, and ask them about their views about the Higher Power:* Since many people struggle with this issue, if you feel you have a lot in common with someone the chances are he or she had the same doubts you have, and if they found a solution that works for them it might work for you, too.

- *Read about it:* There is some good material about this in various places: in the AA Big Book's *Chapter to the Agnostic,* in other books in sections of bookstores devoted to both religion and addiction and recovery, in workbooks, and in some pamphlets that are available at some meetings.

- *Design your own God:* Think about what you were taught about God, then ask yourself what kind of God would make sense to you and how people might be able to see that God at work in the world: in other words, what would the evidence be? Then wait and see.

- *Bring the subject up at a meeting:* If one person raises the topic and says he or she is having trouble with the concept of a Higher Power, others will respond to say "me, too," or to share their experience in resolving this dilemma. There's nothing wrong with having doubts and questions, and in a healthy group they will be respected and accepted, though others may disagree and share their own views hoping you can find something in them with which you agree.

- *Talk about it with your sponsor:* If you have chosen a sponsor with whom you feel comfortable and with whom you have much in common, he or she may have gone through just the same struggle and have found some solutions you can use.

Resistance to Change

Deep down, many of us find that there are many parts of ourselves and our addictive lifestyles we really don't want to let go of. Here are some ways others have successfully tackled this problem:

- *"I want to want to":* If we can't honestly say we want to change something, at least we can often say we wished we wanted to change it. That's a good start—give yourself credit for effort and keep working on it.

- *Accept the feelings, but control the actions:* Sometimes we can't leave a character trait behind as long as we're trying to get rid of it. We can control the action, and that may be all for a while. And that's okay—but once we accept it with the hope that it will leave us one day but the view that we're okay where we're at for today, it often does start changing.

- *Find replacement activities:* Often it isn't the chemical itself we crave, but something else that happened when we consumed it. Find new ways to get that something else. (Think about the class on Lifestyle Changes: Alternatives to Substance Abuse.) Figure out what the payoff was, and find another way to get it without such a high price tag.

- *Set small goals and reward yourself:* This is a good way to build new habits. It takes about three weeks of practice for most people to get a new habit formed; give yourself little rewards several times during that period for sticking to it. Give yourself time!

- *Hang around with people who are the way you want to be:* You'll learn things from them, and some of their attitudes and habits may rub off on you.

Anger, Fear, and Hopelessness/Depression

One of the reasons people use and drink is to block negative emotions, and when people first quit it can seem as if they're spinning out of control. To get through this phase, try some of these approaches:

- *Talk about the feelings:* With a trusted friend or at a good meeting, if you talk about it you'll understand it better and feel more peaceful, and chances are someone else will say "me, too!" and add some insights that may help you even further.

- *Take care of yourself:* If you eat a healthy diet, get enough sleep, and get regular exercise in a way you enjoy, all of these emotions will diminish and be more manageable.

- *Give yourself at least one good laugh a day:* Hearty laughter changes your brain chemistry the same way as getting some hard exercise, like some prescription drugs—it releases natural antidepressants and painkillers, with no side effects. You might think about collecting some comedy videos or books, and turn to them when you're having a bad day.

- *Look out for distorted thinking:* Think out loud and get feedback from a friend, or listen to yourself, and figure out what beliefs are behind your negative feelings. Often we are trying to live up to some ridiculous rules and expectations we haven't really thought about. When we get them into consciousness and take a close look at them, a lot of negative feelings may go away.

- *Get some counseling:* See a therapist. He or she may be able to help you get past the negative feelings.

- *Give yourself some time:* Remember that this is a normal, but temporary, part of recovery, and it won't last as long as it seems. You've been emotionally numb, and now things are coming back to life. Think about what happens when your leg "goes to sleep," then gets its circulation back—it feels crazy, but only for a short time.

Relationships with People

Some of these people (significant others, family, friends, supervisors, and coworkers) may be angry, hurt, and suspicious because of our past actions, or they may like us better sick and undermine our recovery, or they may just not understand and cause us problems for that reason. Often they are trying to decide whether to stay in relationships with us, and when they see us start changing it's both hopeful and frightening for them. They may also have their own drug and alcohol problems, which make our recovery seem threatening to them. These are some time-tested solutions to these relationship problems:

- *Listen to them and let them vent:* Give them a chance to tell you how they feel about whatever may have happened between you and them. Don't argue, explain, or defend yourself: just listen closely, then tell them what you believe you heard them say. They will either agree, disagree and correct you, or stay mad and keep blasting you. Keep listening and reflecting back what you hear, and they will run out of steam, usually sooner than you expect, and start noticing the changes in you.

- *Help them understand:* Explain to them what you are doing, as far as you feel safe trusting them with that information—but if they knew about your addiction, you might as well tell them about your recovery. Give them the chance to read some literature about what you are doing. Invite them to attend open meetings with you.

- *If they seem interested, encourage them—gently, in a non-pushy way—to get involved in their own recovery programs* such as Al-Anon, AlaTeen, CoDependents Anonymous, and so forth.

- *Make your amends, and give them time:* As you change, most people will eventually come around to seeing, accepting, and trusting the new you. Some may not, but that's beyond your control.

- *Take care of yourself:* Don't put yourself in situations where you are being used or abused, or where your recovery is being undermined. Take action to avoid, change, or leave those situations.

Work, Money, and Time Management Problems

These problems can seem overwhelming, especially when they are requiring you to make major changes in your habits. It can be very difficult to adjust, especially when your body is still getting used to being without the drug, your schedule may be busier than it's ever been, and you're trying to juggle work with meetings and other activities. Here are some ways to make this easier:

- *Make your routine consistent:* Give yourself a regular schedule—structure lowers your stress level by reducing the number of little decisions you have to make. If you always get up at the same time, you don't have to decide when to get up; if you always go to the same meeting, you don't have to decide what to do at that time; etc. Also, in a short time the new routine will become as strong a set of habits as the old one was.

- *Get help from others:* It helps to have other people both encouraging us and depending on us—get a workout partner, join a car pool, seek the advice of someone wise you trust, get others (sponsor and program friends) to help you by pointing it out to you if they see you straying from your plan and when they see you doing well at it.

- *Reward yourself for success:* Give yourself little rewards often as you score small victories. Mention them at meetings, take yourself for a walk, treat yourself to a movie and dinner if you can—and don't wait to do it until you accomplish something great, do it after some of the baby steps you take. And as always, give yourself some time to adjust.

- *Get organized:* Get and use a notebook-type organizer, a calendar, a filing system: schedule regular times for things like paying the bills, balancing the checkbook, and so on. Make yourself checklists for things you have to do. Set aside time at the beginning or end of the day to go over what you need to do or what you've done that day.

Legal Problems

It is best to tackle legal problems head on and get them over with (and we often have no choice, because they tackle us). As long as these are hanging over our heads, we have a hard time relaxing and being comfortable with ourselves, and our stress level stays higher than if they were dealt with. If you have legal problems, talk with your lawyer and do what you have to do to get them resolved and over and done with, if you can. Sometimes your willingness to face them and deal with your problems will make a strong favorable impression on people and show them you're changing, too.

Health Problems

Hopefully once your system is drug-free these will clear up quickly. If not, go see a doctor and take care of yourself. If your physical health is not good, it will make the rest of your recovery more difficult. It's important to eat a healthy diet and get enough rest and exercise, and it's a good idea to have at least one good hard laugh every day if you can.

CONCLUSION

Review the following key points:

1. There are common problems, experienced by many people getting clean and sober, which can trigger relapses and cause other problems if not faced and dealt with.

2. Because so many people have faced the same problems, there are many solutions gained from the experience of recovering people over decades.

REVIEW LEARNING GOALS

1. Upon completion of this presentation, group members will demonstrate understanding of common problems and issues in recovery by listing, without notes or references, at least four common problems encountered by many newly recovering alcoholics and addicts.

2. Upon completion of this presentation, group members will demonstrate understanding of common problems and issues in recovery by listing, without notes or references, at least one coping skill and/or resource to use in handling each problem/issue they list in their answers to the first learning goal.

QUESTIONS/DISCUSSION BEFORE POSTTEST

ADMINISTER POSTTEST

QUESTIONS/DISCUSSION AFTER POSTTEST

INTRODUCTION

Very briefly review the information covered in the presentation on the process of relapse. Ask group members to give reasons why it is important to create a relapse prevention plan. Write answers on a board, flip chart, or transparency sheet. It may be useful to list components of all prevention plans (e.g., fire prevention): warning signs of a problem, risk factors, ways to prevent the problem occurring, and backup plans if one method of prevention does not work. Facilitate a brief discussion of some areas to address in making a relapse prevention plan. Explain that this presentation is about the early warning signs of relapse and some common relapse triggers.

LEARNING GOALS

Explain to group members that they will be evaluated on their accomplishment of the following goals:

1. Upon completion of this presentation, group members will demonstrate understanding of the types of issues that may trigger relapse in a newly recovering alcoholic or addict.

2. Upon completion of this presentation, group members will be able to identify their own relapse triggers and warning signs.

QUESTIONS

As the presenter, you may ask group members to hold their questions until the end or to ask them at any time during the presentation. If participation is a high priority, we recommend allowing questions at any time; if brevity is more important, it works better to hold questions until the end.

PRETEST/POSTTEST

Pass out the pretest if you choose to use it. You may have the group members fill out and turn in pretests without putting names on them as a general measure of baseline knowledge. Explain that the same test will be given as the posttest at the end of the presentation.

BACKGROUND AND LEAD-IN

Explain to group members that relapse is part of addiction and that every recovering person runs the risk of relapse. Some recovering people succeed at avoiding relapse, some relapse and then succeed in achieving long-term sobriety, and some relapse but fail to get clean and sober again. Reemphasize that the process of relapse starts well before the first drink or drug use or compulsive action, and that the time to work on preventing relapse is before the process gets that far.

Ask group members to name lifestyle changes that are part of recovery. List their answers on a board, flipchart, or transparency sheet and facilitate a short discussion about what early indicators of relapse might show up in areas related to their answers. Reiterate that relapse, like recovery and addiction, is a process that can be changed or interrupted at any time, the earlier the better.

CAUSES AND TRIGGERS OF RELAPSE

Personal Issues

Personal issues may contribute to relapse. These are some problems that may make a person more vulnerable to a relapse. Awareness of these issues and of coping tools to handle them can help avoid relapse. Issues include:

- *Internal issues:*

    Cravings and urges to drink or use

    Loneliness and fear of abandonment

    Experiencing painful emotions without "anesthetic" of alcohol or other drugs

    Sexual issues

    Medical problems and chronic pain

    Distorted thinking

- *External or situational issues*:

    Romantic, family, and other relationship conflicts

    Financial problems

    Legal problems

    Employment problems

    Addictive environment: being around people, places, sights, sounds, smells, or tastes associated with past drinking/using experiences

Identifying General Trigger Situations

Being prepared for problems gives people a better chance of avoiding relapse. Many people fail to plan ahead and try to handle things as they come up. Others believe that their desire to remain clean and sober is the only preparation they need. It may help to start a short discussion by asking, "Has anyone here intended to stay clean and sober but found that they relapsed because of personal problems they weren't ready for? What happened?"

Ask group members to think about their own relapse triggers by making individual lists of the following types of situations:

- Times and situations when they often used/drank in the past

- Situations likely to place them in conflict with family or friends

- Life events or losses they feel they couldn't handle clean and sober

- Situations that make them angry

- Situations that make them lonely

- Situations that scare them

- Situations that depress them

- Situations that make them overconfident

- Situations that make them anxious

Drawing on the information discussed in this section, have each group member make lists of his or her own likely relapse triggers, first for the Personal Issues and then for the General Trigger Situations.

WARNING SIGNS OF IMPENDING RELAPSE

Refer group members back to the presentation on the process of relapse and the ways in which people's thoughts, feelings, and behaviors can change even before actual drinking or drug use. Many of these signs will show up before use occurs. If people are alert for the warning signs that point to impending relapse, their chances of avoiding relapse are much better. Otherwise, once the process of relapse begins denial may keep the individual from seeing what is happening. General signs of impending relapse include:

Dishonesty	Complacency and procrastination
Exhaustion	Expecting too much from others
Denial returning	Neglecting daily routine and structure
Argumentativeness	"Testing" recovery by exposure to risky situations
Depression	Expecting too much change too quickly
Frustration	Not participating in aftercare and/or meetings
Self-pity	Needless risk-taking—"It can't happen to me" syndrome
Overconfidence	Irregular eating and sleep patterns

Many newly recovering people are scared when they have cravings and dreams about drinking or using, fearing this means they are close to relapse. In fact, these are common experiences. Many clean and sober people experience these things, sometimes long after they quit drinking and using, but are able to avoid relapse. Even though cravings and dreams are not signs of impending relapse, the best thing to do is to talk about them with friends in recovery, sponsors, and counselors.

Know Your Own Warning Signs

If some group members have already entered recovery and then relapsed, ask them to identify any early warning signs in addition to those listed above that they experienced before their returns to substance abuse. For those group members who have not relapsed since entering recovery, have them think about times that they felt strong urges to use. Ask the group to collectively identify as many potential early warning signs as they can beyond the list above, drawing on the following: their own experiences; the experiences of others, especially people with whom they identify; and readings, classes in treatment, and other documentation.

Individualizing Awareness of Early Warning Signs

Drawing on the information discussed so far in this section, ask each group member to make an individual list of his or her own likely early warning signs of relapse.

CONCLUSION

Review the following key points:

1. Relapse is part of the disease of addiction and all recovering people are at risk of relapse.

2. There are common conditions, both internal and situational, that increase the risk of relapse.

3. There are also common early warning signs of relapse that can be seen in people's feelings, thoughts, and behavior before they actually return to using alcohol or other drugs.

4. By knowing their own trigger conditions and early warning signs and being alert and prepared for them, recovering people can greatly reduce their risk of relapse and increase their chances of staying clean and sober.

REVIEW LEARNING GOALS

1. Upon completion of this presentation, group members will demonstrate understanding of the types of issues that may trigger relapse in a newly recovering alcoholic or addict.

2. Upon completion of this presentation, group members will be able to identify their own relapse triggers and warning signs.

QUESTIONS/DISCUSSION BEFORE POSTTEST

ADMINISTER POSTTEST

QUESTIONS/DISCUSSION AFTER POSTTEST

INTRODUCTION

Begin by asking the group, "Why should you make a relapse prevention plan?" Write group members' responses on a board, flip chart, or transparency sheet. Ask, "Who wants to maintain sobriety from all mind-altering substances?" Explain that the purpose of this presentation is to help newly recovering people choose and carry out effective strategies to avoid relapse into the use of alcohol or other drugs.

LEARNING GOALS

Explain to group members that they will be evaluated on their accomplishment of the following goals:

1. Upon completion of this presentation, group members will demonstrate understanding of effective relapse prevention strategies for high-risk situations, both expected and unexpected, for use alone or with the help of others.

2. Upon completion of this presentation, group members will develop a plan of action for coping with situations that create a high risk of relapse.

QUESTIONS

As the presenter, you may ask group members to hold their questions until the end or to ask them at any time during the presentation. If participation is a high priority, we recommend allowing questions at any time; if brevity is more important, it works better to hold questions until the end.

PRETEST/POSTTEST

Pass out the pretest if you choose to use it. You may have the group members fill out and turn in pretests without putting names on them as a general measure of baseline knowledge. Explain that the same test will be given as the posttest at the end of the presentation.

BACKGROUND AND LEAD-IN

Guide the group in a very quick review of the process of relapse and of the early warning signs that a relapse may be taking place, including individual members' work from the *Relapse Prevention Planning, Part I* presentation. Explain that this presentation will help individual group members do more planning for their own situations and get feedback from other group members about effective versus ineffective strategies and possible alternatives. Point out that a relapse prevention plan needs constant maintenance and improvement; as they move ahead in their recovery, they will need to add or change items and strategies as they and their situations change.

ACTIONS/STRATEGIES TO PREVENT RELAPSES

Brainstorm

Draw a large box on the board, flipchart, or transparency sheet, and divide it into quarters. At the top of the left column, write "with others," and over the right column write "alone." At the edge of the upper row, write "expected," and at the edge of the lower row write "unexpected."

Ask a group member to choose one of the relapse trigger situations discussed in the first presentation on relapse prevention, then have group members brainstorm ways to cope with that specific trigger, both with the help of other people and alone. Generate as many responses as possible for each square in the grid. Ask group members to do this individually for each of the triggers, pressures, and high-risk situations they identified for themselves. Sometimes it's useful to divide the group into smaller teams and have members work together to fill in their own columns. Reconvene the whole group and have a sampling of members share their results.

Generally Useful Strategies

Group members may have already generated some of these options; share those not mentioned yet and have members add whichever they would find useful to their own columns. Point out that each person should list items and actions that are realistic for him or her to do in the present situation, because choosing options that aren't practical will set them up for failure.

1. *Talk to others:* Have group members list who they have available to talk with if needed. Plan how they will ask others for help. Preplanning this reduces stress.

2. *Stay active:* Have group members list three activities they can use to take their mind off using or drinking.

3. *Use positive affirmations:* Suggest positive thoughts to replace negative thoughts, for example, replacing "I can't stand this anymore" with "I can do this for today." Have group members list three positive thoughts.

4. *Use substitute rewards:* List ways that people can reward themselves: watching a movie, taking a walk, calling a friend, eating a favorite food, taking a bath, listening to a favorite CD, taking a nap, cooking a meal, exercising, watching TV, reading a book or magazine. Have each group member list three rewards for himself or herself.

5. *Go to a support group meeting:* Have group members specify how many meetings they will attend, where, and what days and times. Planning this out ahead of time gives the individual something to look forward to and reduces the stress of having to decide on a daily basis.

6. *Find and work with a recovery program sponsor.*

7. *Read program or spiritual literature.*

8. *Say the Serenity Prayer or other helpful prayers or slogans.*

9. *Start and end each day with recovery-oriented activity:* Many recovering people who set aside a few minutes for meditation and prayer at the beginning and end of every day find it helps them manage stress and keep anxiety down.

10. *Make a gratitude list.*

11. *Make a list of the good things about being sober.*

12. *Stay in the present:* Focus on what's going on around them and the next task in front of them, instead of worrying about things in the past they can't change or things in the future that may not happen.

13. *Avoid difficult situations when possible:* For parties and so on, ask "Do I really want to go? Do I need to go, or can I skip it?"

14. *Prepare for challenging situations that can't be avoided:* Talk about them in advance with a sponsor, recovering friends, or home group, and give them a report of how things went afterward.

15. *Keep a cell phone and a list of phone numbers of support people handy.*

16. *Plan how to leave situations that make them uncomfortable or stressed:* For example, take their own cars to parties where difficult situations may come up so they can leave whenever they need to. For many situations, people may want to plan on making a short appearance and then leaving quickly.

17. *Don't go into tough situations alone if it can be avoided:* For expected trigger situations, it can help to ask another recovering person to come along for support.

18. *Plan sober activities or celebrations for holidays or other difficult times.*

INDIVIDUALIZED PLANNING

Drawing on all the material in this presentation, have each group member complete a personal relapse prevention strategy grid with all four sections filled in, and choose at least one strategy for each individual relapse trigger on the list he or she made for the first relapse prevention exercise.

CONCLUSION

Review the following key points:

1. Relapse prevention planning makes it much easier to avoid relapse and stay clean and sober.

2. A good relapse prevention plan is never finished, but is always being improved and updated.

3. A good relapse prevention plan includes strategies for use both with the help of others and alone, and for use in both expected and unexpected relapse trigger situations.

REVIEW LEARNING GOALS

1. Upon completion of this presentation, group members will demonstrate understanding of effective relapse prevention strategies for high-risk situations, both expected and unexpected, for use alone or with the help of others.

2. Upon completion of this presentation, group members will have developed a plan of action for coping with situations that create a high risk of relapse.

QUESTIONS/DISCUSSION BEFORE POSTTEST

ADMINISTER POSTTEST

QUESTIONS/DISCUSSION AFTER POSTTEST

INTRODUCTION

Ask how many group members feel they have the knowledge they need to take good care of themselves physically and emotionally, then ask what impact this might have on their ability to stay clean and sober. Explain that this presentation will cover the basics of physical and emotional self-care because there is a strong link between how well recovering people take care of themselves and how successful they are at staying clean and sober.

LEARNING GOALS

Explain to group members that they will be evaluated on their accomplishment of the following goals:

1. Upon completion of this presentation, group members will demonstrate understanding of the basics of physical self-care by listing, without notes or references, at least four considerations in physical self-care.

2. Upon completion of this presentation, group members will demonstrate understanding of the basics of emotional self-care by listing, without notes or references, at least four considerations in emotional self-care.

QUESTIONS

As the presenter, you may ask group members to hold their questions until the end or to ask them at any time during the presentation. If participation is a high priority, we recommend allowing questions at any time; if brevity is more important, it works better to hold questions until the end.

PRETEST/POSTTEST

Pass out the pretest if you choose to use it. You may have the group members fill out and turn in pretests without putting names on them as a general measure of baseline knowledge. Explain that the same test will be given as the posttest at the end of the presentation.

BACKGROUND AND LEAD-IN

Ask the discussion question "What is self-care?" List group members' answers on a board, flip chart, or transparency sheet and facilitate a brief discussion. Then give the group the following working definition: *Self-care is composed of two elements: One is positive, providing for one's own needs, and one is negative, preventing harm to oneself.*

Physical self-care involves providing for needs. Ask group members to list physical needs. Write their answers on the board, flipchart, or transparency sheet, then add any of the following that they omit and briefly discuss each:

1. *Nutrition:* Point out that studies of people completing treatment and monitored for one year afterward showed lower relapse rates for those eating healthy diets and higher relapse rates for those eating more junk food.

   - *Balanced diet:* Low fat, moderate lean protein, moderate carbohydrates, avoid sweets.

   - *Nutrients:* Take vitamins; eat fruits and vegetables, low-fat dairy products.

- *Fluids:* Lots of water; describe the dehydrating effects of alcohol and some other drugs, including caffeine.

2. *Environment:* Shelter, clothing—protection from the elements

3. *Hygiene:* Vital for protection from disease and parasites

4. *Sleep:* Sleep deprivation weakens the body's immune system. Give group members the following tips:
   - Keep as regular a schedule as practical.
   - Avoid caffeine for several hours before sleep.
   - Avoid vigorous aerobic exercise for 2 to 3 hours before sleep.
   - Avoid long mid-day sleep periods (catnaps don't usually interfere).
   - Eat only mild foods before bedtime.
   - Arrange for a quiet period to collect thoughts—write in journal, read, meditate.
   - Keep paper and pen near bed to write down troubling thoughts.
   - Screen out distractions—use ear plugs and sleep mask if necessary.
   - Create a "sleep routine" to prepare for bed.

5. *Exercise:* Regular exercise keeps the body working at its best, helps optimize weight, improves appearance and endurance, improves moods, raises one's energy level, and increases resistance to illness.
   - Set up a regular routine, getting the advice of someone qualified if you are not familiar with the type of exercise program you are starting.
   - Find an exercise partner to keep each other motivated. Some forms of exercise are unsafe alone.
   - Do 20 to 30 minutes of some aerobic exercise three to five times each week—walk, run, swim, bike, play basketball, play a racket sport. Pick something you enjoy and something that fits your schedule and lifestyle.
   - Frequency is more important than length or intensity.
   - Avoid over-strenuous exercises (too long, too hard, overstressing specific parts of your body).
   - Use the right equipment; get training as needed.
   - Stretch, warm up, and cool down.
   - Back off at signs of impending injury or strain.
   - Include adequate time for muscles to rest and loosen up before more exercise.
   - Be extra careful regarding sun, heat, cold, dehydration.

Types of physical harm we may be able to prevent include:

1. *Injuries:*
   - Avoid high-risk behaviors and situations—this includes being in abusive relationships!
   - Use protective equipment where appropriate (seat belts, sports equipment, etc.) Use sunscreen and avoid dehydration, overheating, getting too cold.
   - Warm up and stretch before strenuous activities.
   - Don't do risky activities alone.
   - Stop if pain indicates possible injury.
   - When hurt, get medical attention as appropriate.

- Be careful regarding medications and the risk of masking pain and increasing injuries.
- People with medical problems should seek a doctor's advice before exercising.

2. *Illness:*

- Keep resistance up with good diet, exercise, rest, and stress management.
- Avoid needless exposures and disease-promoting actions (e.g., smoking).
- Take protective measures: practice safe sex; hand washing; inoculations; proper protective clothing and equipment when needed.
- Get regular physical exams. Catch hard-to-spot problems earlier (for example, high blood pressure and many cancers are not detectable without medical attention).
- Get medical attention when needed, and follow the doctor's instructions.

There are interactions between substance abuse and medical problems. Substance abuse may cause medical problems, for example:

- Accidents, fights, and so on while under the influence
- HIV, herpes, and other STDs resulting from unsafe sex while under the influence and judgment is impaired
- Illness because of substance abuse damaging the immune system and reducing the body's resistance to getting sick
- Direct tissue damage from substance abuse, such as cirrhosis of the liver from chronic excessive drinking

Medical problems may contribute to substance abuse, for example:

- Pain leading to self-medication with alcohol or other nonprescribed drugs
- Abuse of prescribed medications for either pain management or pleasure-seeking
- Becoming addicted to prescribed meds after long use

Emotional self-care involves providing for needs. Ask group members to list what they consider their emotional needs to be; write these below the previous answers and facilitate a brief discussion. Add whichever of the following they do not have listed:

1. *Feeling of being loved, accepted, and valued:* We can increase this by seeking out supportive relationships with people who treat us well and show they care about us.

2. *Feeling of having some ability to control events around us:* We can gain this by planning, having a routine, and avoiding no-win situations when possible.

3. *Feeling of competence and that our activities are worthwhile:* This is often based on a person's job but can stem from volunteer activities, hobbies or clubs, and family activities; again, avoid no-win situations when possible.

4. *Feeling of emotional safety:* We can increase this by avoiding needless risky situations such as destructive relationships.

What are the types of emotional harm we may be able to prevent? It is important to watch for these situations and get help if needed to avoid them, end them, or change them:

1. *Emotional abuse or neglect by others or self:* Don't do it and don't tolerate it. If you have questions about what's abusive or negligent, discuss it with at least two people you consider wise and trustworthy.

2. *Isolation:* Avoid this by staying connected to important others.

3. *Depression, anxiety, etc.:* These can have physical causes also; it is important to get help as needed, including appropriately prescribed medication. (Make sure the doctor knows you're a recovering alcoholic or addict.)

4. *Burnout at work or in other situations:* This can lead to relapse. It is vital to keep balance in one's life.

5. *Distorted thinking:* Check with healthy people for feedback.

OVERALL TOOLS AND RESOURCES

The following are useful in all kinds of self-care:

- Personal relationships that provide support and feedback.
- Recovery support groups and other community activities or programs.
- Fitness centers and other facilities for exercise and recreation.
- Sources of medical information and treatment including public health offices, doctors, nurses, clinics, and hospitals.
- Therapy.
- Literature and other sources of information.

CONCLUSION

Review the following key points:

1. Physical and emotional self-care directly affects one's chances of success in staying clean and sober.

2. Self-care consists of both positive aspects, meeting one's needs, and negative aspects, preventing or avoiding harm.

3. Several types of widely available tools and resources are useful in both physical and emotional self-care.

REVIEW LEARNING GOALS

1. Upon completion of this presentation, group members will demonstrate understanding of the basics of physical self-care by listing, without notes or references, at least four considerations in physical self-care.

2. Upon completion of this presentation, group members will demonstrate understanding of the basics of emotional self-care by listing, without notes or references, at least four considerations in emotional self-care.

QUESTIONS/DISCUSSION BEFORE POSTTEST

ADMINISTER POSTTEST

QUESTIONS/DISCUSSION AFTER POSTTEST

INTRODUCTION

Ask whether group members have noticed any connection between stress and their own drinking or other drug use; list their responses on a board, flip chart, or transparency sheet. Explain that this presentation will help them increase their ability to cope with stress without using alcohol or other drugs so that they can stay clean and sober and have a reasonable quality of life.

LEARNING GOALS

Explain to group members that they will be evaluated on their accomplishment of the following goals:

1. Upon completion of this presentation, group members will be able to identify one physiological, two mental/emotional, and two behavioral symptoms of stress.

2. Upon completion of this presentation, group members will be able to describe the relationship between stress and self-medication leading to chemical dependency.

3. Upon completion of this presentation, group members will be able to identify at least eight healthy and nonaddictive ways recovering people can cope with stress.

QUESTIONS

As the presenter, you may ask group members to hold their questions until the end or to ask them at any time during the presentation. If participation is a high priority, we recommend allowing questions at any time; if brevity is more important, it works better to hold questions until the end.

PRETEST/POSTTEST

Pass out the pretest if you choose to use it. You may have the group members fill out and turn in pretests without putting names on them as a general measure of baseline knowledge. Explain that the same test will be given as the posttest at the end of the presentation.

BACKGROUND AND LEAD-IN

Facilitate a brief discussion of how stress affects addictive behavior. Point out that all people experience stress in their daily life, and that early recovery from addictions brings greater stress because of the many changes taking place in life. Since many people began drinking or using to relieve stress in the first place, this makes coping with recovery's stresses on top of the stresses they already had especially hard. Explain that alcohol and other drugs are short-term solutions, but that the problems causing the stress are usually ongoing. When the chemicals wear off, the problems are still there. Eventually drinking or using stops working to reduce those stresses and instead creates more stress. Managing stress in early recovery is an important part of avoiding a return to use and maintaining a program of recovery.

WHAT IS STRESS?

Explain that definitions of stress include words like strain, pressure, urgency, and tension. A useful visual metaphor for stress is to hold up an uncooked spaghetti noodle between two fingers. Show the group what happens to the noodle if a moderate amount of stress is put on it by lightly pressing the fingers together so that the noodle bends a bit. Ask the group what will happen if the stress is relieved, then show that it will return to its original shape. Now ask them to visualize what happens to the noodle if too much stress is applied—show that the noodle will snap into pieces. Ask the group to talk about some of the ways that people can "snap." Now ask them to think of things that are more capable of standing up to stress than the noodle, and what qualities make this so. They may list qualities like greater strength and greater flexibility. Explain that the methods to be discussed in this presentation are meant to help people achieve both greater strength and greater flexibility.

To understand stress more completely, we must look at stressful situations and their effects on the body, mind, and spirit. Have group members generate a list of stressful situations, and record their answers on the board, flip chart, or transparency sheet. Explain that stress can be both positive and negative. Negative stress, sometimes called *distress,* is the result when people feel overwhelmed and the impact in their lives is destructive; positive stress, also known as *eustress,* can get people's attention, motivate them to make healthy changes and perform better, and have a helpful effect overall.

Examples of stressful situations include:

Meeting new people

Change in employment status (new job, fired, layoff, promotion, demotion, retired)

Breaking up of significant relationship

Getting married

Losing your house key or car keys

Graduating

Entering or leaving treatment

Going to your first support group meeting

Finding and talking with a sponsor

Taking a test

Talking in a group

Moving (short or long distances)

Symptoms of stress can include any of the following physiological, mental/emotional, and behavioral responses. These are useful in watching out for increased stress, either in oneself or in others.

Physiological Symptoms of Stress
- Muscle tension
- Aches and pains, especially in the head, neck, and back
- Rapid pulse and breathing
- Trembling or shaking
- Indigestion

Mental/Emotional Symptoms of Stress
- Anger or irritability
- Lack of motivation
- Confusion
- Fatigue
- Anxiety and worry

- Tearfulness
- Increased emotionality, hypersensitivity

Behavioral Symptoms of Stress
- Increased argumentativeness
- Withdrawal, isolating from peers or activities
- Sleep problems—insomnia or oversleeping
- Becoming more accident-prone
- Inattention, short attention span, difficulty concentrating
- Return to old self-defeating behaviors
- Overeating, loss of appetite, smoking

MANAGING STRESS

Stressful situations are common in early recovery. Any or all of these situations can be very difficult to handle. Even thinking about them can trigger stress symptoms. For example:

- Giving up old acquaintances and developing healthy sober friendships
- Addressing old or new challenges for the first time without a chemical filter
- Communicating with your family on issues you previously avoided
- Experiencing intense feelings, and often mood swings, without being able to numb them

Addictive behaviors aren't the only self-destructive responses to stress. Here are some other methods that people often use because they seem to relieve the feelings of stress for the short term, but that make things worse in the long run:

- Avoiding the situation by leaving or not becoming emotionally involved
- Creating win-lose situations (fighting) and using control to win
- Tackling the situation indirectly or "sideways"; an example would be reacting to financial stress by yelling at the kids, or by doing things that get on coworkers' nerves. This is often referred to as a passive–aggressive way of managing stress.

Here are some responses that will relieve the symptoms of stress without causing more trouble later on:

- *Get some physical exercise:* Work it off. Taking a walk can be enough: strenuous exercise is not necessary.
- *Talk with others:* Share your concerns with others you trust. This may be a way to get feedback and also to see that you may not be alone in what you feel, and it can improve relationships by reducing isolation and increasing trust and understanding.
- *Let go and accept the situations and events that are out of your control:* People spend a lot of time, energy, worry, and stress on things in their lives that they can't change. Use the Serenity Prayer.
- *Get enough sleep and nutrition:* Our bodies and minds need these to work efficiently. Without enough rest, people are unable to deal with stress effectively. Normal sleep patterns may take several months to return in early recovery, so avoid the intake of stimulants. What you put into your body will influence how you handle stress.
- *Help someone else:* It makes a big difference to get your attention off yourself.

- *Be honest:* Often during the time you were drinking or using you spent a lot of time hiding, making excuses, covering your tracks; learning to live honestly reduces the worry and stress associated with dishonesty.
- *Focus on the present:* Avoid dwelling on guilt over past situations or worrying about the future.
- *Learn effective relaxation techniques:* Give yourself a break by taking a five-minute vacation. Relaxation and visualization techniques can provide great relief from stress, depression, anxiety, and even symptoms of medical problems.
- *Practice patience and flexibility:* Learning to admit mistakes, accepting other people's rights to their own opinions, and giving up the need to be right or control events is vital to achieving peace of mind. Many people recovering from addictions feel that they need to be further along than they are. It is important to point out that long-term positive changes come with learning new skills and practicing consistently over time. Many recovering people want to perform perfectly and when they do not, they experience stress and frustration.
- *Learn to laugh at yourself and life's problems.*
- *Avoid competitiveness:* comparing yourself with other people and always wanting to win or come out on top is a guaranteed recipe for frustration and feeling inadequate.
- *Act; avoid procrastination.*
- *Confront your fears:* When we don't confront our fears, they grow, and the fear itself can become a bigger problem than the things the fear is focused on.
- *Ask for help:* Often, there are solutions to our difficulties, but they can't be carried out alone. Many people drink and use in isolation; break this old pattern and reach out to the people and resources around you.
- *Practice time management:* Keep a reasonable daily schedule and routine. Often, people need to learn how to prioritize tasks and accept that they can't do as much as they want to in the time they have.

CONCLUSION

Review the following key points:

1. Stress is a normal part of life, and healthy stress management is necessary for recovery from addiction.
2. Stress has clear-cut symptoms that show up in people's bodies, thoughts and emotions, and behavior.
3. There are both unhealthy and healthy ways to relieve the symptoms of stress. Learning effective stress management techniques can enable people to handle hard situations and keep their peace of mind.

REVIEW LEARNING GOALS

1. Upon completion of this presentation, group members will be able to identify one physiological, two mental/emotional, and two behavioral symptoms of stress.
2. Upon completion of this presentation, group members will be able to describe the relationship between stress and self-medication leading to chemical dependency.
3. Upon completion of this presentation, group members will be able to identify at least eight healthy and nonaddictive ways recovering people can cope with stress.

QUESTIONS/DISCUSSION BEFORE POSTTEST

ADMINISTER POSTTEST

QUESTIONS/DISCUSSION AFTER POSTTEST

INTRODUCTION

Start with a practical example: Ask whether all group members have pens or pencils, and pass them out to any who don't. Pass out blank pieces of paper and explain that you will give instructions and will give up to two clarifications of the instructions if anyone wants you to do so. Ask whether everyone is ready, then begin by telling group members, "I entail that each of you suscitate a papyrus monoplane of your own delineation."

If someone says that they don't understand, tell them, "I mendicate that you fabricate vellum aeronautical transports of whatever conceptions you desiderate."

If someone wants more explanation, say "Your undertaking is to contrive an avion of foolscap."

If no one has figured it out after the third try, tell them that the group has failed the exercise, and then explain that what you meant was, "I want you to make a paper airplane."

Ask the group members for comments about what has just happened. Write their answers on a board, flip chart, or transparency sheet. Ask how many know how to make a paper airplane, are willing to make one, and want to succeed in this program. Then ask what went wrong. They will point out that they didn't know what to do. Reply that the presenter gave them instructions. They will reply that the instructions weren't in a form most people could understand.

Acknowledge that the task was not presented clearly, and ask whether it wasn't really the presenter who failed. Point out that the presenter knew exactly what the group members were supposed to do, and that they would have done it if they'd understood the instructions. Note that the problem was not inability or unwillingness or that the presenter didn't give them the needed information, but that the information was not given in a useable form.

Then ask how many times the group members have experienced or seen anger and frustration caused when someone failed to communicate clearly. Ask for a show of hands of group members who have seen relationship problems that could have been avoided with clearer communication. Ask how many think the stress of relationship problems could be a trigger for relapse. Explain that this presentation will be about communication skills and ways to improve communication, to help people avoid relapse by reducing stress caused by poor communication.

LEARNING GOALS

Explain to group members that they will be evaluated on their accomplishment of the following goals:

1. Upon completion of this presentation, group members will demonstrate understanding of communication skills by listing, without notes or references, the four necessary basic elements of the communication process.

2. Upon completion of this presentation, group members will demonstrate understanding of communication skills by listing, without notes or references, four skills related to effective communication.

3. Upon completion of this presentation, group members will demonstrate understanding of communication skills by demonstrating use of a specific active listening and feedback process.

QUESTIONS

As the presenter, you may ask group members to hold their questions until the end or to ask them at any time during the presentation. If participation is a high priority, we recommend allowing questions at any time; if brevity is more important, it works better to hold questions until the end.

PRETEST/POSTTEST

Pass out the pretest if you choose to use it. You may have the group members fill out and turn in pretests without putting names on them as a general measure of baseline knowledge. Explain that the same test will be given as the posttest at the end of the presentation.

BACKGROUND AND LEAD-IN

Refer to the introductory exercise and restate that this was an example of poor communication. Ask the group to list forms of communication, write answers on a board, flip chart, or transparency sheet, and facilitate a brief discussion. Possibilities include:

1. Verbal, through choice of words and manner of speaking

2. Written

3. Nonverbal, including facial expressions, gestures, posture, and other actions

4. Omission, or what is not said, written, or done

Ask the group to list causes of poor communication, and again write answers on a board, flip chart, or transparency sheet, and facilitate a brief discussion. Possibilities include:

1. Language differences or lack of shared vocabulary

2. Failure to listen

3. Unclear expression of ideas

4. One person expecting another to be a mind reader

5. One person thinking he or she already knows what the other person thinks before being told

6. Fear of speaking directly

7. Lack of desire to communicate

8. Deliberate dishonesty

COMMUNICATION SKILLS

Present items below that are basic elements of the communication process. Then ask group members for examples of how these might be lacking and facilitate a brief discussion of each one:

Sender: The sender must have a message and the desire and ability to send it. Lack of a sender with all of those factors makes communication impossible.

Receiver: The receiver must have the willingness and ability to receive the message. Lack of a receiver with these traits also makes communication impossible.

Message: The message must contain information in a form having a meaning known to both sender and receiver. If the message lacks information, is in a form that is not understandable to both parties, or has different meanings to the two parties, accurate communication will not take place.

Medium: The medium must be useable by both sender and receiver; if it is not, the message cannot be carried from one to the other.

Guidelines for effective communication include:

1. *Stay as calm and positive as practical:*

   • Give other people credit for having good intentions unless they've proven they don't. Remember, what others say and do makes sense from where they stand.

- Criticize actions but don't attack people.
- When possible, offer solutions.
- If you feel as if you're about to lose your temper, stop and take a few deep breaths and make yourself relax, especially the muscles in your face and shoulders.
- Use the "sandwich method" for criticism or correction—say something positive, then offer the criticism or other information likely to be perceived as negative, then finish with another positive statement. Example: A shop teacher says to a student: "I like the energy and enthusiasm you bring to this class. I would like you to be more careful, because this morning when you were so eager to get to work on your project, you didn't put on your safety goggles before you started using the drill press. However, I know you try really hard to do things the right way and you're a fast learner, so I have a lot of confidence that you'll remember and not make that mistake again."

2. *Be clear and specific:*

- Make your point clearly—ask for what you want, tell how you feel.
- If you quote someone's words, be accurate.
- If you talk about other's actions, be specific—give times, dates, and places.
- Stick to what's relevant—don't talk about more than one thing at a time.
- Ask for feedback—"Please tell me in your own words what you believe I meant."
- Rephrase/restate your message if necessary until the other understands.

3. *Talk from your own point of view:*

- When you talk about someone else, talk about what he or she actually said or did, not what you believe he or she was thinking or feeling, since there's no way you can ever know those things for certain.
- Own your own feelings—say "I felt _____", rather than "you made me mad/sad/etc."
- Use "I" statements.

4. *Keep the conversation a two-way process:*

- Stop often enough to let others respond while they can remember what's on their minds.
- Make one point at a time.

5. *Stay on the subject:*

- Organize your thoughts in a clear order before starting.
- Discuss one topic at a time.
- If you feel the need to talk about other issues, save them for other conversations.

6. *Be a good listener:*

- Try to put yourself in the other person's place and understand how he or she is experiencing the situation—try to see it through that person's eyes as well as your own.
- Listen with full attention, rather than rehearsing your response. Wait until the other person has finished what he or she is saying and you're sure you understand it correctly before starting to think about what you will say in reply.
- Actively listen. Pay attention to posture, tone, expression, as well as words.
- Don't interrupt.
- Ask questions when you aren't sure you understand something.
- Give feedback—paraphrase message back to sender, and ask if you understood the meaning correctly; if not, ask for a restatement.

- When someone tells you what they think or feel, you can let them know you understand their thoughts and feelings without that meaning you agree with them.

A STRUCTURED COMMUNICATION PROCESS: ACTIVE LISTENING AND FEEDBACK

Explain that this process is useful when people need to discuss subjects that bring up strong emotions. When the navy taught it to couples in a premarital communication skills course, it resulted in those couples having a lot fewer arguments and a divorce rate over the next 10 years that was only half the average for navy marriages.

Preparation

1. *Make an appointment:* Agree to discuss an issue at a time when both people are ready to do so.

2. Decide who will take the first turn as the sender (speaker) and who will start out as the receiver (listener). Both people will get turns in both roles.

Process

1. The sender speaks: He or she makes a brief (one- or two-sentence) statement, on one topic, being specific and using the A-B-C format (event, result, emotions: "When you did A, B happened, and I felt C.").

2. The receiver listens closely without interrupting while the sender speaks, then gives feedback, that is, responds by rephrasing the sender's message in the receiver's own words and asking whether it is accurate—this doesn't mean the receiver is agreeing, just that he or she understands! During this stage, the receiver doesn't answer, explain, defend, or argue. His or her turn is coming to present the other side.

3. The sender responds to the receiver's feedback: If it is accurate, the sender says so. If it is inaccurate or incomplete, the sender restates any part that wasn't understood, and the receiver responds again.

4. Switch places once the receiver gives accurate feedback to the sender, and repeat the process.

Results

People say they have the following experiences with this method:

- Less frustration—both people feel they have been heard and understood.

- Getting communication out of argument ruts.

- Clearing up or avoiding misunderstandings.

- Avoiding angry blowups.

- Greater empathy both ways and feeling closer to one another.

COMMUNICATION MISTAKES TO AVOID

Explain that conflict is a natural part of any relationship between two people, and that when people get into a conflict they tend to have two conflicting desires: to solve the problem, and to win the argument. Point out that they have to choose, and if they would rather solve a problem than make an argument worse, they should avoid the following mistakes, which tend to make arguments worse instead of ending them.

- *Always/never statements:* "You always do this," "you never do that," etc.

- *Attacks:* Yelling, name-calling, and sarcasm.

- *Stating thoughts as feelings:* "I feel that . . ." is not a feeling! Feelings are emotions, not views or opinions.

- *Kitchen-sinking:* Starting out to talk about one issue, then bringing more and more problems into the discussion.

- *Blaming:* "You made me do _____", "you made me feel ____", etc.

- *Interrupting.*

- *Monopolizing:* Not giving the other person a chance to talk.

- *Mind reading:* Telling other people you know what they think or feel.

- *Fortune-telling:* Telling other people what you think they are going to do.

- *Hinting:* Expecting the other person to know what you think or feel without your telling them; saying things like "If you cared about me you'd know why I was upset," etc.

- *Exaggerating or minimizing:* Either someone else's behavior or your own.

CONCLUSION

Review the following key points:

1. There are four elements that are needed for communication to take place:
   - A *sender* with a message and the ability and willingness to communicate it.
   - A *receiver* with the ability and willingness to receive the message.
   - A *message* that has a shared meaning for both the sender and receiver.
   - A *medium* that both the sender and receiver can use.

2. Effective communication skills include the following:
   - Stay as calm and positive as practical.
   - Be clear and specific.
   - Talk from your own point of view.
   - Keep the conversation a two-way process.
   - Stay on the subject.
   - Be a good listener.

3. There is a structured communication process that helps reduce communication problems in emotional situations.

4. There are a number of mistakes to avoid, which will make arguments worse instead of solving problems.

REVIEW LEARNING GOALS

Upon completion of this presentation, group members will demonstrate:

1. Understanding of communication skills by listing, without notes or references, the four necessary basic elements of the communication process.

2. Understanding of communication skills by listing, without notes or references, four skills related to effective communication.

3. Understanding of communication skills by demonstrating use of a specific active listening and feedback process.

QUESTIONS/DISCUSSION BEFORE POSTTEST

ADMINISTER POSTTEST

QUESTIONS/DISCUSSION AFTER POSTTEST

INTRODUCTION

Ask each group member to briefly state the three most important changes he or she hopes to see in his or her life as a result of becoming clean and sober. List answers on a board, flip chart, or transparency sheet, indicating duplications by putting check marks next to answers given by more than one person.

Facilitate a brief discussion of how many of the changes listed have to do with relationships (romantic, family, friendship, or work). Ask group members how many of the desired changes are likely to occur if they stop using alcohol or other drugs but make no other major changes in their lifestyles, then briefly discuss the idea that recovery involves many changes above and beyond abstinence from psychoactive substance use.

LEARNING GOALS

Explain to group members that they will be evaluated on their accomplishment of the following goals:

1. Upon completion of this presentation, group members will demonstrate understanding of healthy relationship skills by listing, without notes or references, at least four skills for finding and developing healthy relationships.

2. Upon completion of this presentation, group members will demonstrate understanding of healthy relationship skills by listing, without notes or references, at least four skills for maintaining healthy relationships.

3. Upon completion of this presentation, group members will demonstrate understanding of healthy relationship skills by listing, without notes or references, at least four specific problem areas to watch for in relationships.

QUESTIONS

As the presenter, you may ask group members to hold their questions until the end or to ask them at any time during the presentation. If participation is a high priority, we recommend allowing questions at any time; if brevity is more important, it works better to hold questions until the end.

PRETEST/POSTTEST

Pass out the pretest if you choose to use it. You may have the group members fill out and turn in pretests without putting names on them as a general measure of baseline knowledge. Explain that the same test will be given as the posttest at the end of the presentation.

BACKGROUND AND LEAD-IN

Ask group members what effects they believe the quality of their relationships might have on their success in recovery and on their quality of life and happiness. Ask how many feel they have all the knowledge and skills they need in this area. Explain that this presentation will give them information and skills that will increase their chances of having healthy relationships, based on the experiences of many others before them.

HEALTHY RELATIONSHIP SKILLS

Refer to the group members' relationship goals listed earlier: Some will probably be directed toward current relationships and some toward future relationships they hope to develop. This first section addresses skills that are useful in starting relationships. In general, these apply not only to romantic relationships but also to other friendships and work relationships.

Become capable of healthy relationships. Relationships can't be any healthier emotionally than the people in those relationships. It is also true that we tend to attract, and be attracted to, others who are at about our own levels of emotional health. Therefore, before we become capable of participation in a good relationship, we must be functioning in a healthy way as individuals on our own. This means using the tools presented throughout treatment and in support groups and allowing time to work on and change our addictive and unhealthy lifestyle patterns. This is why sponsors and others often advise newly recovering people to avoid making major relationship decisions or commitments for at least their first year of recovery. It takes most people at least that long to become stable enough to make healthy choices.

Select and screen partners and friends. There is nothing wrong with being cautious and picky, or with screening people out when we feel they aren't right for us. Many people who become alcoholics or addicts grew up in situations where they may not have learned that they had the right to say no. It's important to remember that *no one is obligated to go out with anyone else, or become romantically or sexually involved, or even to become friends, just because the other person wants this or is in need.* We meet many people who are truly needy but who are not able to be in healthy relationships. We have the right to say no to any relationship we feel is unhealthy, unsafe, or inappropriate. Also, a relationship that may seem to start out well can later change for the worse. Again, we have the right at that time to end those relationships, or to reduce our level of involvement in them.

Control pace and stages in relationship development. Rome wasn't built in a day, and neither was any healthy relationship. A common pattern in unhealthy relationships is "moving too fast"—a rapid progression to high levels of emotional and/or sexual intimacy. This is not safe. It takes time to know another person well enough to tell how stable and dependable he or she is. By contrast, a healthy relationship develops slowly enough that both partners are able to get to know one another at deeper and deeper levels of intimacy and trust and let the levels of openness and vulnerability in the relationship increase only as that trust based on knowing the other person deepens.

Risk management is the art of being neither too reckless nor too cautious as a relationship develops, so that we don't get hurt too badly too often, but we don't deny ourselves the chance to experience good relationships. There are two key principles here:

1. *Don't risk more than you can afford to lose.* Don't make yourself physically or emotionally vulnerable unless you can accept the chance that the other person will let you down and unless you can handle the effects on you if he or she does so.

2. *Don't risk much more than the other person is risking.* If you are making yourself very open emotionally, sharing your secrets, feelings, dreams, and fears, and the other person is withholding this type of disclosure, something is out of balance. An imbalance of vulnerability creates an unhealthy imbalance of power in a relationship.

Watch for repetition of unhealthy patterns. Many of us find, reviewing our lives, that we have certain patterns of behavior that have caused us problems over and over. In relationships, these can be patterns such as being drawn to certain types of people who hurt us or engaging in certain types of relationship-destroying behavior of our own. It is wise to first review our own pasts to identify such patterns, then to watch for patterns coming up again and to get the feedback of others we trust to help us do this watching. If we see the old patterns being replayed, we have two choices: We can either do something different (cut the relationship short or keep it at a different level from past patterns, or choose to change our own behaviors as the relationship develops) or we can do the same thing again *and probably get the same results we have gotten in the past.*

Know when to back away. There are some near-universal signs that a developing relationship is unhealthy. One of the skills in finding and developing healthy relationships is identifying these signs and getting some distance or getting completely out of the relationship, whichever is most appropriate. Some warning signs are:

1. You and the other person want significantly different types of relationship (e.g., you want a nonromantic friendship and he or she wants to become lovers), and neither of you is willing to change your goals for the relationship.

2. The other person becomes abusive, intrusive, manipulative, demanding, or controlling. This includes physical and sexual coercion, pressure, or violence; open or implied threats; guilt-inducing statements such as anything starting with "If you care about me . . ." or similar words; demands or pressure to account for time or activities; or inappropriate jealousy, such as demands or pressure to cut back or give up other family or friendship relationships or other activities.

3. The other person becomes consistently needy and you find yourself frequently rescuing him or her, solving his or her problems, or otherwise "fixing" the person.

4. You become aware that the other person is being dishonest, sneaky, secretive, or unethical in other ways and is unwilling to discuss this and/or change these behaviors.

5. Friends or family whom you consider to be healthy and to have good judgment perceive the other person as unhealthy or unsafe.

6. You find yourself doing things you don't really want to do in the relationship out of a feeling of obligation or pity. This includes situations in which you feel pressure to violate your values for fear of losing the relationship. It is best to let it go and find someone with whom you can be yourself and still be in a relationship.

MAINTAINING HEALTHY RELATIONSHIPS

For group members who are in relationships they wish to make or keep healthy, the following skills are important.

- *Communication skills:* Communication is the most important area in most relationships, and the most common source of trouble. We learn to talk more or less automatically as children, but we don't learn good communication skills automatically unless our parents or caregivers model them for us. These are covered in detail in separate presentations. Good communication skills include:

  1. Active listening and feedback skills

  2. Staying positive

  3. Being clear and specific

  4. Staying on the subject

  5. Avoiding "you" statements, mind reading, and attacks

- *Acceptance and being supportive:* We often find that when a partner or friend tells us about a problem, we feel obligated to solve it. Often we know we can't. This can lead to the following problems:

  1. The listener feeling guilty or inadequate and changing the subject

  2. Cutting off the person who is speaking and giving advice

  3. Minimizing, comparing, or belittling the problem

What people usually want from their friends or partners is not a solution, but support. In a healthy relationship, partners practice listening, offering understanding and support, and letting the other person find his or her own solution. This is also much easier than trying to solve another person's problems for him or her.

- *Balancing togetherness and individuality:* In a healthy relationship, there are three categories of time and activities: yours, mine, and ours. Partners in friendship or love do some things together and others on their own; they have some mutual friends and some friends they don't share.

- *Being interdependent:* We all want to feel needed, but none of us has the strength or resources to adequately manage more than one life at a time. In a healthy relationship, there is a balance of needs with neither partner being consistently more needy than the other.

- *Balancing work and play:* In a healthy relationship, work and play are both important, and partners share some of both. Work is necessary for both partners to contribute to the relationship (work can be anything from a paid job to maintaining a household), and shared play is necessary to keep love and enjoyment of one another active.

- *Handling conflicts:* Every relationship includes conflict. Having conflict does not mean a relationship is unhealthy. In healthy relationships, people accept that conflict is natural and find ways to resolve it so that both partners are satisfied with the results over time, and they remember that although they are in conflict they care about each other more than they care about the conflict. This means that in a healthy relationship, partners can disagree, argue, and work out conflicts in a loving and respectful way. This is also addressed in detail in separate presentations. Some specific conflict management skills are:

  1. Checking for misunderstanding and clarifying when it is found
  2. Working to see the other's point of view
  3. Seeking compromises acceptable to both partners
  4. Practicing putting the relationship ahead of winning the conflict
  5. Using time-outs to allow tempers to cool when necessary
  6. Making appointments to discuss touchy topics at times when both partners are prepared to do so
  7. Working on one area of conflict at a time

DEALING WITH SPECIFIC PROBLEMS

Some particular types of problems occur in many relationships. Here are some of these specific problems:

- *Misunderstandings and disappointments:* If you have chosen a partner who is dependable and honest, then problems of this type will probably result from poor communication and expectations that aren't realistic or that weren't made clear to each other. The primary solutions in a healthy relationship are to practice good communication skills and to check our own thinking about our partners to make sure our expectations are reasonable and based on our experiences with those partners rather than on our untested ideas or impressions about them, especially when a relationship is new and we don't know each other very well yet.

- *Violations of rights or boundaries:* If you have chosen a healthy partner, when these happen they will usually result from honest mistakes such as poor communication and differing expectations. Two partners may have grown up in families with different rules about rights, roles, and boundaries between partners. And again, the healthy relationship solutions are good communication and frequent self-examination of motives, expectations, and beliefs.

- *Jealousy and possessiveness:* This is an unhealthy pattern, but is present to some degree in nearly every relationship, even comparatively healthy ones. It is typically based on insecurity and fear of abandonment. The healthy solution is for partners in a relationship to address these underlying fears, as well as the jealous and possessive behavior, and resolve both in a way that both people are satisfied with.

- *Children:* We and our partners will always have different experiences, beliefs, and expectations about proper child rearing because of having grown up in different families that did things different ways. In a healthy relationship, these differences are openly addressed, preferably before having children, and resolved by finding compromises acceptable to both partners.

- *Money:* Again, we and our partners are likely to have learned different habits and views about managing money, and in a healthy relationship will discuss this openly and reach a compromise acceptable to both partners. If either or both partners lack skills or experience in managing money, information and training are available from community agencies.

- *Change in general:* Changes are always stressful, and because we and our partners are different people, we see and experience these changes differently. This sometimes leads to honest differences of opinion about how to handle them. Because people are less patient and tolerant when under more stress, and because change is stressful, this can trigger emotional conflicts. In a healthy relationship, partners work at their conflict management skills, use them to handle conflict resulting from change, and anticipate problems when they know major changes are coming in their situation.

CONCLUSION

Review the following key points:

1. Most recovering people have important goals in relation to present or future relationships.

2. Creating and maintaining healthy relationships takes specific skills.

3. It is possible for newly recovering people to learn these skills and improve their chances of succeeding in recovery and having better quality of life.

REVIEW LEARNING GOALS

1. Upon completion of this presentation, group members will demonstrate understanding of healthy relationship skills by listing, without notes or references, at least four skills for finding and developing healthy relationships.

2. Upon completion of this presentation, group members will demonstrate understanding of healthy relationship skills by listing, without notes or references, at least four skills for maintaining healthy relationships.

3. Upon completion of this presentation, group members will demonstrate understanding of healthy relationship skills by listing, without notes or references, at least four specific problem areas to watch for in relationships.

QUESTIONS/DISCUSSION BEFORE POSTTEST

ADMINISTER POSTTEST

QUESTIONS/DISCUSSION AFTER POSTTEST

INTRODUCTION

Ask group members what they think this topic has to do with staying clean and sober, other than the obvious answer that staying clean and sober is a goal in itself. Ask each member to name a goal that is important to him or her, and write their answers on a board, flip chart, or transparency sheet. Facilitate a brief discussion of how they have gone about achieving goals in the past and how successful they have been. Explain that this presentation will give them information about skills in setting and achieving goals to help them succeed in staying clean and sober and having a good quality of life.

LEARNING GOALS

Explain to group members that they will be evaluated on their accomplishment of the following goals:

1. Upon completion of this presentation, group members will demonstrate the ability to define the steps in setting a reasonable and worthwhile goal.

2. Upon completion of this presentation, group members will demonstrate the ability to define at least five qualities of a well-defined goal.

3. Upon completion of this presentation, group members will demonstrate the ability to define eight steps in the process of achieving a goal.

QUESTIONS

As the presenter, you may ask group members to hold their questions until the end or to ask them at any time during the presentation. If participation is a high priority, we recommend allowing questions at any time; if brevity is more important, it works better to hold questions until the end.

PRETEST/POSTTEST

Pass out the pretest if you choose to use it. You may have the group members fill out and turn in pretests without putting names on them as a general measure of baseline knowledge. Explain that the same test will be given as the posttest at the end of the presentation.

BACKGROUND AND LEAD-IN

Ask these discussion questions: What is the difference between a goal and a simple desire or wish? How do successful people set and achieve their goals? Record their answers on a board, flip chart, or transparency sheet. As the presentation progresses, refer back to them as applicable.

STEPS IN SETTING A REASONABLE AND WORTHWHILE GOAL

If group members follow these steps when they think about goals they want to achieve, they will improve their chances of success:

1. State the goal clearly and visualize it. If you can't put your goal into words, clearly enough for someone else to understand it, you probably won't achieve it. Can you state it clearly? In other words, what do you want to have happen? Can you picture it clearly? If you succeed, what will it look like? How will your life change?

Reality check: Is this goal possible and practical, in your situation? Do you know what will have to be done, and can you do it?

2. State your reasons or motives. Why do you want to achieve this goal? What's wrong with the way things are now? Will achieving your goal change that? What are any possible reasons or motives *not* to make this change?

3. Think about the other likely results. What is the downside? What will be the negative results if you achieve your goal? What will the ripple effects be? What other changes will these changes cause in turn?

4. Check your motivation. How much do you want it? Do you want it enough to do whatever it takes for you to achieve it? Do you want it enough to accept the downside and the ripple effects? If the downside or ripple effects turn out to be worse than you expected, where do you draw the line and decide the goal is not worth it after all? In other words, what price would be too high for you to pay for this goal?

5. If you are sure your goal is reasonable and you want to achieve it, you should make and use a written plan to carry out whatever action is needed.

QUALITIES OF A WELL-DEFINED GOAL

As a check to see whether you've done a good job in choosing and defining a goal, make sure it meets the following requirements:

1. *It is conceivable.* You can clearly picture it and understand it. You can see the result you want in detail in your imagination. You can clearly explain it to someone else.

2. *It is believable.* You believe you can do it. It is not asking too much in too short a time. It doesn't require abilities or resources you don't have and can't get. You have confidence in your own ability to do it.

3. *It is controllable.* Either you can do whatever is needed without help, or if it requires the help of anyone else, you know they will help you.

4. *It is measurable.* You can measure your success in some way that will let you know clearly whether or not you have succeeded.

5. *It can be stated as a single goal.* No "ands" or "ors." Planning gets too complicated if a goal isn't stated as one single desired outcome; different goals should be planned for separately.

6. *It is positive and good for you.* Be sure that you will be better off if you get what you want.

AN EIGHT-STEP APPROACH TO GOAL ACCOMPLISHMENT

1. *Visualize the goal in detail:* Create a clear mental picture of the result you want to achieve. Create a clear description in words. Write it down.

2. *Set subgoals as needed:* Set one subgoal for each specific action needed. If some subgoals have to be completed before others can be done, spell out the sequence. Set a target time and date for each subgoal.

3. *Analyze obstacles:* Figure out how hard the necessary tasks will be. What problems will get in the way? Identify factors that are beyond your control. Identify the resources you will need to overcome the problems and cope with the factors beyond your control.

4. *Analyze your resources:* Personal *internal* resources such as determination, self-discipline, courage, intelligence, strength, talents. Personal *external* resources such as money, connections, tools, free time. Where are things you need that you can get from other people or other sources?

5. *Analyze and choose your methods:* Research to find out how others have achieved similar goals before you. Brainstorm ways you could achieve the result you want. Evaluate the pros and cons of each option you have. Choose the option that looks best after this evaluation.

6. *Carry out the chosen methods:* Gather needed resources. Follow time lines and sequences. Use affirmations for positive thinking and positive self-talk.

7. *Check your results as you go and correct your methods as needed until finished:* How will you check results while you are working toward the change? How will you know when you're done?

8. *Review and compare with your original vision:* Have you accomplished your starting goal? Did you do it the way you planned? Did you meet your planned timetable? Are the downside and ripple effects what you planned for? Are any other changes now needed because of the changes you made?

CONCLUSION

Review the following key points:

1. Success in setting and achieving goals is important in getting clean and sober and staying that way.

2. Using specific skills to plan and work toward goals increases the chance of success.

REVIEW LEARNING GOALS

1. Upon completion of this presentation, group members will demonstrate the ability to define the steps in setting a reasonable and worthwhile goal.

2. Upon completion of this presentation, group members will demonstrate the ability to define at least five qualities of a well-defined goal.

3. Upon completion of this presentation, group members will demonstrate the ability to define eight steps in the process of achieving a goal.

QUESTIONS/DISCUSSION BEFORE POSTTEST

ADMINISTER POSTTEST

QUESTIONS/DISCUSSION AFTER POSTTEST

INTRODUCTION

Ask group members to think about problems and people they know who seem to have either more or less than their share of problems. Then ask them to compare, and identify what separates the people with few problems from those with many. Usually the difference is not that fewer problems come up for some people, but rather that some are more skilled at solving problems than others, so they deal with them more quickly and easily.

LEARNING GOALS

Explain to group members that they will be evaluated on their accomplishment of the following goals:

1. Upon completion of this presentation, group members will demonstrate the ability to define eight steps in the process of solving a problem.

2. Upon completion of this presentation, each group member will demonstrate the ability to explain how he or she could apply the steps of this problem-solving method to a situation in his or her own life.

QUESTIONS

As the presenter, you may ask group members to hold their questions until the end or to ask them at any time during the presentation. If participation is a high priority, we recommend allowing questions at any time; if brevity is more important, it works better to hold questions until the end.

PRETEST/POSTTEST

Pass out the pretest if you choose to use it. You may have the group members fill out and turn in pretests without putting names on them as a general measure of baseline knowledge. Explain that the same test will be given as the posttest at the end of the presentation.

BACKGROUND AND LEAD-IN

Ask these discussion questions, then give these answers after facilitating a brief discussion on each question:

- *What is a problem?* Definition from Webster's Unabridged Dictionary: "a question, matter, situation, or person that is perplexing or difficult." What is it that makes a thing perplexing or difficult? Again solicit group members' answers and facilitate a discussion.

- *When is a problem not a problem?* Answer: when a person has sufficient skills and resources that for him or her it is not "perplexing or difficult." To make this clear, ask the group whether reading a clock is a problem; then ask them, how about for a two-year-old? The difference is the skill: for the child, it is perplexing and difficult because he/she doesn't yet know how. Explain that the goal of this presentation is to give group members a generalized problem-solving method they can use for many problems to take those problems out of the "perplexing or difficult" category.

THE EIGHT-STEP PROBLEM-SOLVING METHOD

Ask a member of the group to come up with a real or imaginary problem and have the group work through these steps together during the presentation using that problem as a case study.

1. *Define the problem:*
   - Put it in perspective—how big/bad/serious/important is it? Have you dealt with equal or worse problems before—if so, how did you do it?
   - Give it an identity—externalize the problem, so you don't feel defective for having it.

2. *Generate solutions:*
   - Brainstorm possible actions: Think of as many ideas as possible as fast as possible, don't evaluate to see if they're any good at this point—nothing is ruled out.
   - Get help from others: A brainstorming session works better the more people are involved (tape ideas as people call them out or have one or two people writing them down).

3. *Think about the solutions' consequences and chances for success:*
   - Look at practical pros and cons—fact-based—for each solution.
   - Consider: What would happen if you did this?
   - For each solution, think about how likely it is to succeed.

4. *Explore feelings about the different solutions:*
   - Look at feelings pro and con about each possible solution.
   - Consider: How would you feel after you did this?

5. *Choose a solution:*
   - Decide how much weight to give practical and feeling pros and cons.
   - Based on the practical and feeling pros and cons, choose the solution that looks the best overall.

6. *Put the chosen solution into action:* Identify the necessary steps to get started, give yourself a deadline, and start doing it.

7. *Evaluate the preliminary results:*
   - Is it solving the problem?
   - Are you satisfied with what is happening overall?
   - Are there unexpected results, and if there are, are they acceptable?
   - If you aren't satisfied with what is happening, how can you improve the solution?

8. *Maintain the change:* What "preventive maintenance" is needed to keep this solution working? Do it. Evaluate continuously and return to Step 1 if you encounter difficulties.

CONCLUSION

Review the following key points:

1. Success in coping with problems depends largely on problem-solving skills.

2. Using a general set of problem-solving skills can improve the chances of overcoming any kind of problem.

REVIEW LEARNING GOALS

1. Upon completion of this presentation, group members will demonstrate the ability to define eight steps in the process of solving a problem.

2. Upon completion of this presentation, each group member will demonstrate the ability to explain how he or she could apply the steps of this problem-solving method to a situation in his or her own life.

QUESTIONS/DISCUSSION BEFORE POSTTEST

ADMINISTER POSTTEST

QUESTIONS/DISCUSSION AFTER POSTTEST

Presentation 7.13 Facilitator's Guide: Coping with Anger and Resentment

INTRODUCTION

Ask group members to name any connections they have noticed between anger and their own using or drinking (e.g., anger resulting in using/drinking; using/drinking resulting in feelings of anger; using/drinking as a method used to cope or avoid anger reactions). Ask members to describe any ways anger has undermined their intentions in recovery or other areas of their lives, and list their responses on a board, flip chart, or transparency sheet. Explain that anger is a feeling everyone has, and that it is normal and in some situations healthy and helpful for survival. Explain that what becomes unhealthy or destructive is the way people handle or deal with feelings of anger, and it is possible for people who have had problems because of their anger to learn different ways to deal with this emotion. Finally, explain that when people don't manage their anger in a healthy way, it sets them up to relapse and to return to other old and self-destructive behavior patterns, and that this presentation will provide some skills for effectively handling anger and resentment.

LEARNING GOALS

Explain to group members that they will be evaluated on their accomplishment of the following goals:

1. Upon completion of this presentation, group members will be able to identify what anger and resentment are and demonstrate an ability to recognize their own symptoms of anger and resentment before a crisis.

2. Upon completion of this presentation, group members will demonstrate knowledge of coping methods to handle anger without causing harm to themselves or others.

QUESTIONS

As the presenter, you may ask group members to hold their questions until the end or to ask them at any time during the presentation. If participation is a high priority, we recommend allowing questions at any time; if brevity is more important, it works better to hold questions until the end.

PRETEST/POSTTEST

Pass out the pretest if you choose to use it. You may have the group members fill out and turn in pretests without putting names on them as a general measure of baseline knowledge. Explain that the same test will be given as the posttest at the end of the presentation.

BACKGROUND AND LEAD-IN

Ask group members to describe the difference between feelings and behaviors, then compare their answers with the following and briefly discuss:

- *Feelings:* Anger is a feeling and is part of us. All feelings or emotions, including anger, are acceptable, although some are destructive in the long run to the people who hold them. Feelings don't always make sense or fit together with each other, as we can have two or three conflicting feelings at the same time. For example, we can feel anger without knowing the specific reason, and we can feel love toward someone we are mad at or who hurts us.

- *Behaviors:* Unlike feelings, not all behaviors are acceptable. Behavior is the way we choose to react to our feelings. We can control our behaviors. We always have choices of which behaviors we will use.

We can change our behaviors, even old behaviors that are strong habits. Although people sometimes use feelings as excuses or justifications for their behaviors, they are still responsible for their actions, because actions are chosen. For example, someone saying "I had to hit him, because he made me angry," does not justify an assault.

What is anger? What is resentment? Ask group members for definitions of anger and resentment, then provide the following definitions from *Webster's Unabridged:* and facilitate a brief discussion:

Anger: "a strong feeling excited by real or supposed injury"; its root word means regret, anguish, or fear.

Resentment: "holding an attitude from something that is in the past; resentment is old anger." Note that the *sent* part of the word *resent* is related to the word *sentiment*, and means "feel," so to resent is to resent, or to re-feel—that is, to replay an old anger.

THE PHYSICAL PART OF ANGER: FLIGHT, FIGHT, OR FREEZE

Anger includes physical reactions. For most of the time human beings have been alive, the most common threats or sources of harm or injury have been physical dangers such as large animals or human enemies, and the best ways to cope were to fight, run away, or freeze in place and stay hidden. Our bodies are still conditioned that way, so when we feel threatened, our brains trigger the release of chemicals (natural drugs) to help, either for fight or flight or for freeze reactions. Unfortunately, most threats today are different. We can't use physical combat, running away, or hiding to deal with overdue bills, the boss, a broken-down car, and so on. These chemicals in the bloodstream help us to react physically with more speed and strength if that's what we need, but they also put stress on the body if we don't use them up through physical action. Anger that is not dealt with actually poisons the body over time.

Identifying Our Anger Early

Note the resemblance of these symptoms to the effects of stimulant drugs: these are signs that a person is feeling anger, even if he or she doesn't consciously realize it. By watching for these signs in ourselves, we can spot anger early and manage it more effectively. Physical symptoms include:

- Muscle tension: Clenched jaw, tightened shoulders and neck, fists, drumming fingers, vibrating feet and legs
- Breathing and heart rate speed up
- Sharpened senses
- Increased energy and reactivity: jumpy, shaky, restless
- Clammy skin: This is caused by the blood moving into deep muscles and key internal organs, both to help them work better and to reduce bleeding from surface injuries
- Possible nausea or "butterflies," resulting from the digestive process being temporarily shut down, along with other body systems not necessary in a fight-or-flight situation, to divert oxygen-carrying blood to the muscles and brain

Mental/emotional symptoms include:

- Increased alertness
- Feeling an urge to attack, to run away, or both; sometimes exhilaration
- Racing thoughts and a sense of urgency, or "brain freeze": either reaction makes clear thinking more difficult
- Vivid memories of past stressful situations

- Feeling of oncoming loss of control
- Thinking shifts to black-and-white, and a person can see fewer options
- Feelings of power and certainty in some people

COPING WITH ANGER WITHOUT HARM TO SELF OR OTHERS

Acknowledge and accept the feelings. Tell yourself what the feeling is and that it's okay to feel that way right now. Remind yourself that feelings and actions are separate, and that feeling anger does not mean you have to act it out—you can stay in control.

Reverse the physical/emotional/mental preparation for fight/flight/freeze. Sit down. Begin breathing slowly and deeply. Relax muscles in one part of the body at a time; it may help to tense extra hard for several seconds and release. Visualize a relaxing scene or memory.

Identify the source and choose an effective response. Find out where anger came from; identify the trigger (Where's the threat?). Is this a safe situation that is just reminding me of another that was a real threat? Let it go. Am I afraid something bad is happening, or something I want isn't happening? Express it. Fear of what will happen in the future? Act *now* to change the odds. Is something bad really likely to happen? How likely is it? If it happens, how bad will it be? Could I stand it? Have I gotten through similar or worse situations before? Consider the consequences of acting from anger: What would happen afterward? What are my other options (time out, talk it out directly or at a meeting, walk away)? Visualize a good outcome: Picture yourself handling the situation successfully.

Carry out a nonharmful solution. Do this in a timely fashion so it does not turn into a resentment. Think about what happened. Relax. Get some physical exercise to burn off the fight-or-flight chemicals in the system. Talk it over with someone you trust. Give yourself credit for what you did well in this situation. Tell someone; this is hard at first but gets easier with practice. Plan for the future: How can I avoid this happening again or be ready for it when it does happen?

A number of factors affect our ability to handle anger including:

General Physical State:

- Sleep deprivation
- Hunger
- Influence of chemicals—judgment is impaired, inhibitions are lowered; body is already in a fight or flight state
- Lack of exercise—accumulation of fight-or-flight chemicals in the bloodstream.

Mental/Emotional Factors:

- Resemblance of the current situation to past stressful situations may set off reaction out of proportion to the here-and-now; this is sometimes referred to as having your buttons pushed.
- Preexisting stress: "I have one nerve left and you're getting on it."
- Reinforcement of negative parts of self-image: another way buttons get pushed.
- Loneliness: lack of emotional support.
- Unrealistic expectations: rules, musts, shoulds. We can only be disappointed if we have expectations that aren't met; if we have expectations that can't be met, we will be disappointed. (Refer to the list of unrealistic thinking that is included in the presentation on depression and anxiety.)

Protect yourself against future problems with anger. Keep your resistance to stress as high as possible by getting:

- Adequate rest
- Healthy diet

- Regular exercise
- Supportive relationships through program meetings and sponsorship

If you are feeling Hungry, Angry, Lonely, and/or Tired (HALT), act to correct the problem. Get in the habit of regular self-checks throughout the day. Correct distorted thinking patterns. Address past resentments: Resentments put recovering people at high risk to relapse.

Practice coping skills. Practice the steps described in this presentation. With input and feedback from people you trust, mentally rehearse situations you would have trouble handling, and plan how you will react in a healthy way to those situations.

CONCLUSION

Review the following key points:

1. Anger and resentment are normal feelings experienced by all people.

2. All feelings are acceptable, but not all actions.

3. Anger has a strong physical element to it, and anger that is not handled effectively can damage the body over time.

4. Use of specific methods to cope with anger can improve people's ability to get rid of their anger in ways that don't cause problems for themselves or for others.

REVIEW LEARNING GOALS

1. Upon completion of this presentation, group members will be able to identify what anger and resentment are and demonstrate an ability to recognize their own symptoms of anger and resentment before a crisis.

2. Upon completion of this presentation, group members will demonstrate knowledge of coping methods to handle anger without causing harm to themselves or others.

QUESTIONS/DISCUSSION BEFORE POSTTEST

ADMINISTER POSTTEST

QUESTIONS/DISCUSSION AFTER POSTTEST

Presentation 7.14 Facilitator's Guide: Coping with Depression and Anxiety

INTRODUCTION

Ask group members how many have felt depressed or anxious often in the past year. Ask them how they think this is connected to substance abuse for them and for people in general. Ask them what they would like to see happen in connection with their feelings of depression and anxiety during the next year. Facilitate a brief discussion of their responses.

Explain that these are common feelings during early recovery. Depression and anxiety are problems whenever they occur, but they are particular problems for someone attempting to maintain sobriety because they can cause relapse. Often, people return to using or drinking as a way to cope with depression and anxiety. The problem is that along with all the other painful results of relapse, using alcohol and other illegal drugs is an ineffective way to manage negative moods and only makes people more depressed or anxious in the long run.

LEARNING GOALS

Explain to group members that they will be evaluated on their accomplishment of the following goals:

1. Upon completion of this presentation, participants will demonstrate understanding of how depression and anxiety affect thoughts, perceptions, and behaviors.

2. Upon completion of this presentation, participants will demonstrate knowledge of skills and resources to cope with depression and anxiety.

QUESTIONS

As the presenter, you may ask group members to hold their questions until the end or to ask them at any time during the presentation. If participation is a high priority, we recommend allowing questions at any time; if brevity is more important, it works better to hold questions until the end.

PRETEST/POSTTEST

Pass out the pretest if you choose to use it. You may have the group members fill out and turn in pretests without putting names on them as a general measure of baseline knowledge. Explain that the same test will be given as the posttest at the end of the presentation.

BACKGROUND AND LEAD-IN

Ask group members for their definitions of depression and anxiety. Write their answers on a board, flip chart, or transparency sheet, then give them the following information and facilitate a brief discussion.

DEFINITIONS

Depression: Webster's Unabridged Dictionary defines depression as "low spirits, gloominess, sadness . . . a decrease in force, activity . . . a feeling of inadequacy . . ." Counselors, therapists, psychiatrists, psychologists, and other professionals define depression using the *DSM-IV-TR* and describe a major depressive episode as experiencing five of the following nine symptoms for two weeks or more:

1. Depressed mood most of the time

2. Loss of pleasure in most/all activities

3. Significant weight loss/gain or a change to appetite

4. Unable to sleep or sleeping too much

5. Physically dragging or agitation

6. Fatigue or loss of energy nearly every day

7. Difficulty thinking/concentrating, indecisiveness

8. Feeling worthless or excessively guilty

9. Recurrent thoughts of death, especially suicidal thoughts, plans, or attempts

   Anxiety: Webster's Unabridged Dictionary defines anxiety as "concern . . . regarding some event, future or uncertain, which disturbs the mind." It is important to note that symptoms of anxiety and depression can range from mild to severe.

TRIGGERS OF DEPRESSION AND ANXIETY

Physical Triggers:

- *Chemical imbalances:* These can be treated with medications. They may be temporary in response to some traumatic event, or permanent, often running in families.

- *Results of substance abuse:* Either during use, as a withdrawal effect, or more long term due to excessive abuse of certain substances. Some drugs are *depressants* (like alcohol), which means they depress functioning in many areas. Other drugs are *stimulants,* which means they stimulate functioning to higher than normal levels; the body tries to restore normal levels, resulting in a depressive rebound effect when the drug is removed from the system. Examples include coming down from methamphetamine use especially after prolonged use over days, or the "crash" associated with cocaine use.

- Other physical causes are sleep deprivation, hunger, physical illness, or chronic pain.

Mental/Emotional/Environmental Triggers:

- *Crisis situations:* where people feel overwhelmed or helpless, in any of these areas: relationships (death, breakup, divorce, children leaving, etc.), job (loss of employment, retirement, change, etc.), financial, legal, loss of structure (move, change of job), health, or high stress of other kinds.

- *Emotional isolation:* which is especially common for adolescents, elderly individuals, and chemically dependent individuals.

- *Distorted thinking patterns:* Explain that many treatments for depression specifically work on identifying thinking patterns that support depression and anxiety. Treatment of depression seeks to change these negative thought patterns, which in turn changes behavior. Basic distortions of reality occur on three levels: unrealistic negative view of self, negative interpretations of events, and unrealistically negative expectations for the future. Several common patterns of distorted thought/perception are:

  (a) Leaping to negative conclusions with little evidence

  (b) Focusing on the bad, ignoring the rest of the picture

  (c) Over-generalizing from one or a few negative incidents to expect every situation to turn out badly

  (d) Magnifying or minimizing the importance of events—typically, magnifying the negative and minimizing the positive events

  (e) Taking everything negative personally, or blaming yourself anytime things go badly

  (f) Thinking in extremes, no gray area: seeing things, situations, and people as perfect/worthless, successes/failures, winners/losers, and so on.

(g) Being sure others are looking down on you or thinking bad things about you

(h) Deciding that because things aren't going well at one time, life will never get better

- *Unrealistic expectations or rules for self, others, and situations:*

    (a) It is not okay for me to feel angry in this situation.

    (b) If I feel angry, I won't be able to control my actions.

    (c) It's not acceptable for me to make a mistake: if I do, I'm a failure.

    (d) It's not okay for me not to know something: if I don't, I'm stupid.

    (e) I'm weak if I need or ask for help.

    (f) If he/she gets mad at me, he/she does not care about me.

    (g) Other people make me unhappy, and I have no control over this.

    (h) My past experiences and events determine my present behavior, and their influence is too strong for me to overcome.

    (i) There is a right, perfect solution to every problem, and I have to find it or the results will be disastrous.

    (j) Other people must treat me fairly; if they don't it is terrible and I can't bear it.

COPING SKILLS FOR DEALING WITH DEPRESSION AND ANXIETY

Correct the Physical Causes

- *Get illicit drugs out of the system:* Allow your body to regain its chemical balance; understand that there are ways to cope with depression and anxiety and that the mood changes caused by drug use or withdrawal are temporary.

- *Practice basic self-care:* Getting appropriate diet, rest, and exercise builds up the body's resistance to mood problems as well as other illnesses.

- *Get medical attention for illnesses or injuries.*

- *You may need to take medications* prescribed by a psychiatrist after a thorough evaluation, especially if you have permanent chemical imbalances.

Correct the Mental/Emotional/Situational Causes

- *Get professional help:* Effective counseling can help people do more to understand their problems and overcome depression, anxiety, and many other problems than they can do alone.

- *Address crisis situations if possible:* Do whatever you can to improve the severe problems that are causing you the most stress. Again, this sometimes means getting help from a professional, whether that be a doctor, counselor, lawyer. Emotional support from friends and family is also important.

- *Reduce emotional isolation:* get more involved with other people. Some opportunities may include supportive family relationships, friendships, organizations, volunteer work, and recovery programs.

- *Correct distorted thinking patterns:* Learn corrective thinking skills and practice them. A good way to help group members practice this is to review the list of unrealistic rules presented earlier in the presentation and replace each with a more realistic rule.

- *Act on positive, healthy thoughts and beliefs:* Identifying your negative thoughts is not enough; sometimes by acting differently, you can change old thinking habits and reinforce new ones. At first you may have to "act as if," or as many people in 12-Step programs say, "fake it 'til you make it," but that's a positive thing to do.

- *Act to solve other nagging problems:* Many times, newly recovering people face many problems that have accumulated as a result of their drinking and using. Worrying about these problems increases depression and anxiety and the feeling of hopelessness, and clearing up the mess makes a big difference.

- *Get more active, especially in activities that are fun:* Activity does more than passivity to improve moods. More activity leads to feeling more energetic, increases motivation, and improves self-image. Plan some activities that you can do alone and some that you can do with others, and *do* them.

- *Make and follow a daily schedule* that is flexible and realistic.

- *Reward yourself* for accomplishing tasks, no matter how small.

CONCLUSION

Review the following key points:

1. Depression and anxiety are common in early recovery.

2. These moods are problems for anyone, but especially dangerous for newly recovering people because they increase the risk of relapse.

3. There are many practical methods people can use to cope with feelings of depression and anxiety.

REVIEW LEARNING GOALS

1. Upon completion of this presentation, participants will demonstrate understanding of how depression and anxiety affect thoughts, perceptions, and behaviors.

2. Upon completion of this presentation, participants will demonstrate knowledge of skills and resources to cope with depression and anxiety.

QUESTIONS/DISCUSSION BEFORE POSTTEST

ADMINISTER POSTTEST

QUESTIONS/DISCUSSION AFTER POSTTEST

Presentation 7.15 Facilitator's Guide: Resisting Pressures to Drink or Use

INTRODUCTION

Ask for a show of hands of group members who don't think they will be confronted with any pressures to return to drinking or drug use, either during or after treatment. If any raise their hands, facilitate a brief discussion among them and those who did not, letting both explain their expectations. Then ask how many think that all of those pressures will be open and easy to identify.

Point out (to whatever degree this applies, depending on treatment setting) that while in treatment, group members may be completely or partially sheltered from pressures to engage in the addictions that brought them there, but they will soon be back in their normal environment, facing pressures that led them to drink and use before.

Ask group members to think about any people they know who either succeeded or failed in maintaining abstinence after treatment and to share their thoughts on what pressures to relapse those people encountered and how they dealt with the pressures.

Point out that many people with intelligence, willpower, and strong motivation to stay clean and sober have left treatment planning to stay abstinent, only to relapse in the face of pressures to return to active addiction; at the same time, others facing the same or tougher pressures have succeeded in resisting. Explain that the key factors are not strength, intelligence, or luck, but information and action: knowing how to identify pressures and what to do or avoid doing.

LEARNING GOALS

Explain to group members that they will be evaluated on their accomplishment of the following goals:

1. Upon completion of this presentation, group members will demonstrate with an accuracy rate of at least 80 percent, knowledge of open and hidden pressures to drink or use by labeling, without notes or references, various situations as open or hidden pressures to relapse.

2. Upon completion of this presentation, group members will demonstrate understanding of techniques of resisting open and hidden pressures to drink or use by listing, without notes or references, at least three sources of support and three strategies to resist either open or hidden pressures to return to addictive behaviors.

QUESTIONS

As the presenter, you may ask group members to hold their questions until the end or to ask them at any time during the presentation. If participation is a high priority, we recommend allowing questions at any time; if brevity is more important, it works better to hold questions until the end.

PRETEST/POSTTEST

Pass out the pretest if you choose to use it. You may have the group members fill out and turn in pretests without putting names on them as a general measure of baseline knowledge. Explain that the same test will be given as the posttest at the end of the presentation.

BACKGROUND AND LEAD-IN

Ask whether anyone in the group has had experience with going back to their normal life after treatment before, and if so, what challenges they ran into. Ask the group the discussion question:

What people and situations may pressure me to relapse, and how might they do so? Write their answers on a board, flip chart, or transparency sheet and facilitate a short discussion.

Open and Hidden Pressures to Drink or Use

There are a number of kinds of pressure to drink or use drugs. *Open pressures* are easy to identify, though they may be either easy or hard to resist. Refer to previous feedback from group members and cover the following types of open pressure to relapse:

1. *Peer pressure:* Individual friends (and family members) with whom a person used to drink or use other drugs may urge the group member returning from treatment to return to the addictive behavior for several reasons:

    • They may be uneasy about their own substance abuse and react defensively when someone they know rejects that behavior; this often takes the form of feeling insulted when someone refuses to drink or use with them.

    • They may sell drugs and see someone else's quitting as a threat to their finances.

    • They may sincerely believe the newly recovering person can drink or use in moderation and that a little bit is harmless and even beneficial.

    • The peer group culture supports and/or promotes use of substances.

2. *Situational pressure:* A social or even a work-related situation may include substance abuse as an important element, creating pressure to drink or use:

    • Group recreational activities may always include alcohol or other drugs.

    • Religious or social rituals may involve consuming alcohol or other drugs, such as sacramental services involving wine and drinking of toasts at weddings.

    • Parties at work (office Christmas parties, etc.) may involve alcohol or other drugs, and the group member may be required or pressured to attend and participate.

    • Group members may not have any social groups or activities that don't involve drinking or using, and it may seem that to be abstinent means to always be alone.

There are also *hidden pressures,* including:

1. *Self-image:* Your own self-image can be a source of pressure to return to drinking or using. Ask group members how many grew up with the idea that drinking or other drug use (including smoking tobacco) was a sign of maturity and sophistication, being a success in life, being attractive to the opposite sex, and so on. Ask how many sometimes feel like failures because they can't be controlled drinkers/users. Ask how many had key role models who drank or used heavily. Note that part of recovery is rethinking these points and creating a new self-image that includes positive views about abstinence and finding new role models that don't drink or use.

2. *Habit:* Often, newly recovering people either relapse or come close to doing so by sheer unconscious reflex, because it is such an ingrained habit or because some situation is such a strong cue for substance use. Ask for examples; provide some if group members don't (the person who always drinks beer at baseball games, the gambler who automatically buys a lottery ticket at the convenience store, etc.)

3. *Rejection:* The newly clean and sober person may encounter painful rejection from others either because they dislike the change or because they refuse to believe that the change is sincere and will last. Because they have grown up believing that they have to please others, many people find this rejection particularly difficult.

4. *Lack of knowledge of alternative ways to feel good or cope with problems:* All alcoholics, addicts, and people engaged in other compulsive patterns of behavior originally did so for similar reasons: They

liked the way it made them feel. Part of recovery is finding new ways to feel good, relieve unpleasant feelings, and cope with situations you used to handle by drinking or using.

Resisting Open Pressures to Drink or Use

- *Awareness/anticipation:* This is the easy part of open pressures. Because they are open, the newly recovering person *knows* he or she is being pressured. By looking ahead and knowing when this is likely to happen, for example, the first time one meets an old using friend after returning from treatment, we can be on guard and have a plan ready.

- *Avoidance when possible:* The easiest and best way to handle open pressure to use or drink is to avoid it if you can: Don't see the person, don't go to the place. But often this may not be possible, so it can't be your main or only strategy.

Coping when avoidance isn't practical. In most situations, the person returning from treatment must face at least some sources of pressure to drink, use, or return to other addictions. When you can't avoid these situations, these coping strategies are useful:

- Preparation: Think about how you will feel and what you will say or do. Very few people do their best thinking or decision making in a hurry or under high stress, so the time to think and decide is in advance, when the pressure is not on yet and you have plenty of time. Talk about your plan with other recovering people and get their feedback.

- *Support:* If possible, make sure someone who supports what you're doing is there when the pressure takes place. If that's not possible, have someone supportive in your life who's easy to get in contact with. The best way to get this kind of support is often to pick someone, tell him or her what you are trying to do together, and ask for the other person's help. Most people feel good about being able to help someone else and will give you their support. This support can come from individuals like friends, individual family members, a sponsor, a coworker, a therapist or counselor, or from groups such as a family, an AA or other 12-Step group, or a therapy group.

Planning specific strategies for coping. These may include:

- Planning to have your own transportation so you can leave a party when you want.

- Planning a reason to leave a situation early.

- Planning what you will say and do if someone challenges or ridicules your refusal to drink or use.

- Planning to consume only nonalcoholic beverages, etc., and bringing your own if necessary; also, never leaving your glass unwatched where someone could put alcohol or something else in it without your knowing.

Resisting Hidden Pressures to Drink or Use

Strategies for coping with hidden pressures are more subtle, like the pressures themselves, and often don't involve direct confrontation, for example:

- *Awareness/anticipation:* This is more tricky but also more important with hidden pressures. The best ways to be aware of and anticipate such pressures are to think about your past patterns of drinking and using and what triggered you before. Discuss this with others who know you and get their ideas, especially before occasions when hidden pressures may arise.

- *Avoidance when possible:* Again, if possible, the simplest and easiest way to handle hidden pressures to drink or use is to avoid them completely. But this is harder to do and will often be impossible, especially for the hidden pressures that come from within.

- *Coping when avoidance isn't practical:* Preparation is even more important with hidden pressures than with open ones. Again, think about how you will feel and what you will say or do. Under stress you may lose awareness of hidden pressures, so plan to give yourself reminders to help you stay alert and on guard.

Support is even more vital in resisting hidden pressures. These pressures are often based on what we think others expect of us, and the power of these pressures comes from our desire to be liked and accepted. When someone shows us that we may be more liked and accepted if we are sober, it gives us a powerful reason to avoid relapse, so it helps to spend as much time as we can around people who value sobriety.

CONCLUSION

Review the following key points:

1. Nearly every newly recovering person faces both open and hidden pressures to return to drinking and drug use.

2. Intelligence, strength of will, and motivation aren't enough to stay clean and sober. Success in resisting these pressures depends on awareness, planning, and use of effective strategies.

3. There are definite methods newly recovering people can use to help them resist pressures to relapse.

REVIEW LEARNING GOALS

1. Upon completion of this presentation, group members will demonstrate with an accuracy rate of at least 80 percent, knowledge of open and hidden pressures to drink or use by labeling, without notes or references, various situations as open or hidden pressures to relapse.

2. Upon completion of this presentation, group members will demonstrate understanding of techniques of resisting open and hidden pressures to drink or use by listing, without notes or references, at least three sources of support and three strategies to resist either open or hidden pressures to return to addictive behaviors.

QUESTIONS/DISCUSSION BEFORE POSTTEST

ADMINISTER POSTTEST

QUESTIONS/DISCUSSION AFTER POSTTEST

Chapter 8

Other Mental Health Issues: Materials for Use in Psychoeducational Groups

In this chapter, we shift our focus to a series of problems that are separate from, but often linked with, substance use problems. By other mental health issues, we are referring to situational problems that may be contributing causes, effects, or both of addiction and abuse. They are dangerous enough in their own right to both the client and others that they demand treatment at the same time as chemical dependence problems, and aside from the dangers they pose in and of themselves, they can thoroughly undermine sobriety and recovery if left unaddressed during drug and alcohol treatment. Because these conditions and problems are so entangled with substance abuse issues, you will encounter some or all of them in many of your clients.

As in Chapters Six and Seven, these presentation materials are primarily cognitive in format and combine the learning modalities of seeing the information, hearing it discussed, and experiencing it kinesthetically through the process of writing key information while filling in the blanks in the handouts.

The materials included in this chapter address the following topics:

To conserve space and provide more material within the practicable scope of this book, only the facilitator's guide for each presentation is included in the text, but the companion CD-ROM also includes a group member's handout, a pre-/posttest, and a Microsoft PowerPoint slideshow for each presentation, as well as an electronic copy of the facilitator's guide included here.

Presentation 8.1 Facilitator's Guide: Family Dynamics

INTRODUCTION

Ask the group how many feel their childhoods were affected by their parents' substance abuse, and how many feel that their parents' drinking or drug use was only part of the problem; finally, ask how many want to avoid passing those experiences on to their own children.

LEARNING GOALS

Explain to group members that they will be evaluated on their accomplishment of these goals:

1. Upon completion of this presentation, group members will demonstrate an understanding of the typical roles and interaction patterns people act out in addictive/alcoholic and other dysfunctional families.

2. Upon completion of this presentation, group members will demonstrate an awareness of healthy alternative interaction patterns and resources available to help people change their learned role behaviors.

QUESTIONS

As the presenter, you may ask group members to hold their questions until the end or to ask them at any time during the presentation. If participation is a high priority, we recommend allowing questions at any time; if brevity is more important, it works better to hold questions until the end.

PRETEST/POSTTEST

Pass out the pretest if you choose to use it. You may have the group members fill out and turn in pretests without putting names on them as a general measure of baseline knowledge. Explain that the same test will be given as the posttest at the end of the presentation.

BACKGROUND AND LEAD-IN

Return to the discussion begun in the introduction. Ask how many group members have seen families in which the parents' problems caused their children to experience any of the following:

- Being abused or neglected, emotionally or physically

- Going without necessities like food, reliable shelter, and safety

- Having to grow up too soon and take on adult responsibilities

- Living in fear of their parents and wanting to get away from them as soon as possible

- Being ashamed of their parents, their families, and their homes

- Promising themselves that they will never be like their parents when they grow up

Ask the question: Who here wants your own children to have that kind of a childhood? Then ask: Do you think any of the parents in those situations planned it or wanted it to be that way, or were happy about it?

Offer the suggestion: They probably wanted the same things for their children that you do for yours, but they couldn't achieve them. How will you succeed where they failed?

Facilitate a brief discussion on these questions. Explain that along with willingness to work for change, they need to know *how* to do things differently, and that's what this presentation is about.

DYSFUNCTIONAL FAMILY ROLES IN ACTION

Here are descriptions of six common roles in chemically dependent families. Encourage group members to think about themselves and members of their families while they listen and talk about these descriptions:

1. *Dependent person:* This is the alcoholic or addict.

2. *Chief enabler:* Often the spouse or partner of the dependent person, this person's role in the family is taking care of the dependent person, cleaning up after him or her, covering up for him or her, and so on, thereby sheltering the dependent person from the consequences of his or her actions. This person is often controlling, full of self-pity and resentment, and burned out.

3. *Family hero:* Often the oldest child, this person makes the family proud and is a superachiever; his or her role is to be the one nobody has to worry about and the one who helps the family look good and healthy to the outside world. This person also tends to take care of the rest of the children and may share common traits with the chief enabler. However, this child often feels inadequate and angry and strives for perfection to feel adequate.

4. *Scapegoat:* Often the second child, this is the person who is always in trouble and may be blamed for the dependent person's using or drinking ("Having a kid like you would make anyone drink!") This child's role is to be the lightning rod, the one who takes the blame for the family's problems, and to distract attention from the dependent person's actions.

5. *Lost child:* Often a middle or younger child, this person has developed the survival tactic of avoiding trouble by being invisible, either not being around or fading into the background when trouble erupts. His or her role is to be the one who makes life easier for the parents by never needing anything or demanding their attention.

6. *Mascot:* Often the youngest child, this is the person who is always clowning around and distracting people from their problems. He or she seems never to be serious about anything, and this person's role in the family is to prevent big scenes and keep people from getting too upset by making them laugh whenever the atmosphere starts to get too tense.

Identifying Interaction Patterns

Ask the group to describe some unhealthy ways the members of a chemically dependent or dysfunctional family relate to one another. Write their answers on the board, then compare with this list of unhealthy behaviors:

- *Dishonesty/denial:* Refusing to admit how bad the problem is, covering up, avoiding confronting problems until too angry to keep silent; blaming others for problems in the family that are clearly the result of substance-abusing behavior.

- *Breaking promises:* Not following through on commitments to children or spouse.

- *Isolating:* Keeping secrets from "outsiders"; not allowing friends to visit so there is no speculation that something is wrong in the family; instilling the "no talk rule"; sometimes withdrawing from other family members who may serve as support for the children but are nuisances for the adults as they may comment on the substance-abusing behavior.

- *Emotional and physical abuse and neglect:* Parents hitting children and each other, yelling, calling names, bullying, belittling, ridiculing, leaving kids alone and unfed, ignoring school problems, ignoring medical needs of children.

- *Parentifying children:* Forcing older children to function as parents and caretakers to younger siblings and possibly to parents when hung over, high, or drunk.

- *Influencing children to be self-destructive:* Pressuring children to drink or use other substances with the parents, role-modeling drunk driving, avoiding addressing problems with children (e.g., shoplifting, truancy), allowing siblings to abuse one another.

Family Rules and Chemical Dependence

Explain that rules are developed in every family system to keep the situation in balance. Roles are adapted to cope with ongoing dysfunction in the family, rules are developed to protect and isolate family members from one another, to prevent family members from sharing their thoughts and feelings with one another and to keep distance. Discuss the following list of rules that often exist in families where a parent is suffering from an addiction:

- It's not okay to talk about problems.

- It's not okay to talk or express any feelings except happiness or anger openly.

- Always be strong, good, and perfect.

- Do as I say, not as I do.

- It's not okay to be a child, to be carefree, or to be playful.

- Don't make waves.

- You can't trust anyone.

- Don't say what you're really thinking—use hints.

- Other people's needs are more important than your own.

Predicting Outcomes

Ask group members to predict what a child in each of the roles will be like as an adult if he or she stayed in those roles. What strengths and problems might he or she have? Again, write their answers on the board, flip chart, or transparency sheet and facilitate a discussion. It is important to discuss the strengths as well as the problems that adult children tend to have as a result of growing up in an alcoholic or drug-dependent home.

Now ask group members how they would expect each of these children to behave with their own children when they are adults; write their answers on the board, flip chart, or transparency sheet and facilitate a discussion. Recall the question about how many group members want to spare their children from experiences like their own and how well they could keep that promise.

Now you can help them personalize their situation:

- *Identify own role:* Ask group members which role(s) they feel best fits their own behavior in childhood, explaining that people often take on different roles at different times.

- *Consider consequences:* Refer to the list of family rules and explore thoughts and feelings about the possibility that group members might be that way with their own children. Ask how it would feel to look in the mirror and see their father or mother.

Changing Role Behaviors

Frequently, group members comment that they do not believe their substance abuse has had any impact on their children because the children are too young or the parents never use substances around them. Other group members will express guilt regarding the evident or likely result of their substance-abusing behavior on their children. Often, parents in treatment have had their children removed from their homes due to legal and/or substance-abusing behavior. They express both guilt and anger regarding this situation and feel that it is impossible to have their children returned to them.

Knowing What We're Trying to Accomplish Is Goals

It does not matter why these rules and roles were developed, the point is that they do not have to be continued. It is important that group members understand that they have choices and can break the unhealthy patterns of the family. For example:

1. *Addressing denial regarding the impact of their own substance abuse:* Discuss the importance to group members of protecting their children from sharing the bad family experiences they had; note that to change these patterns, it is important (and painful) to take responsibility for substance-abusing behavior. Point out to group members that despite the excuses that their use did not impact their children, children are aware that parents are different when high or drunk; that the children's needs for healthy parents who are fully available to them did not get met; and that home did not feel safe and stable for the children. To help their children, parents must recognize addiction or substance abuse as a family illness that needs family treatment.

2. *Behavior changes:* Ask group members to list healthy behaviors they would like to substitute in their own lives for the unhealthy behaviors listed and to describe any experiences they've had when they've acted out these healthy behaviors. To get the conversation started, offer these examples: replace the "no talk rule" with open communication where children are encouraged to express their feelings and thoughts; avoid physical or verbal threats; avoid name calling; and make home a safe place.

3. *Tools and support:* Poll group members for knowledge of community and personal resources to help stay clean and sober and also to start making these changes, then offer these ideas:

   * *Individual friends and relatives* (if they respect the recovering person's intentions).
   * *Support groups:* Al-Anon, AlaTeen, Codependents Anonymous, Adult Children of Alcoholic and Dysfunctional Families; less formal organizations.
   * *Other sources:* There are a lot of books on family dynamics and related issues; most large bookstores have a good selection. Two particularly useful workbooks are *Repeat After Me* by Claudia Black and *The 12-Steps: A Way Out for Adult Children* (anonymous author(s)).
   * *Therapy:* Especially for some severe problems related to intense abuse from parents or residual effects that damage relationships, coping abilities, and self-image.

   How can people systematically plan and carry through changes in these types of behaviors? Here are some suggestions:

1. Ask for input, then refer group members to steps 4 through 9 of 12-Step Programs.

2. What have group members done already to make these kinds of changes, and what do they plan to do?

3. When will they start?

CONCLUSION

Review the following key points:

1. The desire to be a good parent is not enough to prevent physical and emotional abuse and neglect of children in families where parents suffer from alcoholism or other forms of addiction.

2. There are common patterns of interaction and individual roles that usually develop in these families as ways to adapt to the addiction's impact.

3. Once people grow into these roles in childhood, they often unconsciously keep acting them out in adult life.

4. The key to avoiding or correcting these problems is awareness, understanding, and knowledge of tools and resources.

REVIEW LEARNING GOALS

1. Upon completion of this presentation, group members will demonstrate an understanding of the typical roles and interaction patterns people act out in addictive/alcoholic and other dysfunctional families.

2. Upon completion of this presentation, group members will demonstrate an awareness of healthy alternative interaction patterns and resources available to help people change their learned role behaviors.

QUESTIONS/DISCUSSION BEFORE POSTTEST

ADMINISTER POSTTEST

QUESTIONS/DISCUSSION AFTER POSTTEST

INTRODUCTION

Ask for a show of hands of group members who have been affected by domestic violence. Explain that there is a strong link between domestic violence and substance abuse, especially the abuse of alcohol and methamphetamine. This is another area where many people look back at their parents and say, "I will never be like that," but unless they learn how domestic violence works and how to do something different, their chances of slipping into the same patterns are great. Every year, thousands of adults and children are killed and injured in domestic violence incidents. Once violence starts in a relationship, it usually continues. Often, it keeps getting worse until it is stopped by the relationship breaking up, by the death or incarceration of one partner, or by the couple or family going into intensive therapy.

LEARNING GOALS

Explain to group members that they will be evaluated on their accomplishment of the following goals:

1. Upon completion of this presentation, group members are able to identify behaviors that constitute domestic violence.

2. Upon completion of this presentation, group members will demonstrate understanding of the two main theories of domestic violence.

3. Upon completion of this presentation, group members will demonstrate understanding of healthy, non-abusive relationship interactions.

QUESTIONS

As the presenter, you may ask group members to hold their questions until the end or to ask them at any time during the presentation. If participation is a high priority, we recommend allowing questions at any time; if brevity is more important, it works better to hold questions until the end.

PRETEST/POSTTEST

Pass out the pretest if you choose to use it. You may have the group members fill out and turn in pretests without putting names on them as a general measure of baseline knowledge. Explain that the same test will be given as the posttest at the end of the presentation.

BACKGROUND AND LEAD-IN

Ask the discussion question: What is domestic violence, and what causes it? Write group members' answers on a board, flip chart, or transparency sheet. Compare the group's answers with the following, and facilitate a brief discussion.

Domestic violence is any use of force or the threat of force in a conflict between members of a family. This includes the following:

- Battering or direct assault: hitting, kicking, shoving, biting, scratching, yanking hair, pinching, choking, burning, spitting, or use of a weapon.

- Grabbing or holding a person against his or her will.

- Forced or coerced sexual intercourse.

- Restricting a person's freedom of movement.

- Using control of money to limit a person's freedom.

- Preventing a person from working.

- Forcing a person to commit a crime.

- Destroying a person's property.

- Intimidation by abusing pets in a person's presence.

- Verbal or gestured threats to do any of the above.

- Using the threat of suicide or self-harm to control another person.

There are two theoretical models explaining ways people understand the causes of domestic violence:

1. *Cycle of abuse model:* This describes abuse as a cycle similar to addictive behavior with a drug.

2. *Power and control model:* As explained in the Duluth model (Pence & Paymar, 1993), this describes abuse as a deliberate way for one person (usually a man, but not always) to control another.

EXPLANATIONS FOR DOMESTIC VIOLENCE

Cycle of Abuse Model

In this view, domestic violence is a compulsive behavior, much like a binge-type pattern of substance abuse. It describes three stages of the cycle of abuse:

1. *Building tension:* The abuser is irritable, critical, and increasingly hard to please; the victim becomes increasingly tense and nervous, trying not to upset the abuser and sometimes going to much trouble to try to please him or her.

2. *Explosion of violence:* The abuser "snaps" over some event, usually minor, becomes violent, and batters the victim. This usually lasts for a fairly short period of time, but it's long enough to kill or badly injure the victim.

3. *"Honeymoon" period:* After the explosion, the abuser feels guilt, shame, and remorse. The abuser tries to compensate for the battering by crying, apologizing, and promising it will never happen again, pampering the victim, giving gifts, tolerating verbal abuse from the victim, and so on. The honeymoon period fades as the abuser again starts to become irritable and harder to please, beginning another cycle with the "building tension" stage.

Over time, the cycle gets faster and more dangerous. The explosions keep getting more violent, often eventually involving the use of weapons, and the honeymoon period gets shorter and eventually disappears, leaving the family in a condition of constant tension relieved for brief periods by increasingly violent explosions.

This model fits the patterns of some violent families but not others. Research and case histories show that violence in many families does fit the cyclical pattern described here, but in others it works differently. The second model, the Duluth power and control model, does a better job of explaining what appears to happen in many of those situations.

Ending the Cycle of Abuse

According to the cycle of abuse model, the way to end the abuse is to teach the violent abuser communication skills, conflict management, and stress and anger management so that he or she is able to stop the buildup of tension and avoid future loss of control.

THE POWER AND CONTROL MODEL

In this model, presented by Pence and Paymar in the manual *Education Groups for Men Who Batter,* domestic violence is not the result of uncontrollable outbursts of emotion. Rather, it is a deliberate method used by one person to try to control another. It is a constant process rather than a cycle.

The Duluth power and control model is based on one partner, most often the man but in some cases the woman, believing the following things:

- They have the right to dominate and control the other person and to be in charge of the relationship. With men, this is often based on the belief that women are inferior.
- They have the right to choose the other person's friends and activities.
- They have the right to use force to exert this control.
- The other person really likes being dominated.
- The other person is manipulative.
- The other person is using them, sees them as a paycheck, etc.
- The other person's role is to serve them.
- They have the right to punish the other person if he or she displeases them.
- If they are angry, they can't help getting violent; it's the other person's fault for making them so angry.
- Destroying property is venting, not abuse, so it's okay to do.

POWER AND CONTROL WHEEL

The power and control model describes eight separate areas of power and control, other than direct physical and sexual violence, which are used to control a partner. This is visualized (Pence & Paymar, 1993) as a wheel with eight sections:

1. Using coercion and threats: making or carrying out threats (e.g., threatening to leave, commit suicide, to make a report to Child Protective Services).
2. Using intimidation: Creating fear by looks, gestures, breaking things, displaying weapons.
3. Using emotional abuse: Put-downs, derogatory comments, name calling, humiliation, mind games.
4. Using isolation: Controlling the other's actions, contacts, activities; using jealousy to control actions.
5. Using minimizing, denying, and blaming: Making light of the abuse, denying the abuse is happening, shifting responsibility, claiming it is the other's fault.
6. Using the children: Threatening to take the children, using the children to deliver messages, making other feel guilty about the children.
7. Using male privilege (obviously, for male batterers): Defining men's and women's roles, treating woman as inferior or as a servant, and so on.
8. Economic abuse: Preventing employment, restricting money.

Ending the Abuse—Shifting to the Equality Wheel

According to this model, the key to ending the abuse is to change the batterer's basic beliefs and attitudes, replacing the beliefs listed earlier with values respecting the partner's rights as a person, giving up the idea of having the right to control the other person, and accepting responsibility for controlling his or her actions regardless of feelings. The result is summed up by an equality wheel, which replaces the power and control wheel and also depicts eight sections:

1. *Nonthreatening behavior:* Talking and acting in ways that allow the partner to feel safe and comfortable doing things and expressing himself or herself.

2. *Respect:* Listening without judgment, valuing the partner's opinions.

3. *Trust and support:* Supporting each other's goals; respect for the partner's right to his or her own feelings, social activities, and opinions.

4. *Honesty and accountability:* Self-responsibility, acknowledging past violence, communicating openly and honestly.

5. *Responsible parenting:* Sharing parenting responsibilities, positive role modeling.

6. *Shared responsibility:* Making family decisions together, mutual agreement on ways household work is done.

7. *Economic partnership:* Making money decisions together, access of both partners to money.

8. *Negotiation and fairness:* Effective conflict management, accepting change, compromising.

WHAT LEADS TO CHANGE

For either model, one question is "What motivates the abusive partner to change?" In cases where change does happen, the motivating factors usually include the following:

- *Legal pressure:* Short of leaving and never coming back, research shows that the single most effective thing a victim of domestic violence can do to prevent recurrence is to call the police, have the batterer arrested, and press charges. Going to jail is a deterrent, and the court system will often order a couple to therapy. However, the longer the violence has been going on, the less effective and the more dangerous this tactic is.

- *The partner's ultimatum:* Sometimes it is also effective for the victim to tell the violent partner that if the abuse ever happens again, he or she will end the relationship—*and to be ready to follow through;* most people can detect a bluff. Again, the longer the violence has been going on, the less effective and the more dangerous this tactic is.

- *The abuser's becoming clean and sober:* This often makes the difference between a person being violent and nonviolent. Impulse control is increased; also, if the violent person is in a 12-Step program, the process of working the steps requires a person to evaluate his or her own actions, make amends, practice the principles of the steps in all affairs, and make every effort to avoid future abusive behavior.

- *Tools and resources:* These consist of therapy programs, support groups, law enforcement agencies, and shelters, as well as informal resources such as supportive family and friends and having separate access to money.

CONCLUSION

Review the following key points:

1. Domestic violence affects millions of families and leads to the injuries and deaths of thousands of adults and children every year.

2. Children who grow up around domestic violence are likely to repeat the pattern in their adult lives unless they work to change it.

3. There are two explanations for domestic violence, the cycle of violence model and the power and control model. Some situations fit one model better, and some situations fit the other.

4. The key to ending domestic violence is understanding it, getting professional help, and taking effective action to end it before someone is seriously injured or killed.

REVIEW LEARNING GOALS

1. Upon completion of this presentation, group members are able to identify behaviors that constitute domestic violence.

2. Upon completion of this presentation, group members will demonstrate understanding of the two main theories of domestic violence.

3. Upon completion of this presentation, group members will demonstrate understanding of healthy, non-abusive relationship interactions.

QUESTIONS/DISCUSSION BEFORE POSTTEST

ADMINISTER POSTTEST

QUESTIONS/DISCUSSION AFTER POSTTEST

INTRODUCTION

Ask for a show of hands of group members who have been affected by a completed suicide, suicide attempt, or suicidal threat or gesture by someone close to them. Ask in how many of those situations drinking or other drug use was a factor. Point out that suicide and substance abuse are often connected. Then ask that, without answering or raising hands, group members think about whether they have ever attempted or seriously considered suicide, and if they have, what role alcohol or other drugs played in their lives at the time.

LEARNING GOALS

Explain to group members that they will be evaluated on their accomplishment of the following goals:

1. Upon completion of this presentation, group members will demonstrate understanding of suicide factors and warning signs by listing, without notes or references, at least four factors in a person's life situation that would increase the risk of suicide.

2. Upon completion of this presentation, group members will demonstrate understanding of suicide factors and warning signs by listing, without notes or references, at least four personal patterns in a person's life that would increase the risk of suicide.

3. Upon completion of this presentation, group members will demonstrate understanding of suicide factors and warning signs by listing, without notes or references, at least four warning signs that might indicate that a person was in increased danger of suicide.

QUESTIONS

As the presenter, you may ask group members to hold their questions until the end or to ask them at any time during the presentation. If participation is a high priority, we recommend allowing questions at any time; if brevity is more important, it works better to hold questions until the end.

PRETEST/POSTTEST

Pass out the pretest if you choose to use it. You may have the group members fill out and turn in pretests without putting names on them as a general measure of baseline knowledge. Explain that the same test will be given as the posttest at the end of the presentation.

BACKGROUND AND LEAD-IN

Ask the discussion question: How many feel you know enough about suicide to be able to tell when someone close to you is in danger of becoming suicidal? Ask how many group members have children, how many have elderly relatives, and how many have family members or close friends who have alcohol or other drug problems. Explain that all three of these categories of people are higher than average risk groups for depression and suicide.

Explain that this presentation will give group members information about the state of mind that leads to suicide and about situations and lifestyle factors that increase the risk of suicide, and will teach them about the warning signs in others' behavior that may indicate greater risk of suicide. Note that after this presentation and the second presentation on suicide, which will cover what to do, the group members will probably have more knowledge on this subject than anyone else in their families or circles of friends, and that their knowledge may save a life.

SUICIDE FACTORS AND WARNING SIGNS

Ask for group members' ideas about what a person might be thinking when he or she commits suicide. Write their answers on a board, flip chart, or transparency sheet and facilitate a brief discussion. Then explain that research and interviews with people who have tried to kill themselves show that the following four factors are almost always present in suicide:

- Intense emotional pain

- A belief that they cannot tolerate or endure this emotional pain

- A feeling that there is no way to escape the emotional pain except by dying

- A feeling of being isolated, that no one understands or cares very much

Note that if any of these factors is reduced or eliminated, the risk of suicide drops dramatically. This can happen in four ways:

1. The emotional pain is relieved.

2. The person comes to believe that he or she can handle the painful situation.

3. The person comes to believe there is a way to reduce or end the emotional pain without dying.

4. The person comes to feel an emotional connection to, and to feel valued by, another person or people.

Life Situation Risk Factors

In general, the risk of suicide goes up in situations that increase the amount of change, stress, and/or emotional pain a person is experiencing, or that reduce his or her ability to cope with stress, or both. These types of situations include the following:

- *Divorce or breakup of a serious relationship:* This is the single highest situational risk factor for suicide.

- *Severe financial problems:* These can affect every area of a person's life and damage his or her self-esteem and feeling of being a competent adult, parent, spouse, and so on.

- *Recent death of a loved one (especially if by suicide), or an anniversary of a death:* Losing a parent, sibling, partner, child, or close friend often triggers the kind of emotional pain that can lead to suicide. If that person died by suicide, it can strongly influence others in the same direction. Anniversaries of deaths are painful reminders, especially for a person whose grief has not healed.

- *Serious illness or physical injury or disability:* Beyond being painful and frightening, and therefore very stressful, medical problems of this kind are devastating to the self-image of many people, when they suddenly see themselves as no longer whole, attractive, or able to do many things they used to do.

- *Loss or threat of loss of a job, demotion, or retirement:* In addition to the financial impact of losing a job, our culture teaches us to base our identity and self-esteem on our work. Feeling like a failure at this important part of life can be devastating. Even retirement can lead to a loss of identity and a feeling that one's main worth in the world is gone.

- *Recent change of jobs, including promotions:* Even a long-hoped-for promotion is stressful, and can be either disappointing or tougher to handle than expected.

- *Recent reorganization or change of supervisor at work:* This is often more stressful than we realize. It requires a lot of adjustment and brings much uncertainty in a relationship with a person who has great power in our lives.

- *Recent geographical move:* This often includes financial stress, a change of job, and a sudden isolation from supportive relationships.

Personal Risk Factors

A number of personal patterns are also related to greater vulnerability to stress and less capacity for coping with difficulties, resulting in higher risk of suicide under any conditions but especially in high-stress situations like those just listed:

- *Heavy use of alcohol and/or other drugs:* A large proportion of suicides are under the influence of alcohol or other drugs when they kill themselves, and a large percentage of alcoholics kill themselves or try to do so. Alcohol is a depressant drug; depressants reduce control over impulses and impair judgment.

- *Serious mental or emotional illness:* Depression, bipolar depression, anxiety orders such as posttraumatic stress disorder, and schizophrenia all increase the risk of suicide by increasing emotional pain and isolation, increasing the number of life problems a person is likely to face, and by reducing his or her ability to cope with those problems.

- *Social isolation:* Being a loner means a person has few supportive relationships to lean on when he or she is in emotional pain. This may also be a source of pain in itself, due to loneliness and feelings of failure and inadequacy.

- *Working in a high-stress job:* Especially in the case of jobs that have a "macho" image and role expectations, such as the military, law enforcement, and corrections, the combination of high stress and the belief that one should not ask others for help with personal problems can be deadly.

- *Frequent conflicts with others:* This can be a sign of ongoing emotional pain, poor "people skills," an attitude of not caring about the consequences of one's actions, poor impulse control, or all of the above.

- *Owning or having easy access to firearms:* Suicide is often an impulsive act, especially in younger people, and having a gun available can make the difference between acting on an impulse or being delayed long enough to have second thoughts.

- *Engaging in high-risk sports or other activities:* Recklessness in other areas and thrill-seeking behavior is often found in people who commit or attempt suicide.

Warning Signs

There are a number of common behavior patterns in people who are thinking about killing themselves or who have decided to do so:

- *Talking or hinting about suicide or death:* Most suicides repeatedly tell people they are thinking about killing themselves before they actually do so. This may take the form of hints such as talking about wanting to go to sleep and never wake up, to go away and never come back, and similar types of remarks. Always take this seriously and ask the person what he or she meant by the remark. Getting the person to talk about it is more likely to keep him or her from acting on the idea than anything else you can do.

- *Planning or preparing for suicide:* This can take the form of getting a gun and ammunition, hoarding medications for an overdose, arranging to be alone so as not to be prevented from carrying out the suicide, and so on.

- *Frequent anxiety, anger, or depression, followed by sudden improvement of mood when the situation has not improved:* This can mean that the person is no longer feeling trapped in the situation because he or she plans to escape by suicide.

- *Frequent preoccupation:* If a person who is in a very stressful situation suddenly becomes absentminded and often seems mentally somewhere else, this in combination with other factors listed can mean the person is considering suicide.

- *Making arrangements for loved ones' needs:* If a person suddenly starts buying personal insurance policies, making a will, settling debts, and doing similar things, these actions may be preparations for his or her own death.

- *Giving away cherished possessions:* This can be a sign that the person believes he or she won't be around much longer.

- *Saying goodbyes:* This may not be put into words, but if a person suddenly starts making visits to favorite people and places, it may mean he or she is saying goodbye.

- *A sudden increase in conflicts with authorities and others:* This can mean a person has stopped caring about consequences because he or she doesn't plan to be around to face them.

- *A sudden increase in drinking and/or drug use:* This can mean that a person is becoming overwhelmed; in any case, it lowers the ability to cope with stress and resist impulses.

- *A sudden increase in risky behavior and/or becoming more accident-prone:* This can be a sign of a person no longer caring what happens to him or her or unconsciously expressing more self-destructive feelings.

It is important to remember that all of these situational factors, lifestyle factors, and warning signs are merely indicators, and many of them may have other explanations. They become most meaningful when several of them are seen together in a pattern, but regardless, when someone is exhibiting one or more of these warning signs, other people should look into the situation and check with the person to see whether he or she is thinking about self-harm.

CONCLUSION

Review the following key points:

1. There is a significant connection between substance abuse and suicide.

2. Other groups such as adolescents and elders are also at greater risk than average for suicide. There are common factors in the state of mind of people who attempt or complete suicide.

3. Both situational and personal factors can increase a person's vulnerability to suicide.

4. There are common warning signs that people usually exhibit when they are considering or planning suicide.

REVIEW LEARNING GOALS

1. Upon completion of this presentation, group members will demonstrate understanding of suicide factors and warning signs by listing, without notes or references, at least four factors in a person's life situation that would increase the risk of suicide.

2. Upon completion of this presentation, group members will demonstrate understanding of suicide factors and warning signs by listing, without notes or references, at least four personal patterns in a person's life that would increase the risk of suicide.

3. Upon completion of this presentation, group members will demonstrate understanding of suicide factors and warning signs by listing, without notes or references, at least four warning signs that might indicate that a person was in increased danger of suicide.

QUESTIONS/DISCUSSION BEFORE POSTTEST

ADMINISTER POSTTEST

QUESTIONS/DISCUSSION AFTER POSTTEST

INTRODUCTION

Ask how many group members feel they have the knowledge and skills to effectively handle a potential or actual suicidal crisis in someone close to them. Review the facts, mentioned in Part I, that substance abusers are at higher than average risk for suicide, also that group members may have family members or friends who belong to other high-risk groups such as teenagers and seniors. Recall any relevant personal experiences group members described in Part I. Note that whereas Part I taught group members about contributing factors and warning signs of suicidal risk, this presentation contains information about what group members can do if and when they see the signs they learned about in Part I.

LEARNING GOALS

Explain to group members that they will be evaluated on their accomplishment of the following goals:

1. Upon completion of this presentation, group members will demonstrate understanding of suicide prevention strategies by listing, without notes or references, at least four actions they can take to safeguard a potentially suicidal person (someone who is considering or threatening suicide, makes a suicidal gesture, or attempts suicide) in the short term.

2. Upon completion of this presentation, group members will demonstrate understanding of suicide prevention strategies by listing, without notes or references, at least four actions they can take to permanently reduce the risk of suicide with a suicidal person after a short-term crisis has passed.

3. Upon completion of this presentation, group members will demonstrate understanding of suicide response strategies by listing, without notes or references, three actions they can take in response to a suicide attempt, gesture, or completed suicide to effectively help family members, friends, and coworkers of a suicidal person.

QUESTIONS

As the presenter, you may ask group members to hold their questions until the end or to ask them at any time during the presentation. If participation is a high priority, we recommend allowing questions at any time; if brevity is more important, it works better to hold questions until the end.

PRETEST/POSTTEST

Pass out the pretest if you choose to use it. You may have the group members fill out and turn in pretests without putting names on them as a general measure of baseline knowledge. Explain that the same test will be given as the posttest at the end of the presentation.

BACKGROUND AND LEAD-IN

Recall the first question asked in the introduction to this presentation, about who feels they have the knowledge and skills to effectively handle a potential or actual suicidal crisis in someone close to them. Ask group members to recall what Part I said was the most common behavior pattern seen as a warning sign that someone was considering suicide. If no one responds with the correct warning sign, supply the answer that the most common warning behavior is talking about suicide, either directly or in hints. Ask group members who they imagine the suicidal person would approach to talk about this; after getting feedback, answer that the typical suicidal person talks about it with people he or she trusts and feels close to, usually family members or close friends. Note that this means that the person who realizes the danger and needs to act will probably be someone like them, a family member or friend, rather than a trained professional. Suggested analogy: Compare this with the fact that most of the time when a person is hurt physically, the first people on the scene are not doctors or nurses or paramedics, but family, friends, and neighbors, and that they can save a life by doing first aid that keeps the person intact until the professionals arrive. Conclude the lead-in by drawing the parallel that the aim of this presentation is to teach them mental and emotional first aid for suicide so they can keep a person intact until the trained professionals have a chance to do their part. Emphasize that this presentation is not meant to make the group members capable of handling a suicidal crisis on their own, but only to give them the tools to keep someone alive long enough to get them to professionals for more in-depth help.

SUICIDE PREVENTION AND RESPONSE STRATEGIES

Here are some short-term strategies to use when someone is considering or threatening suicide, makes a suicidal gesture, or attempts suicide:

First, we will define some terms:

- *Considering suicide* means just that: it is a serious option a person may decide to act upon.

- A *suicide threat* is a statement not yet put into action.

- A *suicidal gesture* is an action that could be harmful, but is taken without the real belief that one will die as a result, such as shallow cuts on a wrist that don't reach any major blood vessels or a small overdose of a non-lethal medicine.

- A *suicide attempt* is an action taken with the sincere belief that one will die as a result, a genuine try at killing oneself.

If a person has a strong feeling that someone may be at risk for suicide, based on the information presented in Part I, there are several things he or she should do:

The first thing anyone must do is choose to act on that feeling. Ask for reasons why people might fail to say or do anything; write answers on the board, then discuss the following:

- Fear of embarrassment (what if I'm wrong and he or she laughs or gets mad?)

- Feeling someone else should do it (especially if they have little in common with the person)

- Feeling that people should be able to handle their own situations

- Fear of making a mistake and making things worse

- Hope it will get better without their needing to act

Ask directly and get them talking. A common fear is that talking about suicide may trigger someone to carry it out, but this is not what happens. Actually, the more a person talks about it once asked, the less likely he or she is to follow through with action. Someone listening in an accepting way reduces one of the four key mental states, the feeling of isolation and not being understood or accepted. It also seems to be partly because in talking about the situation, the person may see hope or options overlooked before. Some guidelines to keep in mind:

- Listening is the most important thing anyone can do, not coming up with answers. The motto here is "Get them talking and keep them talking."

- Don't argue, belittle the person's feelings, make comparisons, or try to use logic. None of these work, and any such response is likely to be seen as rejection. Just listen and make occasional comments reflecting what they've said or asking for clarification.

- In as calm and matter-of-fact a way as possible, ask for details about the person's suicidal thinking. Do they have a specific method planned? How lethal or dangerous is the method they have thought about? Do they have the means? How quickly can they act on it? The more specific, lethal, and available their planned method, the more danger they are in. For example: A person who has thought about "ending it all" but has not come up with a specific plan is in much less danger than the person who replies that he would shoot himself with a pistol and that he has the loaded pistol in the glove compartment in his car.

Offer understanding encouragement. Don't tell the person he or she shouldn't feel that way, but do the following:

- Encourage the person to remember past hard times and how he or she got through them.

- Help the person remember situations where he or she is helpful to others and needed and loved by them.

- Say things like, "I'm glad you told me," and "I think this was a healthy way of connecting with someone else to keep yourself safe."

Make it safe. If possible, persuade the person to turn over any weapons, and remove dangerous items such as broken glass or alcohol or other drugs. Set up safeguards to keep the person away from windows and balconies if on an upper floor.

If the person is actively thinking about suicide, don't leave him or her alone! Either call for professional help and wait until it arrives, or go with the person to a hospital or other place where he or she will definitely be safe.

Make an anti-self-harm contract. It helps to ask the person to agree that before acting on any desire to kill or hurt self, he or she will talk with the person intervening and/or a professional or crisis hotline worker. If possible, put this in writing and get the person to sign it.

Long-Term Strategies for Reducing the Risk of Suicide

Once an immediate crisis is past, you may feel relief, but unless long-term change occurs, the risk may rise instead of decreasing. The person's problems are probably unchanged, and he or she may even feel embarrassment and a sense of failure at not having successfully committed suicide. Family and friends can contribute to the kind of long-lasting change that really will reduce the danger by doing the following:

- *Stay in connect, keep checking back:* Following through on the initial interest will go a long way to permanently break down that sense of isolation.

- *Get other friends and family involved:* When we hear about someone close to us having a serious problem, how do we feel? Most of us want to help in some way. Others feel the same, and the caring they show will also reduce isolation.

- *Keep the person busy:* Having something constructive to do keeps the mind busy so there is less time to dwell on problems and reduces the feeling of helplessness and uselessness to others that contributes to the risk of suicide.

- *Help the person stay clean and sober:* Reducing or eliminating use of alcohol or other drugs will automatically lower suicide risk by a large margin.

- *Help the person learn needed skills:* For example, if someone has financial problems and never learned how to manage money, teaching him or her how to balance a checkbook and how to manage credit cards may do more good than years of counseling. The same can apply with communication skills, parenting skills, job skills, and so on.

- *Encourage basic self-care:* Just getting proper rest, food, and exercise makes a big difference in ability to handle stress.

- *Encourage getting professional help:* Counseling or therapy may be a big help in dealing with the underlying problems that trigger a suicidal crisis.

- *Encourage increased social activity:* This will help keep the person busy and break down his or her emotional isolation.

Strategies for Effective Response to Help Friends, Family, and Coworkers after a Suicide Threat, Gesture, Attempt, or a Completed Suicide

If any group members have described being strongly affected by another's suicidal speech or actions, recall their experiences: if not, emphasize that suicide has a devastating and lasting impact on those left behind. Those people commonly experience many disturbing emotions and thoughts, including any of the following:

- Feelings of responsibility and self-blame
- Blaming others in the family/group
- Guilt
- Anger
- Hurt
- Shame
- Embarrassment
- Confusion
- Intensified grief
- Thoughts of suicide of their own

To minimize the negative impact on the other people affected, some simple steps are very helpful:

- *Encourage them to talk about their thoughts and feelings:* This is especially important with children, who are even more likely than adults to blame themselves for what happens around them.

- *Encourage them to seek professional help if necessary:* The people close to a suicide may need counseling of their own to overcome their emotional pain in the aftermath.

- *Emphasize supportive relationships:* This helps others avoid the feelings of isolation that contribute to suicidal thinking and behavior.

CONCLUSION

Review the following key points:

1. Family members and friends can do a lot to prevent suicide and to help reduce the risk of future suicidal incidents, even though they aren't professionals.

2. The role of friends and family is not to substitute for professionals but to provide mental and emotional first aid to someone who is suicidal until the professionals can work with him or her.

3. There are both short- and long-term responses to the risk, threat, or attempt of suicide.

4. There are also important things that should be done for family, friends, and coworkers of anyone who makes a suicidal threat, gesture, attempt, or a completed suicide.

REVIEW LEARNING GOALS

1. Upon completion of this presentation, group members will demonstrate understanding of suicide prevention strategies by listing, without notes or references, at least four actions they can take to safeguard a potentially suicidal person (someone who is considering or threatening suicide, makes a suicidal gesture, or attempts suicide) in the short term.

2. Upon completion of this presentation, group members will demonstrate understanding of suicide prevention strategies by listing, without notes or references, at least four actions they can take to permanently reduce the risk of suicide with a suicidal person after a short-term crisis has passed.

3. Upon completion of this presentation, group members will demonstrate understanding of suicide response strategies by listing, without notes or references, three actions they can take in response to a suicide attempt, gesture, or completed suicide to effectively help family members, friends, and coworkers of a suicidal person.

QUESTIONS/DISCUSSION BEFORE POSTTEST

ADMINISTER POSTTEST

QUESTIONS/DISCUSSION AFTER POSTTEST

INTRODUCTION

Ask the group for definitions of trauma, and write their responses on a board, flip chart, or transparency sheet. Then ask for a show of hands from those who feel their lives have been seriously affected by some kind of trauma; from those who raise their hands, ask how many feel there is a connection between their experience of trauma and their problems with alcohol and other drugs. Facilitate a brief discussion of how these things might be connected. Explain that this presentation will give the group information about trauma, posttraumatic stress disorder (PTSD), and the connection between these things and substance abuse, with the aim of helping them avoid or cope with the effects of past or future trauma and avoid relapses related to trauma.

LEARNING GOALS

Explain to group members that they will be evaluated on their accomplishment of the following goals:

1. Upon completion of this presentation, group members will demonstrate understanding of the nature of trauma and be able to give examples of at least four different types of traumatic experiences.

2. Upon completion of this presentation, group members will describe at least three symptoms of PTSD.

3. Upon completion of this presentation, group members will describe at least three resources or methods for coping with trauma and avoiding or relieving the symptoms of PTSD.

QUESTIONS

As the presenter, you may ask group members to hold their questions until the end or to ask them at any time during the presentation. If participation is a high priority, we recommend allowing questions at any time; if brevity is more important, it works better to hold questions until the end.

PRETEST/POSTTEST

Pass out the pretest if you choose to use it. You may have the group members fill out and turn in pretests without putting names on them as a general measure of baseline knowledge. Explain that the same test will be given as the posttest at the end of the presentation.

BACKGROUND AND LEAD-IN

Refer back to the opening question about the definition of trauma. Give the group these definitions from *Webster's Unabridged Dictionary*: "in medicine, (a) an injury or wound violently produced; (b) the condition or neurosis resulting from this. In psychiatry, an emotional experience, or shock, which has a lasting psychic effect." Compare the group's definitions with this one, then ask the group what they think of when they hear the term posttraumatic stress disorder or PTSD. Again, write their answers on the board, flip chart, or transparency sheet, and ask the discussion question: What does this have to do with addiction or with staying clean and sober? Continue the discussion briefly, then explain that this presentation will answer these questions.

TRAUMA AND ITS EFFECTS

Referring to these definitions and to those provided by the group, note that the common elements in both physical and mental or emotional trauma are that they result from a violent and shocking experience and that the effects can be long-lasting. Some of the experiences that can traumatize people include the following:

- Experiencing military combat in which a person is badly wounded, is in great danger, and/or sees other people killed or badly wounded

- Experiencing domestic violence, either spousal abuse or child abuse, as either the victim or a witness

- Being the victim or a witness of a violent crime such as a murder, rape, assault, or armed robbery

- Being a victim or witness of a terrorist attack

- Being caught in a natural disaster such as a hurricane or tornado, earthquake, flood, fire, lightning strike, or other disaster

- Being a victim or witness of a violent accident such as a bloody car crash, a plane crash, a boat sinking, a household or workplace accident in which someone is killed or badly hurt

- Suffering from a life-threatening illness

- Doing work that involves repeated exposure to other people's traumatic experiences, such as being a police officer, firefighter, paramedic, emergency room worker, therapist

The short-term effects of trauma can include going into shock physically if injured, and into a mental and emotional condition resembling shock in response to intense fear, horror, or grief. Either kind of shock can include a numbing of pain, a withdrawal into a dazed condition, and a kind of collapse into a weakened state. Physical shock can kill people even when their injuries are easily survivable, by causing their breathing and heartbeat to become irregular or stop and other bodily functions to stop or be impaired. Mental and emotional shock doesn't cause physical death by itself, but it can place a person in greater physical danger by reducing his or her ability to avoid or cope with further trauma.

Physical shock seems to pass without long-term effects, but some of the effects of mental and emotional shock can last a lifetime. When a person suffers serious long-term mental and emotional damage because of a traumatic experience, he or she may be suffering from something called posttraumatic stress disorder or PTSD.

WHAT IS PTSD AND HOW DOES IT AFFECT PEOPLE

PTSD is a pattern of long-lasting traumatic effects in a person who has experienced a situation in which he or she felt overwhelming fear, helplessness, or horror. Usually this is a violent experience involving the threat of death or serious physical harm to oneself, with or without actual injury, or the threatened or actual death or serious injury of someone close. This can be either a loved one or someone who is literally physically nearby. It seems to be more damaging if the situation doesn't make sense to the person, and/or if the trauma is the result of hostile human action. Talking with people who have experienced this kind of trauma or seen it up close, words like *haunted* and *scarred* are often heard. A common theme is feeling trapped in the experience, as expressed by statements like "I can't get over it," and "If I shut my eyes, it's right there."

Symptoms of PTSD

People with PTSD experience some or all of the following symptoms. If this has gone on for at least 30 days, the diagnosis of PTSD can be made if:

1. He or she has recurring, distressing, intrusive memories of the event, including images, thoughts, or perceptions. The memories disrupt the person's activities, mood, and train of thought.

2. He or she has recurring nightmares about the event or about similar situations.

3. He or she has episodes of acting or feeling as if the event is happening again. These may range from feeling the same emotions and physical reactions all the way to flashbacks in which the person has a hallucination and thinks he or she is actually back in the situation.

4. He or she feels intense distress (panic, rage, grief, etc.) when reminded of the event by internal or external "cues" that are reminders of the situation, such as being in an elevator for a person who was assaulted in an elevator; a certain smell, sound, song, physical sensation, and so on. The distress includes physical reactions—sweating, shaking, nausea, heart pounding, hyperventilation, and so on.

5. The person tends to avoid things that remind him or her of the traumatic event.

6. He or she tends to become emotionally numb in general and becomes cold and distant in relationships.

7. The person may not be able to remember all or part of the traumatic event.

8. The person has difficulty falling or staying asleep.

9. He or she is much more irritable and/or has outbursts of anger.

10. He or she has difficulty concentrating.

11. He or she is "hypervigilant," always very alert and watching whatever is going on around him or her, sometimes seeming to expect something bad to happen at any time.

12. He or she is easily startled and reacts in extreme ways to being startled.

Other Names for PTSD

This pattern has been recognized by the mental health profession and given the name PTSD only since about the era of the Vietnam War, but it has always been part of human experience. People have seen it and described it since ancient times, calling it by names including hysteria, shell shock, battle fatigue, war neurosis, and the "thousand-yard stare." Because PTSD can have many causes, although many people think of it as related to military combat, names for it have also included terms like rape crisis syndrome, battered woman syndrome, and child abuse accommodation syndrome.

The symptoms of PTSD can affect every part of life—mental, emotional, physical, spiritual, and interpersonal. It often leads to other mental, emotional, and medical problems, and is a strong contributing factor in addictions in particular, as well as in crime, homelessness, and suicide. Although it is highly treatable and most often responds well to treatment, it does not usually get better if it is not treated. Individuals vary in the particular ways they experience the symptoms of PTSD, and those symptoms range in intensity from moderately troubling to devastating and life-disrupting. No definite statistics are available to tell us what percentage of people suffer from PTSD today or in the past, but most helping professionals who work with people suffering from PTSD would agree that it is widespread. Today, PTSD is an under-diagnosed problem that may be as widespread as depression. Fortunately, today we also know more about PTSD and how to deal with it than we've ever known, and we're learning more every year.

PTSD increases the risk of addiction, and vice versa. Some people suffer a trauma and fall into addiction by using alcohol or other drugs to self-medicate their PTSD symptoms. Other people suffer traumatic experiences because of their substance abuse and develop PTSD because of those experiences. In either case, when a person has both addictive problems and PTSD, the addiction must be overcome first before any progress can be made in relieving the symptoms of the PTSD.

Avoiding, Preventing, and Treating PTSD

Two people may experience similar events and respond very differently, with one developing PTSD and the other coping and adapting without life-disrupting consequences. This is because just as with physical

8.25

diseases, some of us are more resistant than others to mental and emotional disturbances, although some experiences are so overwhelming that no one can go through them unaffected.

Anyone can increase his or her resiliency. Specifically, we can proactively do the following to protect ourselves in each of the following areas:

- *Danger or occurrence of death or serious harm:* We can reduce our risk by examining our lifestyles and making fewer high-risk choices. Getting clean and sober and staying that way will obviously increase our ability to cope with a traumatic situation if it comes up. We can also avoid being in places where traumatic events are more likely to take place, and getting clean and sober will help with this too.

- *Experience of intense fear, helplessness, or horror:* We cannot eliminate these responses from our minds and bodies, but having a spiritual belief system centered on faith in some Higher Power and the belief that we are cared for by that Higher Power seems to insulate us against much of the terror we might otherwise feel in these situations. It's also useful to practice calming and positive self-talk and other thinking techniques aimed at keeping or quickly regaining our perspective and focusing on what we can do rather than on what we can't do.

- *The experience not making sense:* This is often the result of unrealistic expectations or beliefs. We can address this by thinking about what we believe the rules are in this world, using our spiritual belief systems and our experience of the world as guides.

- *Emotional isolation:* The best protection against this problem is to build and nurture an emotional support network of people whom we trust, feel close to, and frequently talk with about whatever is on our minds and hearts. If we regularly do some sort of work in service to others, such as volunteer work, we further strengthen our network and tap into the strength and caring of others.

- *Trauma resulting from hostile human action:* Most of us tend to take things personally. If we can shift to a view of others and their actions in which we don't take things personally, we will be less deeply wounded when others choose to harm us. We will recognize that although we are affected, it is a reflection of what is going on inside the other person, not us.

We can increase our resistance to trauma the same way we would increase our resistance to any other illness or harm, by practicing as healthy and self-nurturing a lifestyle as we can. If we are physically strong, practice good self-care, and use stress management methods, we will be more stable and resilient in the face of serious trauma.

Effective action after trauma can reduce the chances of developing PTSD. Not all trauma can be avoided, and some will be so painful or frightening that we will be severely affected no matter how resilient we may be or what coping skills and resources we may have. However, there are some ways to greatly reduce our chances of suffering PTSD after a trauma, including the following:

1. *Critical incident debriefing:* This procedure is often done as a group but can be done with individuals, couples, or families. It usually takes only two to three hours, is a one-time event, and reduces the number of people who end up with PTSD in any given group by about 90 percent. It is not therapy, but involves talking about what has happened, with the discussion in several stages. The end result is that the person or people who have experienced the trauma understand the situation better, understand how it has affected them, have more resources to cope, and know that others understand and care.

2. *Counseling or therapy:* Working with a mental health professional or clergy person can also be very useful in improving understanding, reducing isolation, and reducing symptoms.

3. *Support groups:* There are also support groups specifically organized for people who have experienced many types of stresses and traumas.

4. *Informal support from family and friends:* Being able to talk about the traumatic experience with people who will accept what they hear calmly and express love, support, and compassion can be very helpful in reducing the severity of long-term PTSD symptoms. If the listener is someone who has been through a similar experience the benefit is much greater.

Effective Treatment of PTSD Once It Has Developed

If a person is already suffering from PTSD, effective treatment is available. If PTSD is not treated it usually doesn't get better and can greatly increase the risk of relapse into addiction. If treated, it usually responds well to effective therapy; PTSD never completely goes away but sufferers can achieve a lot of relief from its symptoms, whether the trauma is recent or decades in the past. The best-proven treatments are *cognitive therapy* and *cognitive/behavioral therapy*. These approaches work by helping people change their perceptions of situations and themselves, their habits of thought, and their actions. In the hands of a good therapist, these tools can also be quite effective, though they tend to require long-term, intensive work.

12-Step and Other Recovery Programs

Although not properly considered treatment or therapy, these are included in this category because over time they often seem to lead to relief of PTSD symptoms. A person who participates wholeheartedly in a 12-Step program, including attending frequent meetings, working the Steps, working with a sponsor, and performing service work, will be practicing a safer lifestyle, becoming more resilient, and making many of the same changes in perceptions and actions that are the goals of the treatment strategies mentioned previously.

CONCLUSION

Review the following key points:

1. Trauma can be physical or mental and emotional, and results from a shocking and violent experience.
2. Traumatic experiences can either lead to, or result from, addictive behaviors.
3. The mental and emotional effects of trauma, when they last longer than 30 days, may be diagnosed as posttraumatic stress disorder or PTSD.
4. There are many things people can do to reduce their risk of experiencing trauma and PTSD and to improve their ability to cope with PTSD if they do experience trauma.
5. To effectively heal PTSD symptoms in a person suffering from both PTSD and an addiction, the addiction must be taken care of first.

REVIEW LEARNING GOALS

1. Upon completion of this presentation, group members will demonstrate understanding of the nature of trauma and be able to give examples of at least four different types of traumatic experiences.
2. Upon completion of this presentation, group members will describe at least three symptoms of PTSD.
3. Upon completion of this presentation, group members will describe at least three resources or methods for coping with trauma and avoiding or relieving the symptoms of PTSD.

QUESTIONS/DISCUSSION BEFORE POSTTEST

ADMINISTER POSTTEST

QUESTIONS/DISCUSSION AFTER POSTTEST

INTRODUCTION

Ask group members to think of the challenges and difficulties they are coming to see connected with overcoming substance abuse problems, then ask them to think instead about the problems facing people who are mentally ill. Then ask them to consider what life is like for people who face both problems together and facilitate a brief discussion on this topic. State that this situation is commonly described as co-occurring disorders or dual diagnosis, and that many people have co-occurring disorders.

Tell the group that this presentation will contain information about how substance abuse problems interact with some common mental disorders. Tell them that the purpose of this information is to enable them to cope more effectively with co-occurring disorders if they face them themselves or if someone they know is in this situation.

LEARNING GOALS

Explain to group members that they will be evaluated on their accomplishment of the following goals:

1. Upon completion of this presentation, group members will demonstrate basic awareness of co-occurring disorders by listing, without notes or references, at least four common mental disorders that frequently coexist with substance abuse problems.

2. Upon completion of this presentation, group members will demonstrate basic knowledge of ways substance abuse and mental illness can be connected by listing, without notes or references, at least four ways one of these problems can cause or intensify the other.

3. Upon completion of this presentation, group members will demonstrate basic knowledge of specific patterns of co-occurring disorders by matching, without notes or references, at least four common mental disorders with the types of psychoactive drugs most commonly abused by people suffering from those mental disorders.

QUESTIONS

As the presenter, you may ask group members to hold their questions until the end or to ask them at any time during the presentation. If participation is a high priority, we recommend allowing questions at any time; if brevity is more important, it works better to hold questions until the end.

PRETEST/POSTTEST

Pass out the pretest if you choose to use it. You may have the group members fill out and turn in pretests without putting names on them as a general measure of baseline knowledge. Explain that the same test will be given as the posttest at the end of the presentation.

BACKGROUND AND LEAD-IN

Ask group members for their estimates as to what percentage of the population suffers significant effects of mental disorders sometime during their lives, then the same question about substance abuse disorders. Tell them that according to one national survey, both categories were at approximately 20 percent of the population.

Next, give them the following statistics: According to the same study, among those diagnosed with serious mental illnesses, 29 percent also had drug or alcohol problems, and of those who had substance abuse disorders, 53 percent also suffered from psychiatric disorders. Other studies reported even higher percentages for people with both types of problems. Finally, note that among people in prisons, mental hospitals (both over 80 percent, meaning that over 80 percent of people who have either problem have both), and nursing homes (over 60 percent), the percentage of co-occurring disorder patients is higher yet. In summary, this is a widespread problem that causes even greater devastation to its victims' lives than either mental illness alone or substance abuse alone.

CO-OCCURRING DISORDERS

Common mental disorders that often coexist with substance abuse and dependence are:

- *Mood disorders:* These are mental disorders in which a person's moods are disturbed to a degree that interferes with his or her life. The disturbance is in the form of general moods that are either too "high" or too "low." The most common examples are bipolar disorder, major depressive disorder, and dysthymia (a chronic and less intense form of depression).

- *Anxiety disorders:* These are similar to mood disorders, except that instead of the person's mood being generally too far up or down, the person's life is disrupted by feelings that are specifically anxious or fearful. Common examples include panic attacks, obsessive-compulsive disorder, and posttraumatic stress disorder (PTSD).

- *Thought disorders:* In a thought disorder, either the person's beliefs and thinking processes are impaired, which is called being delusional, or his or her sensory experiences are distorted (hallucinations), such as hearing imaginary voices or seeing things that aren't there. The most common form of thought disorder is schizophrenia.

- *Personality disorders:* A personality disorder is a rigid, distorted, and dysfunctional style of relating to others, the self, and the world. The example most commonly found coexisting with abuse of alcohol and other drugs is antisocial personality disorder, which, as its name indicates, is demonstrated by actions that consistently show disregard for law, consequences, and the rights and feelings of other people.

Substance abuse and mental illness affect each other in many ways. Substance abuse can lead to mental illness. Sometimes the use of alcohol and other drugs contributes to mental illness. This can happen in more than one way:

1. *Increased vulnerability:* People under the influence of alcohol and other drugs are much more likely than sober people to get into dangerous situations, and less capable of coping with those situations when they happen. This can lead to traumatic experiences that contribute to mental illness.

2. *Direct causation:* Drugs can also directly create forms of mental illness, such as psychosis induced by various drugs, especially hallucinogens and stimulants. When you consider that the definition of psychosis describes it as distortion in thinking, sensory perception, or both, and consider that drugs often cause exactly those effects, you can say that drugs cause temporary psychosis, which under some conditions can become permanent.

Mental illness can lead to substance abuse. Different forms of mental illness often lead to substance abuse either because the person is self-medicating, seeking relief of symptoms of mental illness, or because the mental illness leads the person to pleasure-seeking or thrill-seeking behavior without regard for consequences; this behavior often includes drinking and other forms of drug use.

Other factors can contribute to both substance abuse and mental illness, including:

1. *Heredity:* Research shows strong indications of hereditary factors in both substance abuse and mental illness. Some people may be more likely to have both problems because they are "programmed" that way by genetics, by their childhood family environments, or by a combination of both.

2. *Other causes:* Traumatic experiences can sometimes create conditions that incline people toward both substance abuse and mental illness. For example, a person who was severely injured in a traffic accident could, as a result, experience both PTSD due to the emotional impact of the experience, and chronic severe physical pain from injuries, which could lead to substance abuse as a form of self-medication for pain.

Co-occurring disorders make treating both problems more difficult for a number of reasons, for example:

1. *Combination of symptoms:* Because the symptoms of both problems can combine to create more problems and make them worse than would be the case with either substance abuse or mental illness alone, the combination is harder to treat, and relapse into both types of problems is a greater problem. Each problem can also conceal and distort symptoms of the other and make accurate diagnosis and treatment more confusing.

2. *Training of therapists:* Many treatment professionals are trained to provide either substance abuse therapy or mental health therapy, but not both, so the person may have to be treated by more than one professional.

3. *Program policies:* Reflecting the same split in thinking as the training of therapists just mentioned, many treatment programs address one problem or the other, but not both, again leading to the client having to seek treatment from more than one source.

PATTERNS OF CO-OCCURRING DISORDERS

Certain types of mental illness are most often found together with the abuse of certain types of drugs; also, some types of mental illness are more likely to coexist with substance abuse than others, such as:

• *Mood disorders:* People suffering from depressions and bipolar disorder most often abuse stimulants as a form of self-medication. Of all the people surveyed who were diagnosed with any mood disorder, 32 percent also had diagnoses of chemical dependence or abuse; for bipolar disorder sufferers in particular, this figure was over 60 percent.

• *Thought disorders:* People suffering from schizophrenia and related disorders most often abuse illegal drugs of various kinds; the fact that the drugs are illicit seems to be the common factor, although a very large proportion of people with schizophrenia also use nicotine, as it improves concentration and relieves some of their symptoms. Forty-seven percent of schizophrenics are also diagnosable with substance abuse disorders.

• *Anxiety disorders:* PTSD sufferers and others with anxiety disorders abuse alcohol and other depressant drugs more often than other types of drugs, as a way of self-medicating their distressing symptoms. For all anxiety disorder sufferers surveyed, the rate of co-occurring substance abuse disorders was around 24 percent.

• *Antisocial personality disorder:* People with this disorder tend to be thrill-seekers who abuse opiates such as heroin and stimulants like methamphetamine, amphetamines, and cocaine. Over 83 percent have co-occurring substance abuse disorders.

WHAT WE CAN DO ABOUT CO-OCCURRING DISORDERS

The most effective approach seems to be to integrate treatment for both problems at once, and to integrate treatment with other activities such as participation in Alcoholics Anonymous or other community support groups. People who suffer from co-occurring disorders can get better treatment by doing the following:

• *Keep treatment providers informed:* Make sure that all doctors, therapists, and other professionals providing treatment know about both the mental illness diagnosis and the substance abuse disorder.

- *Get integrated treatment:* If possible, seek treatment programs and professionals that work with both issues in an integrated way.

- *Participate in community support groups* specifically for people with co-occurring disorders, such as Double Trouble.

CONCLUSION

Review the following key points:

1. Co-occurring disorders, or the experience by one person of both a serious mental illness and a substance abuse problem, affect a substantial portion of the population and can intensify the problems and suffering of those who experience this as well as others affected by those people.

2. Certain mental disorders are more likely to be connected to abuse or dependency on certain types of substances.

3. Co-occurring disorders can also make therapy more difficult for both problems.

4. Integrated treatment for both problems gives the best results in treating people with co-occurring disorders.

REVIEW LEARNING GOALS

1. Upon completion of this presentation, group members will demonstrate basic awareness of co-occurring disorders by listing, without notes or references, at least four common mental disorders that frequently coexist with substance abuse problems.

2. Upon completion of this presentation, group members will demonstrate basic knowledge of ways substance abuse and mental illness can be connected by listing, without notes or references, at least four ways one of these problems can cause or intensify the other.

3. Upon completion of this presentation, group members will demonstrate basic knowledge of specific patterns of co-occurring disorders by matching, without notes or references, at least four common mental disorders with the types of psychoactive drugs most commonly abused by people suffering from those mental disorders.

QUESTIONS/DISCUSSION BEFORE POSTTEST

ADMINISTER POSTTEST

QUESTIONS/DISCUSSION AFTER POSTTEST

INTRODUCTION

Ask group members for their definition of the term "codependency." Write answers on a board, flip chart, or transparency sheet. Then offer this definition: *Codependency is a pattern of trying to control others for their own good, which ends up being bad for yourself and for the relationship.* Compare this with the group's answers, looking for common points. Ask group members what kinds of actions would be examples of codependent behaviors, and facilitate a brief discussion. Finally, ask group members how these behavior patterns might affect their ability to remain clean and sober.

LEARNING GOALS

Explain to group members that they will be evaluated on their accomplishment of the following goals:

1. Upon completion of this presentation, group members will demonstrate understanding of codependency by listing, without notes or references, at least four typical codependent behavior patterns and at least four healthy relationship behaviors as counterparts to those codependent behavior patterns.

2. Upon completion of this presentation, group members will demonstrate understanding of codependency by listing, without notes or references, at least three sources of information and help for people seeking to change codependent behavior patterns into healthy patterns.

QUESTIONS

As the presenter, you may ask group members to hold their questions until the end or to ask them at any time during the presentation. If participation is a high priority, we recommend allowing questions at any time; if brevity is more important, it works better to hold questions until the end.

PRETEST/POSTTEST

Pass out the pretest if you choose to use it. You may have the group members fill out and turn in pretests without putting names on them as a general measure of baseline knowledge. Explain that the same test will be given as the posttest at the end of the presentation.

BACKGROUND AND LEAD-IN

Refer to the impact of codependency on recovery, as briefly discussed in the introduction. Explain that codependent behavior by family and friends, though well-intentioned, can delay a person's getting clean and sober and can contribute to relapse, especially in early sobriety. Explain that this presentation will give the group information on how they and their families can avoid undermining their recoveries by continuing or falling into codependent or addictive relationship patterns.

CODEPENDENCY

What causes codependency? In the definition above, we said that *Codependency is a pattern of trying to control others for their own good, which ends up being bad for yourself and for the relationship.* The key phrase regarding cause is "for their own good." When codependent people engage in the behaviors we will discuss in a moment, they are usually trying to help the alcoholics, addicts, or other compulsive people with whom they are in relationships. The roots of codependency are often in the following feelings and beliefs:

- The desire to help a suffering loved one

- A sense of responsibility, usually caused by feeling that something needs to be done and no one else is doing it

- A belief that the alcoholic or addict is not capable of getting along without the codependent person

- A belief that it is important to protect the image of the family, the couple, and/or the other person by hiding problems

- A belief that the codependent person can change the addicted person and a sense of having both the right and the duty to do so

- A feeling that the codependent person has no right to say no or to withhold help

- The codependent person basing his or her self-esteem on doing things for others

- The codependent person experiencing a feeling of superiority and strength when he or she rescues others or cleans up after them

Typical codependent behavior patterns and healthy counterparts include:

- *Enabling/rescuing (protecting the addiction):* Codependent people usually go to great lengths to clean up after alcoholics or addicts and rescue them from the consequences of their own addictive behavior. The result is to make it easy and convenient for the addicted person to keep on behaving the same way, so this actually delays that person's getting uncomfortable enough to change the behavior. *The healthy counterpart* to this is to let others clean up their own messes as much as possible.

- *Over-responsibility and martyrdom:* The codependent person takes on responsibility for the actions, feelings, and thoughts of others, then feels as if he or she is being victimized by the problems those others create. *The healthy counterpart* to this is to take responsibility for yourself and expect other adults, and children as far as is reasonable, to do the same.

- *Manipulation and control:* A natural result of feeling responsible for others is a tendency to try to control their behavior, either without letting them know (manipulation) or by direct command (control). *The healthy counterpart* to this is mutual respect and self-determination, with partners openly asking for what they want and accepting the other's decision rather than trying to trick or bully the partner into acting as they wish.

- *Parentification of children:* Children in these families tend to grow up early, especially older children, and end up taking over the responsibilities of the adults much of the time. *The healthy counterpart* to this is for adults to handle their responsibilities and let children be children without expecting them to take on adult concerns.

- *Isolation and family secrets:* The belief that the family's image must be protected leads to restricting contacts with "outsiders" and teaching children to "keep things in the family" even when there are obviously problems with which the family needs help. *The healthy counterpart* to this is a balance between privacy and openness, with the freedom to go outside the family for help if necessary and to have healthy friendships outside the family.

- *Denial and "no-talk" rules:* Even within the family, many subjects are off-limits, and often the codependent person will not acknowledge even obvious problems, leading to the "elephant in the living room" syndrome (a huge problem no one talks about because no one wants to bring it up, but everyone sees it and has to keep walking around it). *The healthy counterpart* to this is for all family members to feel free to bring up problems and concerns and talk about them.

- *Resentment and self-pity:* Because the codependent person is doing so much for others (whether they want it or not) and feels unappreciated, he or she often comes to feel burned out, resentful, and self-pitying. *The healthy counterpart* to this is a refusal to take on others' responsibilities, thus avoiding these reactions.

- *Undermining of recovery:* Although the codependent person may say, and believe, that he or she wants the recovery of the alcoholic or addicted partner very much, when this starts to happen the codependent person may (without realizing it) act in ways that undermine the recovery and push the other back toward addictive behaviors. *The healthy counterpart* to this is to treat recovery as a team effort and work on one's own issues while being supportive of positive changes in others.

SOURCE OF INFORMATION, HELP, AND SUPPORT FOR HEALTHY CHANGE

- *Therapy:* Group, couple, family, or individual therapy or counseling may be a big help in identifying codependent patterns and learning healthy behaviors to change those patterns.

- *12-Step groups:* Just as Alcoholics Anonymous, Narcotics Anonymous, Cocaine Anonymous, and other 12-Step groups exist to help alcoholics and addicts, there are 12-Step groups to help their families and friends with issues of codependency. These include *Al-Anon, Nar-Anon, Sex and Love Addicts Anonymous, CoDependents Anonymous,* and *Adult Children of Alcoholics.*

- *Other support groups:* Many communities have other support groups for help with relationship issues, usually listed in newspapers. They will have names such as *Women Who Love Too Much* and *Addictive Relationships.*

- *Healthy examples:* If you know people who have relationships that match the characteristics listed above as healthy counterparts to codependency, seeking their advice or just spending time with them and learning from their examples may be useful.

- *Self-improvement literature:* A wide array of information on this subject is available in popular books and workbooks, videotapes, audiotapes, and on the Internet.

CONCLUSION

Review the following key points:

1. Codependency is a pattern of trying to control others for their own good, which ends up being bad for oneself and the relationship.

2. Codependent behavior is usually based on good intentions, but can actually do great harm by delaying and undermining recovery and by poisoning relationships.

3. The key to avoiding continuing or falling into codependent patterns, especially in early recovery, is to be alert for codependent patterns and know the healthy alternatives.

REVIEW LEARNING GOALS

1. Upon completion of this presentation, group members will demonstrate understanding of codependency by listing, without notes or references, at least four typical codependent behavior patterns and at least four healthy relationship behaviors as counterparts to those codependent behavior patterns.

2. Upon completion of this presentation, group members will demonstrate understanding of codependency by listing, without notes or references, at least three sources of information and help for people seeking to change codependent behavior patterns into healthy patterns.

QUESTIONS/DISCUSSION BEFORE POSTTEST

ADMINISTER POSTTEST

QUESTIONS/DISCUSSION AFTER POSTTEST

INTRODUCTION

Ask the group what connections they think may exist among grief, loss, and substance abuse. Write their answers on a board, flip chart, or transparency sheet. If it is not given as an answer, ask how many group members drank or used to cope with unhappy feelings, and ask how many feel that there is some event that would be so upsetting that they would feel they had to drink or use to handle it. If anyone says there is, ask what that event would be. Tell the group that the purpose of this presentation is to explain the process of grief experienced by most people after significant losses so that when (not if) they find themselves grieving, they can better understand what they are going through and how to cope with it in nonself-destructive ways.

LEARNING GOALS

Explain to group members that they will be evaluated on their accomplishment of the following goals:

1. Upon completion of this presentation, group members will demonstrate understanding of grief and loss by listing, without notes or references, at least four types of losses that often cause intensive grief.

2. Upon completion of this presentation, group members will demonstrate understanding of grief and loss by listing, without notes or references, the five typical stages of grieving over loss described by Elisabeth Kübler-Ross.

3. Upon completion of this presentation, group members will demonstrate understanding of grief and loss by listing, without notes or references, at least four healthy coping skills for dealing with grief and loss.

QUESTIONS

As the presenter, you may ask group members to hold their questions until the end or to ask them at any time during the presentation. If participation is a high priority, we recommend allowing questions at any time; if brevity is more important, it works better to hold questions until the end.

PRETEST/POSTTEST

Pass out the pretest if you choose to use it. You may have the group members fill out and turn in pretests without putting names on them as a general measure of baseline knowledge. Explain that the same test will be given as the posttest at the end of the presentation.

BACKGROUND AND LEAD-IN

Many newly recovering people feel that they would be unable to remain clean and sober if some particular event happened to them. Most often, this event is a loss of some kind, such as a death of someone they love or the loss of a relationship. In many cases, this is a loss that is guaranteed to happen eventually, such as the death of a parent. Point out that this means that these people have already made a plan to relapse. The only thing they don't know is when. In other cases, the losses feared aren't inevitable, but it is beyond their power to prevent them. Even here, they are giving away their choice between sobriety or relapse to the control of people or situations outside themselves. The goal of this presentation is to enable group members to cope with losses while maintaining their sobriety and abstinence, not only from substance abuse but from other self-destructive behavior.

GRIEF AND LOSS

Ask group members to name types of events they would consider significant losses, ones that would cause feelings of intense loss. Write their answers after other class feedback written down earlier, then discuss connections. Add any of the following that the group misses, after checking each one to see whether the group agrees that it belongs on the list:

- *Death of a spouse or partner, other family member, friend, or other significant person:* This is the most obvious answer and will probably be the first response. Discuss the idea that the pain and loss felt are less for the dead person, who is not suffering, than for oneself and the loss of having that person in one's life.

- *Miscarriages and abortions:* These are often ignored or minimized as losses, but are often felt as deeply as the loss of a child carried to term, even in the case of voluntary abortions. Acknowledging the loss and experiencing the grief seem necessary here as much as in other deaths.

- *Divorces and other relationship endings:* Again, this will probably have been given as a response by group members. Note that after death of a spouse, divorce is often considered the second most stressful life event people experience. The effects of a divorce or breakup of a relationship equivalent to marriage may last for years.

- *Loss of a job:* This is also a highly stressful event that affects self-esteem deeply as well as forcing changes and secondary losses in other areas such as security, work friendships, and plans and goals.

- *Death of a pet:* People become strongly attached to animals, and their deaths often result in grief as intense as that resulting from human deaths, but society is less likely to recognize and respect this kind of grief.

- *Major illness or injury to oneself or a loved one:* Even when no one has died, the loss of physical strength and health, sometimes the permanent loss of abilities, has a deep impact on the person suffering the loss and others close to him or her.

- *Geographical moves:* Loss of familiar places and routines, even when replaced by new ones just as satisfactory, is a major life change and often triggers significant grief, sometimes called homesickness. This can be confusing because we may not be able to understand where the feeling of loss comes from.

- *Retirement:* This is a major loss of identity, often a loss of self-esteem, sometimes a serious loss of financial and material security. The period shortly before and after retirement is a time of increased risk of suicide, especially in cultures like ours that place great emphasis on our work as the most important thing about us.

- *Other major life transitions:* Changing from one stage of life or situation to another is always a loss, even when the change is one we want and have worked to bring about. This applies to graduation, marriage, the birth of a child, job promotion, and other similar events. Even when we have also gained, we have lost whatever is left behind, and we seem to need to go through a grieving process even in these cases.

- *Giving up an addiction:* Yes, this is a loss! An addiction is a major part of a person's life. It may have provided a big part of his or her identity and is almost always the primary coping tool for dealing with many situations. Even when we recognize that the use of alcohol or other drugs (or a compulsive behavior such as gambling) has stopped being a source of pleasure and has become painful and destructive, we often feel a terrible sense of loss at giving it up. This is normal. It does not mean we are "doing recovery wrong" or that we are going to relapse.

STAGES OF GRIEF

Elisabeth Kübler-Ross studied people who were dying of fatal illnesses to find out how they adapted to their own impending deaths. She found that the people she talked with usually experienced five stages of grieving, and that these seem to apply in other situations of loss as well. People may not experience these stages in exact sequence, and they may move forward and backward in the process, slipping back into an earlier stage at times. Some people, because of insufficient time or because they resist the process, are unable to complete the stages of grieving and remain stuck somewhere in the midst of the process, sometimes until they die. Some people don't go through all of them. Her five stages are:

1. *Denial:* A common first reaction to loss, either one that has happened or one that is coming, is to refuse to believe it, or to refuse to believe that we will be seriously affected by it. This may be hard to understand for others watching this reaction. This is a first way to control the experience and avoid feeling the pain and fear, but it doesn't usually last long because the denial is difficult to maintain in the face of facts, unless a person is delusional or becomes delusional and therefore seriously mentally ill.

2. *Anger:* The most common second stage, once denial starts to wear off, is anger. This anger may be felt toward anyone or anything. We often feel angry at doctors and other medical professionals working with a dying or dead person; at other people, often family members or friends; at ourselves; and often at the person or thing that is being lost. Often, this anger is intense even though we know that it doesn't make sense. This is a second way to keep the pain away, which can last longer than the denial but usually breaks down in turn.

3. *Bargaining:* In this common stage, we may try to "make a deal" with God, fate, or some person we feel has the power to keep the loss from happening: "God, if you let my wife live, I'll do anything." This is still another attempt to control the situation and avoid the loss. This stage also tends to end when we see that this tactic is not preventing the loss, and sometimes we slip back into anger at this realization.

4. *Depression:* This is the stage we reach when all our efforts to avoid experiencing the loss fail and we realize that we can't escape this painful experience. Depression may be experienced not only as a "down" mood, but as apathy, withdrawal, loss of interest in many parts of life, loss of energy, loss of appetite or increase in eating, changes in sleep patterns, difficulty thinking or concentrating, self-hatred, and/or thoughts of death or suicide. People in this stage often become worried that they are falling apart or "going crazy," that their feelings will never return to normal, and that they are not reacting normally, but this is a common experience. After a time, as we adjust to the loss we are experiencing and it starts to become a normal part of our world, we can move on to the final stage (though, as mentioned, in many cases, people fail to reach the last stage for various reasons).

5. *Acceptance:* This is the last stage, in which our feelings begin returning to normal. We get to be comfortable with the knowledge that we will die, or a loss we have experienced becomes part of the past and the new version of our world becomes what we think of as normal. Thinking of the loss becomes less painful, though it will probably still cause sad feelings for a long time, possibly for the rest of our lives.

It is important to emphasize that grief is a very personal process. How someone goes through the process is also very personal.

CONNECTIONS AMONG GRIEF, LOSS, AND SUBSTANCE ABUSE

As was mentioned previously, the very act of giving up the use of alcohol and/or other drugs is one of the losses alcoholics and addicts must experience as part of early recovery.

Accepting pain, anger, and depression and dealing with them drug-free may be very difficult, if only because it's a new task and the newly recovering person may never have done it before.

In many cultures, and many subcultures including families, there may be traditions of drinking or other drug use at times of loss. Beyond this, our culture generally encourages looking for quick fixes and escaping pain and discomfort in any way we can rather than accepting them as normal parts of life.

Maintaining abstinence can be difficult without the support of others, especially early in recovery. Because our culture is uncomfortable with loss, even others who would be supportive in some situations may avoid a person who is grieving a loss, and people may minimize the loss, tell the grieving person he or she needs to "put it behind you and get over it," refuse to discuss the loss, or avoid contact with the grieving person. This can undermine an important resource for staying clean and sober just at a time when stresses that can influence a recovering person toward relapse are heightened.

HEALTHY COPING SKILLS FOR GRIEF AND LOSS

Having healthy alternatives is one of the most effective factors in maintaining abstinence from addiction and other compulsive behaviors, and that is true in this area as in others. Some healthy coping skills for grief and loss, which can reduce the risk of relapse, include the following:

- *Build, maintain, and rely on a support system:* Both within a recovery program such as Alcoholics Anonymous and in other situations, it is vital to find people who are supportive, who will listen to and spend time with someone who is suffering, and to turn to them when one has the kind of painful feelings that led to drinking, drugs, or other excesses. For some of us, our habit has been to isolate ourselves, and it may take deliberate and uncomfortable effort to go to others. It is especially helpful to join with others feeling the same loss for mutual support.

- *Understand and accept the grieving process:* Learn about the information in this presentation, and understand that feeling as if you are falling apart or going crazy is normal and not a sign that you aren't handling the situation adequately.

- *Remind yourself that the pain is temporary:* As people often say, "This, too, shall pass." It does not lessen the hurt in the present to remember this. However, a dangerous aspect of depression is the feeling that life will always be sad and painful, and this can lead to despair. Remembering how past pains healed can be a source of hope and strength.

- *Slow down:* When we are grieving, we don't function as well in any area of life. We are less effective at work, more prone to problems in relationships, more likely to get physically sick, and more accident-prone. It is important not to expect as much of ourselves as we normally would.

- *Concentrate on basics:* We may tend to neglect self-care in times of grief. It is important at these times to make sure we eat properly, get enough rest, and get regular exercise of some kind. Failure to do these things makes us vulnerable to stress and depression even under normal conditions. In a time of loss this failure can set us up for relapse.

- *Turn to spiritual sources of support:* Whether through participation in an organized religion or a private relationship with a personal higher power, faith and reliance on something larger than oneself for support can be a literal lifesaver. In circumstances of loss, the application of some of the tools and principles of 12-Step recovery programs can be as useful to cope with grief as to avoid relapse.

CONCLUSION

Review the following key points:

1. Many people believe that there are losses that they could not experience without relapsing into drinking or using.

2. Because some of those losses are inevitable and others may happen no matter what a person does to try to prevent them, a person who believes they would have to drink or use if he or she experienced one of these losses has set up a plan to relapse eventually.

3. Grief is a normal process after a loss. It has distinct stages and it passes with time.

4. There are a number of coping skills that will help recovering people get through losses and periods of grieving without relapse or other self-destructive behaviors.

REVIEW LEARNING GOALS

1. Upon completion of this presentation, group members will demonstrate understanding of grief and loss by listing, without notes or references, at least four types of losses that often cause intensive grief.

2. Upon completion of this presentation, group members will demonstrate understanding of grief and loss by listing, without notes or references, the five typical stages of grieving over loss described by Elisabeth Kübler-Ross.

3. Upon completion of this presentation, group members will demonstrate understanding of grief and loss by listing, without notes or references, at least four healthy coping skills for dealing with grief and loss.

QUESTIONS/DISCUSSION BEFORE POSTTEST

ADMINISTER POSTTEST

QUESTIONS/DISCUSSION AFTER POSTTEST

CD-ROM Information

CD-ROM Table of Contents

CD-ROM Information

4.13	CH0410.DOC	Treatment Termination Warning
4.14	CH0411.DOC	Treatment Termination Notification
4.15	CH0412.DOC	Treatment Discharge Summary
4.16	CH0413.DOC	Request for an Accounting of Disclosures
4.17	CH0414.DOC	Disclosure Tracking Log
5.11	CH0501.DOC	Outcome Measurement Tracking Form
5.12	CH0502.DOC	Informed Consent for Participation in Outcome Assessment
6.3	CH0601.DOC	Psychopharmacology, Part I, Facilitator's Guide
	CH0601a.DOC	Psychopharmacology, Part I, Group Member's Handout (CD-ROM)
	CH0601b.DOC	Psychopharmacology, Part I, Pretest/Posttest (CD-ROM)
	CH06PPa.PPT	Psychopharmacology, Part I, Slideshow (CD-ROM)
6.9	CH0602.DOC	Psychopharmacology, Part II, Facilitator's Guide
	CH0602a.DOC	Psychopharmacology, Part II, Group Member's Handout (CD-ROM)
	CH0602b.DOC	Psychopharmacology, Part II, Pretest/Posttest (CD-ROM)
	CH06PPb.PPT	Psychopharmacology, Part II, Slideshow (CD-ROM)
6.16	CH0603.DOC	The Process of Addiction, Facilitator's Guide
	CH0603a.DOC	The Process of Addiction, Group Member's Handout (CD-ROM)
	CH0603b.DOC	The Process of Addiction, Pretest/Posttest (CD-ROM)
	CH06PPc.PPT	The Process of Addiction, Slideshow (CD-ROM)
6.20	CH0604.DOC	The Process of Relapse, Facilitator's Guide
	CH0604a.DOC	The Process of Relapse, Group Member's Handout (CD-ROM)
	CH0604b.DOC	The Process of Relapse, Pretest/Posttest (CD-ROM)
	CH06PPd.PPT	The Process of Relapse, Slideshow (CD-ROM)
6.23	CH0605.DOC	Addiction and Contemporary Culture, Facilitator's Guide
	CH0605a.DOC	Addiction and Contemporary Culture, Group Member's Handout (CD-ROM)
	CH0605b.DOC	Addiction and Contemporary Culture, Pretest/Posttest (CD-ROM)
	CH06PPe.PPT	Addiction and Contemporary Culture, Slideshow (CD-ROM)
6.27	CH0606.DOC	Switching Addictions: Other Compulsive Behaviors, Facilitator's Guide
	CH0606a.DOC	Switching Addictions: Other Compulsive Behaviors, Group Member's Handout (CD-ROM)
	CH0606b.DOC	Switching Addictions: Other Compulsive Behaviors, Pretest/Posttest (CD-ROM)
	CH06PPf.PPT	Switching Addictions: Other Compulsive Behaviors, Slideshow (CD-ROM)
7.3	CH0701.DOC	The Process of Recovery, Facilitator's Guide
	CH0701a.DOC	The Process of Recovery, Group Member's Handout (CD-ROM)
	CH0701b.DOC	The Process of Recovery, Pretest/Posttest (CD-ROM)
	CH07PPa.PPT	The Process of Recovery, Slideshow (CD-ROM)
7.8	CH0702.DOC	Recovery Programs and Resources, Facilitator's Guide
	CH0702a.DOC	Recovery Programs and Resources, Group Member's Handout (CD-ROM)
	CH0702b.DOC	Recovery Programs and Resources, Pretest/Posttest (CD-ROM)
	CH07PPb.PPT	Recovery Programs and Resources, Slideshow (CD-ROM)
7.13	CH0703.DOC	Lifestyle Changes, Facilitator's Guide
	CH0703a.DOC	Lifestyle Changes, Group Member's Handout (CD-ROM)
	CH0703b.DOC	Lifestyle Changes, Pretest/Posttest (CD-ROM)
	CH07PPc.PPT	Lifestyle Changes, Slideshow (CD-ROM)
7.16	CH0704.DOC	Common Problems and Issues in Recovery, Facilitator's Guide
	CH0704a.DOC	Common Problems and Issues in Recovery, Group Member's Handout (CD-ROM)
	CH0704b.DOC	Common Problems and Issues in Recovery, Pretest/Posttest (CD-ROM)
	CH07PPd.PPT	Common Problems and Issues in Recovery, Slideshow (CD-ROM)
7.22	CH0705.DOC	Relapse Prevention, Part I, Facilitator's Guide
	CH0705a.DOC	Relapse Prevention, Part I, Group Member's Handout (CD-ROM)
	CH0705b.DOC	Relapse Prevention, Part I, Pretest/Posttest (CD-ROM)
	CH07PPe.PPT	Relapse Prevention, Part I, Slideshow (CD-ROM)
7.26	CH0706.DOC	Relapse Prevention, Part II, Facilitator's Guide
	CH0706a.DOC	Relapse Prevention, Part II, Group Member's Handout (CD-ROM)

CD-ROM Information

	CH0706b.DOC	Relapse Prevention, Part II, Pretest/Posttest (CD-ROM)
	CH07PPf.PPT	Relapse Prevention, Part II, Slideshow (CD-ROM)
7.29	CH0707.DOC	Physical and Emotional Self-Care, Facilitator's Guide
	CH0707a.DOC	Physical and Emotional Self-Care, Group Member's Handout (CD-ROM)
	CH0707b.DOC	Physical and Emotional Self-Care, Pretest/Posttest (CD-ROM)
	CH07PPg.PPT	Physical and Emotional Self-Care, Slideshow (CD-ROM)
7.33	CH0708.DOC	Stress Management, Facilitator's Guide
	CH0708a.DOC	Stress Management, Group Member's Handout (CD-ROM)
	CH0708b.DOC	Stress Management, Pretest/Posttest (CD-ROM)
	CH07PPh.PPT	Stress Management, Slideshow (CD-ROM)
7.37	CH0709.DOC	Communication Skills, Facilitator's Guide
	CH0709a.DOC	Communication Skills, Group Member's Handout (CD-ROM)
	CH0709b.DOC	Communication Skills, Pretest/Posttest (CD-ROM)
	CH07PPi.PPT	Communication Skills, Slideshow (CD-ROM)
7.43	CH0710.DOC	Healthy Relationship Skills, Facilitator's Guide
	CH0710a.DOC	Healthy Relationship Skills, Group Member's Handout (CD-ROM)
	CH0710b.DOC	Healthy Relationship Skills, Pretest/Posttest (CD-ROM)
	CH07PPj.PPT	Healthy Relationship Skills, Slideshow (CD-ROM)
7.48	CH0711.DOC	Setting and Achieving Goals, Facilitator's Guide
	CH0711a.DOC	Setting and Achieving Goals, Group Member's Handout (CD-ROM)
	CH0711b.DOC	Setting and Achieving Goals, Pretest/Posttest (CD-ROM)
	CH07PPk.PPT	Setting and Achieving Goals, Slideshow (CD-ROM)
7.51	CH0712.DOC	Problem-Solving Skills, Facilitator's Guide
	CH0712a.DOC	Problem-Solving Skills, Group Member's Handout (CD-ROM)
	CH0712b.DOC	Problem-Solving Skills, Pretest/Posttest (CD-ROM)
	CH07PPl.PPT	Problem-Solving Skills, Slideshow (CD-ROM)
7.54	CH0713.DOC	Coping with Anger and Resentment, Facilitator's Guide
	CH0713a.DOC	Coping with Anger and Resentment, Group Member's Handout (CD-ROM)
	CH0713b.DOC	Coping with Anger and Resentment, Pretest/Posttest (CD-ROM)
	CH07PPm.PPT	Coping with Anger and Resentment, Slideshow (CD-ROM)
7.58	CH0714.DOC	Coping with Depression and Anxiety, Facilitator's Guide
	CH0714a.DOC	Coping with Depression and Anxiety, Group Member's Handout (CD-ROM)
	CH0714b.DOC	Coping with Depression and Anxiety, Pretest/Posttest (CD-ROM)
	CH07PPn.PPT	Coping with Depression and Anxiety, Slideshow (CD-ROM)
7.62	CH0715.DOC	Resisting Pressures to Drink or Use, Facilitator's Guide
	CH0715a.DOC	Resisting Pressures to Drink or Use, Group Member's Handout (CD-ROM)
	CH0715b.DOC	Resisting Pressures to Drink or Use, Pretest/Posttest (CD-ROM)
	CH07PPo.PPT	Resisting Pressures to Drink or Use, Slideshow (CD-ROM)
8.3	CH0801.DOC	Family Dynamics, Facilitator's Guide
	CH0801a.DOC	Family Dynamics, Group Member's Handout (CD-ROM)
	CH0801b.DOC	Family Dynamics, Pretest/Posttest (CD-ROM)
	CH08PPa.PPT	Family Dynamics, Slideshow (CD-ROM)
8.8	CH0802.DOC	Domestic Violence, Facilitator's Guide
	CH0802a.DOC	Domestic Violence, Group Member's Handout (CD-ROM)
	CH0802b.DOC	Domestic Violence, Pretest/Posttest (CD-ROM)
	CH08PPb.PPT	Domestic Violence, Slideshow (CD-ROM)
8.13	CH0803.DOC	Suicide Awareness and Prevention, Part I, Facilitator's Guide
	CH0803a.DOC	Suicide Awareness and Prevention, Part I, Group Member's Handout (CD-ROM)
	CH0803b.DOC	Suicide Awareness and Prevention, Part I, Pretest/Posttest (CD-ROM)
	CH08PPc.PPT	Suicide Awareness and Prevention, Part I, Slideshow (CD-ROM)
8.18	CH0804.DOC	Suicide Awareness and Prevention, Part II, Facilitator's Guide
	CH0804a.DOC	Suicide Awareness and Prevention, Part II, Group Member's Handout (CD-ROM)
	CH0804b.DOC	Suicide Awareness and Prevention, Part II, Pretest/Posttest (CD-ROM)
	CH08PPd.PPT	Suicide Awareness and Prevention, Part II, Slideshow (CD-ROM)

Introduction

This appendix provides you with information on the contents of the CD that accompanies this book. For the latest and greatest information, please refer to the ReadMe file located at the root of the CD.

System Requirements

- A computer with a processor running at 120 Mhz or faster
- At least 64 MB of total RAM installed on your computer; for best performance, we recommend at least 128 MB
- A CD-ROM drive.

NOTE: Many popular word processing programs are capable of reading Microsoft Word files. However, users should be aware that a slight amount of formatting might be lost when using a program other than Microsoft Word.

Using the CD with Windows

To install the items from the CD to your hard drive, follow these steps:

1. Insert the CD into your computer's CD-ROM drive.
2. The CD-ROM interface will appear. The interface provides a simple point-and-click way to explore the contents of the CD.

If the opening screen of the CD-ROM does not appear automatically, follow these steps to access the CD:

1. Click the Start button on the left end of the taskbar and then choose Run from the menu that pops up.
2. In the dialog box that appears, type *d*:\setup.exe. (If your CD-ROM drive is not drive d, fill in the appropriate letter in place of *d*.) This brings up the CD Interface described in the preceding set of steps.

What's on the CD

The following sections provide a summary of the software and other materials you'll find on the CD.

CD-ROM Information

CONTENT

All author-created material from the book, including 131 forms in Word format and 29 PowerPoint presentations. Word files contain clinical documentation for every phase of treatment, as well as facilitator guides, group member handouts, and tests for each of the 29 psychoeducational presentations on chemical dependence and related topics. The Microsoft PowerPoint slideshow file for each presentation can be used to print transparencies or alternative handouts or used with a projector connected to a computer. All documentation is included in the folder named "Content."

APPLICATIONS

The following applications are on the CD:

Adobe Acrobat Reader

Adobe's Acrobat Reader is a freeware viewer, to allow for viewing files in the Adobe Portable Document format.

Microsoft Word Viewer

Microsoft Word Viewer is a freeware viewer that allows you to view, but not edit, most Microsoft Word files. Certain features of Microsoft Word documents may not display as expected from within Word Viewer.

Microsoft PowerPoint Viewer

Microsoft PowerPoint Viewer is a freeware viewer that allows you to view, but not edit, Microsoft PowerPoint files. Certain features of Microsoft PowerPoint presentations may not work as expected from within PowerPoint Viewer.

OpenOffice.org

OpenOffice.org is a free multi-platform office productivity suite. It is similar to Microsoft Office or Lotus SmartSuite, but OpenOffice.org is absolutely free. It includes Word Processing, Spreadsheet, Presentation, and Drawing applications that enable you to create professional documents, newsletters, reports, and presentations. It supports most file formats of other Office software. You should be able to edit and view any files created with other Office solutions.

Shareware programs are fully functional, trial versions of copyrighted programs. If you like particular programs, register with their authors for a nominal fee and receive licenses, enhanced versions, and technical support.

Freeware programs are copyrighted games, applications, and utilities that are free for personal use. Unlike shareware, these programs do not require a fee or provide technical support.

GNU software is governed by its own license, which is included inside the folder of the GNU product. See the GNU license for more details.

Trial, demo, or evaluation versions are usually limited either by time or functionality (such as being unable to save projects). Some trial versions are very sensitive to system date changes. If you alter your computer's date, the programs will "time out" and no longer be functional.

User Assistance

If you have trouble with the CD-ROM, please call the Wiley Product Technical Support phone number at (800) 762-2974. Outside the United States, call 1(317) 572-3994. You can also contact Wiley Product Technical Support at **http://www.wiley.com/techsupport**. John Wiley & Sons will provide technical support only for installation and other general quality control items. For technical support on the applications themselves, consult the program's vendor or author.

To place additional orders or to request information about other Wiley products, please call (800) 225-5945.

CUSTOMER NOTE: IF TH[...] PLEASE READ THE
FOLLOWING BEFORE OP[...]

This software contains files [...] npanying book. By
opening the package, you ar[...]

This software product is p[...] he author, John Wiley
& Sons, Inc., or their lice[...]rs. You are [...] to use this [...] on a single computer. Copying
the software to another medium or format for use on a single computer does not violate the U.S.
Copyright Law. Copying the software for any other purpose is a violation of the U.S. Copyright Law.

This software product is sold as is without warranty of any kind, either express or implied, including
but not limited to the implied warranty of merchantability and fitness for a particular purpose. Neither
Wiley nor its dealers or distributors assumes any liability for any alleged or actual damages arising
from the use of or the inability to use this software. (Some states do not allow the exclusion of
implied warranties, so the exclusion may not apply to you.)

WILEY
Publishers Since 1807